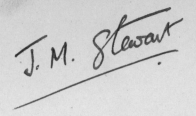

J. M. Stewart

Page 51. Northumberland's plans - Lady Jane Grey.
Page 55. Sir Thomas Wyatt.

D1387868

ELIZABETH AND LEICESTER

By the Same Author:
SIR WALTER RALEIGH

ROBERT DUDLEY, EARL OF LEICESTER
From the National Portrait Gallery.   Painter unknown.

ELIZABETH
AND LEICESTER

MILTON WALDMAN

THE REPRINT SOCIETY
LONDON

THIS EDITION PUBLISHED BY THE REPRINT SOCIETY LTD.
BY ARRANGEMENT WITH WM. COLLINS SONS AND CO. LTD.
1946

To

ALAN McGLASHAN

friend and healer

PRINTED IN GREAT BRITAIN
BY COLLINS CLEAR-TYPE PRESS: LONDON AND GLASGOW

CONTENTS

5

LIST OF ILLUSTRATIONS

Foreword

THIS book began many years ago as a biography of the Earl of Leicester. There seemed at the time two good reasons for attempting one. Of all the prominent Elizabethans he was the most enigmatic and elusive ; and biographers had somehow almost entirely fought shy of him. But presently the first reason began to explain the second. More and more his elusiveness seemed to arise from the fact that as a subject for biography he was incomplete. Unlike Cecil and Walsingham and others of his contemporaries who, however subordinate to Elizabeth in their actions, still displayed personalities of their own, Leicester's personality often curiously merges with Elizabeth's, whose " creature " in a very special sense both of them realised him to be. So familiar were their relations that their business was frequently carried on by private conversation, with little in the way of records to distinguish between what he felt and she felt. For a great many years the prime object of his life was to marry her, an important element in hers to keep him from doing so without finally refusing him, and of this lengthy, politically momentous and not always loverly transaction there was naturally very little preserved in documents. There was little need for him to communicate with a world which almost universally hated him as long as he could satisfactorily communicate with her in whose love and favour he had his being and without whom he would have been nothing. And so the projected biography of Leicester inevitably, almost imperceptibly evolved into this more narrowly personal essay on Elizabeth and Leicester.

All the relevant material listed in Mr. Conyers Read's invaluable *Tudor Bibliography* has, I think, been consulted. I have gratefully to acknowledge Professor J. E. Neale's kindness in calling my attention to Leicester's letter to Douglass Sheffield recently identified by Mr. Read in the Huntington Library and to *The Black Book of Warwick* ; and to thank Professor G. M. Trevelyan, O.M., and Mr. A. L.

Rowse for much friendly encouragement which I hope they will not think misplaced.

Note to second edition : I have also to thank Professor Neale for uncovering and correcting various errors in my first edition.

Chapter One

ELIZABETHAN PANORAMA

IN ALL fascination there is an element of mystery ; and perhaps the abiding fascination of the Elizabethan Age lies in the fact that something so well known can be so little understood. By comparison with most periods of the remoter past its documentation is remarkably complete. We know its buildings and its streets, their very smells even ; the characteristic faces of its people, their dress, their coiffures, their cosmetics, their scent ; its household furniture, its food and drink, the wares in its shops and storehouses, its methods of producing and exchanging, of transporting and using them, its preoccupations and diversions and speculations. In fact, from the richly assorted products of its toil and its play that have come down to us, we can pretty well construct the whole range of properties, physical and mental, with which it carried on the business of living. And yet it somehow remains bathed in that atmosphere of strangeness, of human unrecognisability almost, so continually remarked by the student and profoundly felt by the ordinary reader. Something eludes us, some vital element needed to bind together and give meaning to this mass of information. We can recover the properties but not the psychology, uncover the achievements but not their sources in human motive and character. We seem to possess every facility for knowing the Elizabethan Age except the power to understand its people.

Study their portraits. Though, like any other collection of faces, they exhibit the endless versatility of their Maker, they possess an unmistakable likeness to one another, a family resemblance sufficient to identify them in time and place even if the jewelled hairdressing, the starched ruffs and other period fripperies had been left out. Almost without exception they reveal pride, boldness, wary distrust. In the fifteenth century the pride would have been compounded with humility, in the seventeenth and eighteenth with sober self-confidence ; in the nineteenth the distrust would have verged upon diffidence. But more even than what they show, those sixteenth century faces are curious for what they do not show. In most portraits at least half the interest lies in what one imagines to lurk beneath the paint, in the impression given by the artist of what he had seen with the eyes of his mind while recording with his hand. There is no such impression here, no suggestion of inner humility or self-doubt to contradict—or complement—the physical mask. It all appears to be on the surface, or, perhaps more exactly, the surface seems to register all that there is.

Or take their language. The common word " greatness," for example. To an Elizabethan it signified high wordly position, to us it conveys moral and intellectual stature. For us it resides within a man, for him it resided without, like the rank, offices, titles and wealth to which it pertained : not a quality, as for us, but an attribute which the owner might lose as easily and by the same process as he might lose the offices and the wealth ; an attribute which the Earl of Leicester, for instance, possessed in conspicuous degree and which William Shakespeare would not have dreamed of claiming. Again the surface seems to be all, what lies inside to be ignored or taken for granted.

Of all the forms in which they expressed themselves, and transmitted to posterity the means of knowing them, the most characteristic and abundant is writing—a medium almost diabolically suited to artless self-exposure. But in that medium they intuitively selected the drama as the vehicle for the highest and most spontaneous expression of their versatile energies. Now drama is of all literary forms the most external and objective. It affords little scope for exposition of the author's self, and little more for his characters' obscurer motives ; the unconscious impulse must be inferred from the conscious action, not deliberately abstracted from it as so often, and increasingly, in the novel, essay, biography or less forensic sort of poetry. What—to take their most prodigious writer—do we know of Shakespeare from the thirty-seven plays, two long poems, 154 sonnets and miscellaneous oddments ? Nothing except that he was a man of towering genius and tireless industry which he devoted, according to the meagre extrinsic evidence, to the deliberate purpose of improving his financial and social status. Not a real glimmer otherwise does the whole corpus of his work throw on the hidden texture of the spirit out of which it was fashioned.

Their essays and their more reflective poetry, like their dramas, stress man's relations with the outer world rather than his relations with himself inside himself. So do their biographies, whether by them about themselves or by others about them. When by them, the interest they display in a contemporary seems in general confined to his or her positive doings and ostensible purposes ; when about them, the available material affords little or no clue to anything else. Their private papers are confidential rather than intimate— no different in manner or substance from their ordinary correspondence and memoranda save for such details as discretion or self-interest rendered impractical to diffuse ; of really intimate records—diaries, memoirs, the unguarded letters of familiars— there is, for an age of such teeming literary productivity, a quite extraordinary dearth. And—what seems even more extraordinary —the few examples of such composition that we have not only refrain from deliberate self-dissection, but avoid to a remarkable degree anything in the nature of unconscious self-revelation. Either the Elizabethans were almost morbidly chary of giving themselves away on paper or singularly free from the impulse to do so.

On the whole the second seems more likely, the freedom than the inhibition. Heaven knows, the Elizabethans were little enough inhibited when it came to saying anything they particularly wanted to say. If they were silent about the secret processes of their souls, it is reasonable to assume that they were not greatly interested in those processes. And the reason for that would seem to be that they were sufficiently absorbed in the external results of those processes ; in what the soul produced, not in how and why it produced them. They did not, like us, separate motive from action and give it independent value, but took it for granted and measured it solely by its outcome in action ; apart from that it seems to have been mere waste product so far as they were concerned.

This habit of mind made for considerable efficiency. It gave the Elizabethans faith in themselves and their ability to deal with the world about them ; it kept them from painful and paralysing doubts about the wisdom of what they wanted. But it also made them difficult for a less extroverted age to understand. Rarely do we discern in them those unmotivated deeds and unfulfilled dreams by which in the moments of insight we see ourselves in others. They knew what they did and why they did it or why they failed ; their surfaces were so brilliant precisely because they were able through some freak of psychic organisation to put so much of themselves into them ; but for the same reason there seems to be no hidden and unexpended residue in them to be accounted for, none of those dispersed desires and unused potentialities by which we seek out that important half of human personality we instinctively think of as the inner or " real " man. The unknown is absorbed in the known, the invisible in the visible, the unachieved in the achieved, leaving a race of creatures as alien to our perception as a race of thorough-going mystics would be of whom the exact opposite were true. The one essential difference is the imprint which the Elizabethan race was able to leave on this its favourite world.

It is not only to posterity that Elizabethan England appears inexplicable ; to her contemporaries as well, though for other reasons, she was a sore puzzle as well as a sore trial. Just as the actions upon which she embarked often exceeded any reasonable calculation of her strength, so the way in which she lived seemed out of all proportion to her visible resources. In an era of continental national expansion she had lost the last of her once vast overseas possessions, so that politically she occupied no more impressive a place in the general scheme of things than nature, isolating her in the stormy, fog-bound waters of the North Atlantic, had allotted her geographically—that of the larger of two smallish kingdoms sharing a somewhat backward island off Europe's less inviting coasts. Visitors from abroad—after a passing tribute to her shipping in the narrow seas and to her capital—found her undercrowded and underdeveloped : her industries in many respects primitive, her arts immature, her roads so few and so bad that all but the most local of her internal traffic could be carried more swiftly and cheaply round by sea. Her population, scattered over an area the same in extent as it is to-day, numbered perhaps three and a half million— less than a fourth that of France or half of Spain's.

Of the people a contemporary Dutch voyager reports :

". . . They are generally fair, particularly the women, who all— even to the peasant women—protect their complexions from the sun with fans and veils, as only the stately gentlewomen do in Germany and the Netherlands. As a people they are stout-hearted, vehement, eager, cruel in war, zealous in attack, little fearing death ; not revengeful, but fickle, presumptuous, rash, boastful, deceitful, very suspicious, especially of strangers, whom they despise. They are full of courteous and hypocritical gestures and words, which they consider to imply good manners, civility and wisdom. They are well spoken and very hospitable. The people are not so laborious as the French and Hollanders, pre-ferring to lead an indolent life, like the Spaniards. The most difficult and ingenious of the handicrafts are in the hands of foreigners, as is the case with the lazy inhabitants of Spain. They feed many sheep, with fine wool, from which, two hundred years ago, they learned to make cloth. They keep many idle servants, and many wild animals for their pleasure, instead of cultivating the soil. They have many ships, but they do not even catch fish enough for their own consumption, but purchase of their neighbours. They dress very elegantly. Their costume is light and costly, but they are very changeable and capricious, altering their fashions every year, both the men and the women. When they go away from home, riding or travelling, they always wear their best clothes, contrary to the habit of other nations. The English language is broken Dutch, mixed with French and British terms and words, but with a lighter pro-nunciation. They do not speak from the chest, like the Germans, but prattle only with their tongue."

The land itself, to eyes fresh from the thriving congestion of the nearer portions of the continent, presented the appearance of having come down from a bygone age, quaintly pleasant though occasionally somewhat uncouth in its almost unmitigated ruscticity. It was still largely an elemental patchwork of green, gold, brown and grey, of vast primeval forests closely enfolding sleek strips of farm and grassy meadows, of desolate moors sharing horizons with the shaggy windswept grazing of the hills and salt marshes ; here intersected by a stream or indented by a natural harbour, there dotted by a village or pitted by a mine. Yet it was from this bucolic inheritance that those three and a half million extracted that " abundance of necessaries " which made them the wonder and envy of every visitor and placed within their reach every known luxury from all the ends of the earth.

The first and by far the most important item in that abundance was food. The amount and variety of it they consumed was staggering not only to the onlookers but often, if their attention was called to it, to themselves. On the scientific interpretation to be placed on this phenomenon opinions differed. According to one school of thought it might be taken as proof of inferior vitality : " they require to be so largely supplied with victuals," argued a foreign diplomat shrewdly interested in the question of English fitness for war, " it is evident they cannot endure much fatigue." According to another, native, opinion it was just the other way round : " The situation of our region, being neere unto the north, doth cause the heate of our stomachs to be of somewhat greater force : therefor our bodies doe crave a little more ample nourishment than the inhabitants of other regions are accustomed withal, whose digestive force is not altogether so vehement because their internal heat is not so strong as ours, which is kept in by the coldness of the air that . . . doth environ our bodies." In other words the same Providence which had endowed the English with the need had also bestowed upon them the ability to eat so much. And to crown its goodness had given them enough and more than enough both to satisfy the need and to test the ability to the uttermost.

But eating was with the Elizabethans no mere act of aboriginal gluttony. It had become an art, with its own formal rules and discipline ; and like most Elizabethan art it contained a strong element of the fantastic. On the higher levels of subsistence, where it naturally reached its most profuse and refined manifestation, it even possessed a tincture of religion and a touch of the restraint characteristic of the greatest arts.

For to the owner of a great house and title custom prescribed that he should twice a day preside over a banquet at which he discharged with an almost riotous punctilio his duty of feeding the stranger while constraining himself to an elegant moderation. At eleven each morning his table—commonly of polished oak with detachable leaves set upon a trestle frame—was laid for dinner by a highly specialised hierarchy of servants, at five each afternoon again for supper. On it was spread a cloth of fine, or if the standing of his invited guests warranted it, of finest damask, seven or eight yards long by three yards wide into which the scutcheon of the host's arms or some heroic tale out of antiquity had been worked. Then would come the various articles of service : " the salts " of which the following from the inventory of the Earl of Leicester's chattels may be taken as a specimen :

" shippe fashion, of the mother of pearl garnished with silver and diverse warlicke engines and ornaments, with xvi pieces of ordinance, whereof ii on wheels, two ancers in the fore parte and on the stearne the image of Dame Fortune standing on a globe with a flagge in her hande " ;

a knife-case such as the same owner's :

" George on horseback, of woode painted and gilte etc., with a case for knyves in the taile of the horse and case for oyster knyves in the breast of the dragon " ;

goblets, pots, jugs and bowls of silver or fine Venice glass, candlesticks of the same materials and if of glass gilded and engraved in fanciful shapes and colours. When all was in order the host and hostess would take their places with their guests, both the invited and the " manie unlooked for," according to rank, the ewers for washing and napkins for wiping the hands would be circulated, grace said and the food brought in.

There were no menus or courses. There was no need to hold back in hope of something better or to stuff in fear of something not so good. Borne by a seemingly endless file of liveried waiters moving smoothly from kitchen to table, the whole stupendous proof that " our tables are more plentifully garnished than those of other nations " broke upon the gaze practically at once : each day and every day

> " not only beef, mutton, veale, lamb, kid, pork, conie, capon, pig, all in season, but also some portion of the red or fallow deer, beside some great variety of fish and wild fowl and imported delicacies brought in by the seafaring Portingale " ;

by way of vegetables, in general not greatly esteemed, there were, *inter alia*, the new-fangled " potatoes and such venerous roots come from Spain, Portugale and the Indies " ; mountains of bread of finest home-grown wheat barely cooled from the oven, so-called manchets of exceeding whiteness and lightness ; by way of sweets, definitely the favourite portion of the meal and the sweeter the better,

> " geliffes of all colours representing sundry flowers, herbs, trees, forms of beasts, fish, fowl and fruits, and thereunto marchpane (marzipan) wrought with no small curiosity, tarts of divers hues and sundry denominations, conserves of domestic and foreign fruits, suckets, dodinacs, marmilats, sugar-bread, gingerbread, florentines and sundry outlandish confections."

The pungent aroma of strong, hot spices from the steaming meats stimulated an anticipation which the sight of the sweets swiftly confirmed—nose combining with eye and the power of surprise to circumvent the danger of surfeit and monotony which, under such a daily regime, must have been the gravest concern of the " musicall-headed Frenchmen " and other Latins who commonly catered for the Elizabethan peerage. Round the table wove an intricate yet orderly pattern of waiters presenting serving vessels of silver—the host being of the degree of baron, bishop or upwards—to each guest in turn in order of rank, the coarser and solider foods first, then the more delicate, to ascertain his preference, which almost invariably fell upon the rarer and more exotic in each category. Meanwhile another troop of servants wove in and out distributing the liquid portions of the meal from jug and pot to bowl and goblet. If one desired wine there were red and white, sweet and strong—strength being the criterion of superiority ; French in several of its fifty-six imported varieties, some of the thirty kinds of Italian, Spanish, Greek or Canary, and even possibly a vintage or two from the declining native growths. If one preferred beer there was the specially fine home-brew to be found only in nobleman's households, fixed and standing at least a year or in rare cases even two.

The last guest having helped himself to his fill, what remained of the food departed for the kitchen, where a first call upon it was made by the chief officers and upper servants of the household as a supplement to their regular allowance, and by " such inferior guests as are not fit to associate with the nobleman himself—commonly forty to sixty persons in these halls, to the relief of such poor suitors and strangers as are otherwise hardly likely to dine." After that it went to the serving-men and waiters, who also had their separate daily allowance, and finally to the poor " which lie ready at their gates in great numbers to receive the same." The drink remained behind and the household had to make do with beer " usually not under a month old " as well as with a darker and heavier sort of bread.

In the houses of the gentry and the more substantial burghers the same routine was followed on a smaller scale, with certain varieties of custom dictated either by small means or special conditions. The gentry, like the nobility and university students in term, dined at eleven and supped at five, the merchants as a rule, especially in London, at twelve and six.[1] Two or three dishes, or even one, sufficed them when alone and four to six when they had " small resort of strangers," though on extraordinary occasions they could rise almost to the opulence of the nobility. In the matter of drink, however, all but the richest of them were rather more careful.

[1] Breakfast was a meal only indulged in by "hungry young stomacks that cannot wait for dinner." University students out of term compromised by advancing their dinner-hour to 10.

The vessels containing it, of earthenware, ordinarily, in " sundry colours and moulds, wherein many are garnished with silver or leastwise in pewter " stood not upon the table but on a sideboard ; and instead of the servants keeping them full each guest " as thirst moved him called for a cup of what he wanted, which, when he had tasted it, he handed back to one of the waiters, who poured what remained back into the original vessel " ; a sound device to discourage excessive tippling, for " if full pots should continually stand at the elbow of the trenchers, divers would alwaies be dealing with them, whereas most drink seldom and only when necessity urgeth and so avoid the note of great drinking or often troubling the servitors with filling of the bols." In such houses the servants enjoyed in addition to the ordinary diet assigned to them the reversion of the left-overs, apart from favoured dishes like cold lamb and venison due to return to the master's table a second time.

Below this level, the variety, in particular the imported delicacies, tended to disappear, though the abundance remained until one reached the " hard and pinching diet " of the poor. In the main white meat, milk, butter and cheese, spurned by the prosperous as " no good appertinent only to the inferior sort," did for the trades-man, artisan and husbandman, together with such other staples as could be easily obtained and quickly prepared. For their ordinary bread, " preferably new as possible so it be not hot," they relied on rye or barley as well as the less finely-milled wheat, though in time of dearth the really poor had often to be content with loaves made of " beans, peason oats with even part or whole acorns." Their drink, apart from the universal beer—" each covetting to have the same as stale as he may so it be not sour " (beer brewed in March of barley malted in the winter being deemed " old " and therefor best)—consisted of local specialities such as the cider of apples and the pirrie of pears in Kent, Sussex and Worcester, the metheglin of Wales, and the east country variety of it called mead, " very good . . . for such as love to be loose-bodied (bowelled) or a little eased of the cough " but otherwise a mere " swish-swash " of honeycomb, water and spices.

To this sort of fare, irregularly supplemented by the products of stream and moor, they sat down contentedly enough if they could afford it at noon and at seven in the evening most days of the year. But now and then they let themselves go, from " the companies of every trade in London " who on their quarter day meetings wined and dined " nothing inferior to the nobility " down to the farm labourers who on their periodic " junkettings " would assemble in the cottage of one of their number bringing whatever flesh, fish and fowl they had been able to gather, legally or other-wise, the host providing only bread, sauce, houseroom and fire, and there " if full of venison and very strong beer or ale . . . not stick to compare themselves with the Lord Mayor." And by another chronicler it is told " that it is very common for a number of them, when they have got a cup too much in their heads, to go up to some belfry and ring the bells for an hour together for the sake of the amusement," being " vastly fond of great ear-filling noises."

Scarcely less remarkable to the outsider than how well the Englishman did himself in the matter of eating was how poorly he did himself in the matter of housing. " The English have their houses of sticks and dirt, but they fare commonly as well as the King." Even the houses of the gentry were still with few exceptions of these rudimentary materials, stout timbers locally cut, covered with thick clay red, white or blue—which last quickly faded on contact with the air—locally dug ; only their size and the greater scope afforded the skilled native carpenters in the working of the timbers distinguished them externally from the houses of the poor. All were of two or more stories, the upper ones overhanging where they faced upon streets. Over the clay was spread an asbestos of lime in most places as a protection against fire, and into it inserted stones or oysters shells, or in Wales " a certain kind of red stone," which received oil and shed water. For roofing there were tiles of wood if suitable timber were handy or of slate if quarries were near ; otherwise straw, sedge or reeds made do. The inner walls consisted of a coat or two of white mortar tempered with hair applied to laths nailed close together : though on top of this, and on the floor, plaster of Paris would often be spread because of its fire-resisting properties and given a smooth finish. It is not hard to understand why these primitive dwellings should have appeared " rude " individually and, owing to the English horror of alignment and uniformity, disorderly collectively to eyes used to the neat stone rows of the Continental towns and villages ; nor why the disparity between English eating and housing—an emphasis on food over other essentials of existence being a generally accepted trait of savages—gave rise to the impression that the islanders were not yet altogether civilised.

Nevertheless in this as in other respects standards were rapidly changing. The well-to-do, fast increasing in number, had taken to building new homes of brick or stone or both ; not only the rusty stone of the West Country, which had always been to some extent in local use, but the white stone of Caen brought by river-barge from Normandy and formerly dedicated to cathedrals, great abbeys and royal palaces alone. The style of building, too, had altered, largely under the influence of imported architects and craftsmen, the ideals of splendour and fantasy (never far from the Elizabethan taste) superseding those of ruggedness and simplicity, yet curiously contriving to include spaciousness, light and convenience in unheard-of degree.

The interiors conformed. The walls received tapestries, once the rare and exclusive embellishment of the very rich, or " painted cloths depicting divers histories, beasts or herbs," or else panelling of domestic oak or " wainscott brought hither out of the eastern countries." Against this background the household attained a standard of profusion, richness and taste to which royalty itself would barely have aspired a generation or two earlier. The carpets, plate, linen and glass in a nobleman's establishment—and he was likely to keep several—were often worth between a thousand and two thousand pounds (with money at perhaps twelve times or more its present value), in that of a gentleman or merchant quite half as much. Nor were the rich the only beneficiaries of this great (though not yet by any means universal) " amendment of living." The more solid sort of artisan and yeoman had almost begun to take for granted real plate in his cupboard, linen napery on his table and beds hung with tapestry or silk. Horn windows were every-where disappearing as glass became cheap and plentiful ; chimneys, formerly not exceeding two or three in a town when " each made his fire against a rere-doose in the hall where he dined and dressed his meat," had become so familiar as scarcely to be remarked except for their novelties of shape and design. The elderly poor looked back with disdain upon the days when " our fathers, and ourselves too, have lien full upon straw pallets, on rough mats covered with a sheet under coverlets made of dogswain . . . and a good round log under their heads instead of a bolster or pillow " ; when if a householder had purchased a mattress or feather bed within seven years of his marriage, and a sack of chaff to put his head on, he " thought himself as well lodged as the lord of the town," as he probably was except for warmth ; when " pillows were thought meet only for women in childbed " and servants thought themselves lucky to have a sheet over them and expected nothing under them more than their own hardened hides to keep them from the pricking straws that ran through the canvas of the pallet. Only when one travelled into the remote and less populous regions of the north did one find the older conditions still prevalent—a fact which helps to explain why the new age, and the Tudor monarchy that symbolised it, had to look for their chief defenders, and in times of crisis their very survival, mainly to the south.

If it ever was true, the dictum that apparel oft proclaims the man was never less true than of the period in which it was coined. Its author probably wrote it with his tongue in his cheek and dis-engaged himself from responsibility by giving it utterance in the mouth of a fool. In Elizabethan eating and housing, however extravagant, there was at least some relation between custom and reason. The table a man kept and the house he lived in at least gave a tolerably accurate indication of his wealth and position. But in the matter of costume fashion took leave of reason altogether. What a man wore furnished little reliable evidence of his rank, means, character, taste or even always of his sex. Of two men in the same social class one with an income of thousands a year might dress in plain velvet or even dark homespun and the other display upon his back the value of several thousand pounds without a farthing in the world outside. Of two men attired in the latest style, one might be a duke, a statesman or a tough old warrior and the other a mountebank, a fop or a professional sodomite without anything to say which was which in the style and colour of their silks and satins or the number and glitter of the jewels that spangled them from top to toe.

It must be remembered that England was going through a "boom" with all the dizziness of pace that accompanies such a period. There seemed no limit to the amount of money within men's reach, and, since the possibilities of financial investment were still very restricted, ready cash spent on personal adornment might turn out to be a good social speculation in view of the possibilities for advancement of late opened to talent, push and cheek. Moreover, by virtue of her growing commercial activity, England was again in easy intercourse with the strange outer world from which she had for nearly a generation remained comparatively estranged, and like a provincial with money in hand was finding its temptations too wonderful to be resisted.

So with "sables about their necks, corked slippers, trimmed buskins and warm Mittens, furred stomachers, long gowns," according to an angry episcopal denunciation, "these tender Parnels must have one gown for the day, another for the night, one long, another short, one for the winter, another for the summer, one furred through, another but faced, one for the workday, another for the holy-day, one of this colour, another of that, one of cloth, another of silk or damask . . . one afore dinner, another at after . . . yes, a ruffian will have more in his ruff and hose than he should spend in a year." Within this abundance reigned a most bewildering variety. "Now Spanish quite, now French toies . . . then high Almain fashion, by and by Turkish manner, the Morisco gown, the Barbarian sleeve, the short French breeches make such a comely vesture that except it were a dog in a doublet, you shall not see any so disguised as are my countrymen of England." Nor were variety and eccentricity all that counted : the careful dresser insisted upon cut as well. ". . . hardly can the tailors please them in the making of it fit for their bodies and how many times must it be sent back to him that made it ! What chafing, what fretting, what reproachful language, doth the poor workman bear away ? And many times when he doth nothing to it at all, yet when it is brought home again it is very fit and handsome ; then must we put it on, must the long seams of our hose be set by a plum-line, then we puffe, then we blow, and finally sweat till we drop, that our clothes may stand well on us."

And not only the clothes. The hair and beard had to stand equally well before the man could be considered correctly turned out. ". . . our heads, which sometimes are polled, sometimes curled, or suffered to grow at length like a woman's locks, many a time cut off above or under the ears round as by a wooden dish . . . our variety of beards, of which some are shaven from the chin like those of the Turks, not a few cut short like the beard of the Marquis Otto (a mere fringe under the chin), some made round like a rubbing brush, others with a pique de vant . . . or now and then suffered to grow long, the barbers grown to be as cunning in this behalf as the tailors. And therefor if a man have a lean and straight face, a Marquis Otto will make it broad and large ; if it be platter-like, a long slender beard will make it seem the narrower ; if he be wesell (weasel) beaked, then much hair left on the cheek will make the owner look big like a bowelled hen and so grim as a goose." Once the shape of the hair and beard were decided, they would be dyed and perfumed to taste. The final effect was often enhanced, even amongst men of unquestioned virility, by earrings of wrought gold, precious stones or drooping pearls.

To the conservative eye the plumage of the women was even more scandalous . . . " such staring attire as in time past was supposed meet for light housewives only, is now become a habit for chaste and sober matrons. What should I say of their doublets with pendant codpieces on the breast, full of jags and cuts and sleeves of sundry colours ? their galligascons to bear out their bums and make their attire sit plum round (as they term it) them ? their fardingales and diversely coloured nether stocks of silk, jersey and such like ? . . . I have met with some of these trulls in London so disguised that it hath passed my skill to discern whether they were men or women. Thus it is now come to pass that women are become men and men transformed into monsters."

It was not only his own sentiments that the Reverend William Harrison was here expressing. Probably the majority of his countrymen no more approved than they emulated the new fashions. His fellow-clerics, reversing the current trend, had discarded the bright colours, the piked shoes, the crisped hair, the fur and lace, silver and gold of Popish times, when " to meet a priest was to behold a peacock that spreadeth his tail when he passeth before the henne," and adopted the simplest and soberest garments possible for the uniform of their profession. The merchant class, blending substance and dignity, went in for a consciously old-fashioned style of which the materials were " fine and costly, yet in form and colours in accord with the ancient gravity pertaining to citizens and burgesses." The mass of peasants and townsfolk still clung to their traditional homespun and worsted, of which the range of patterns and quality had of late, in particular in the towns, sensibly increased.

To this sturdy majority the latest fashions seemed frivolous, indecent and downright ugly in themselves and even worse for the pagan cosmopolitanism which they represented. Piety and superstition abhorred them as signs of a state of national sin which Providence would not let go unpunished; in April of 1562, records Hayward, himself a courtier and a man of fashion, many calves and lambs were born " having collars of skin growing about their necks, like the double ruffs that were then in use. In May a man child was born in Chichester, the head, arms and legs like an anatomy, without any flesh ; the breast and navel monstrous big, a long string hanging from the navel ; about the neck grew a collar of flesh and skin, pleated and folded like a double ruff, and rising up into the ears, as if nature would upbraid our pride in artificial bravery by producing monsters in the same attire."

Even the government, many of its members also courtiers and men of fashion, were gravely troubled by the outbreak of sartorial excess and tried hard to restrain it. A typical proclamation issued by Elizabeth—whose own wardrobe so gorgeously illustrated all criticism as positively to stupefy it—and subscribed by her Council early in her reign decreed that no man under the degree of earl might wear imported wool ; under that of knight, unless he had £200 a year clear, any velvet in his gown or coat or other outer garment, nor any manner of embroidery or picking with gold, silver or silk in any part of his apparel or that of his horse or mule ; no Englishman under the degree of knight's son might wear silk in his hat, night-cap, girdle, scabbard or shoes, on pain of three months' imprisonment and a fine of £10 for each day the offence was perpetrated. But neither this effort to place extravagance within social bounds nor other similar edicts were of any more avail than sumptuary laws usually are unless accompanied by strong religious sanctions. The Renaissance had started an impulse which the Reformation could not control and of which an aspect so important as scarcely to be exaggerated was the conviction that to be inconspicuous was practically equivalent to not being alive.

There was a further reason why many hated and feared the new fashions. Not only, wrote William Cecil, principal minister of state during practically the whole of the reign, were they " false and deceitful, serving rather for the gaze than any good use ; " but they took " substantial staple wares " out of the realm. In other words, they were not simply fripperies, they were foreign ; in the opinion of Cecil and the very powerful element in the country who thought like him, harmful to the country's economy as well as its morality.

That economy was still predominantly insular and self-sufficient. It presupposed a domestic production of all the common necessities broad enough in quantity and low enough in price both to supply and protect the home market. Since the kingdom possessed no investments nor performed any services to speak of abroad, its luxuries, few of which were indigenous, had to be paid for out of its native " abundance of necessaries," with the result that the necessaries tended to rise in price, the abundance to diminish and the country to become more and more dependent on its foreign trade. This, in fact, had already begun to happen. The conflict had already set in between the economy of goods and an economy of money, between the conception of a tight little kingdom and a maritime empire—the rival conceptions of which William Cecil and the Earl of Leicester evolved into respective champions.

As with every such revolutionary conflict, the real causes were as obscure to the participants as the inevitable outcome. Looking round, it was unarguable that England had plenty and to spare for all her reasonable needs. Of the food required to nourish her on the scale described above, none had to be brought from abroad except such secondary wants as spices, cane-sugar, semi-tropical fruits, oil, most of her wine and part of her hops; all the familiar varieties of grain and meat (the latter of choicest quality, due perhaps to the quality of the home-grown feeding stuffs), fruit, vegetables, honey, dairy products, etc., her own soil regularly produced with a large enough margin for comfortable export. In addition she possessed an apparently inexhaustible supplement to her larder in her moors, forests and a deep-sea fishing industry, parent of a brisk trade in salted fish for export, which the government did its best to foster by restoring the Papist obligation to abstain from meat on Fridays. From its wealth of grazing stock the country derived a by-product of leather enough both to supply itself and maintain a constant foreign demand because of its excellence, while its surplus of wool constituted one of the principal raw materials in the markets of the world; against this it had to import for its own textile requirements only a few specialities like cloth of gold and silver, its articles of mercery and the bulk of its linens, and certain dyestuffs like woad and madder. Tin and lead abounded in Wales and Cornwall, iron in Wales and the neighbourhood of Manchester with smaller mines in Kent, Sussex, Shropshire and the region of the Mendips, coal in the North and West as much " as may suffice for all the realm : so must they do hereafter, indeed, if wood be not cherished better than it is at this present." From the tin and an alloy of " kettle brass " was derived the pewter that served so many purposes, the best of it " esteemed overseas . . . as a like amount of fine silver." Coal, in addition to its value for export, was beginning to be used in conjunction with iron, especially in its immediate neighbourhood as a substitute for peat, though the famous iron-works of Sussex and Hampshire still clung to charcoal because of heavy transport costs ; in general the home-made steel was not yet considered equal to the better foreign. Besides the baser metals, including copper, whose mining had been resumed after a lapse, there was also a trickle of gold and silver. " It was not said of old without great reason, that all countries have great need of Britain and Britain itself of none," and unless the definition of need were to include the desire for luxury, the saying still appeared to be true.

But though not visibly it was in fact already hopelessly untrue. Three principal factors had conspired to make it so—the demand for wool, the supply of silver and the stimulus given by the relation between them to the system of enclosures. By ancient custom the small farmer enjoyed grazing as well as other rights over the common land of which the greater part of England of old consisted, and could in consequence decide in what proportion to keep cattle and sheep and in which proportion to rear his sheep for wool or for meat. But these rights had during the past century come into conflict with the interests of various local magnates impressed by the rising price—stimulated of late by the influx of the monetary metals from the new world—of raw wool. To increase their available supply of it they had to have more land, and the common land stood temptingly convenient. Many of these land-hungry magnates had already fleshed their teeth on the abbey-lands, also jointly enjoyed by those who worked them till confiscated by Henry VIII, and their appetite had grown with eating. One way and another they pushed their boundaries out to enclose the common lands, paying when they had to : though the small sum he received outright did little to compensate the peasant for his permanent loss, especially in the face of the swift ensuing rise in the cost of living.

For as farms grew scarcer rents multiplied three and four times over, causing ejections wholesale for non-payment. The rise in rents coupled with the decrease in crops and the number of animals available for slaughter sent the price of food soaring still further. To the landlords, on the other hand, the innovation proved such a success in terms of money that they hastened to extend it in all directions. They fenced in streams and coverts from which the poor man had eked out his diet, cut down forests which from time immemorial served to provide him with timber and fuel and to shelter the fruits of his husbandry against the blasts of the winds ; and out of these acquisitions fashioned not only additional sheep-walks but, with an eye to the features of the landscape, stately private parks fenced with oak palings and stocked with strange exotic animals ; for with the growth of money incomes had arisen exciting new possibilities of personal display. In places whole villages were pulled down to make way for still more sheep and still grander parks. The dispossessed, the homeless unemployed, straggled towards the cities to seek work as unskilled labourers or swelled the growing and dangerous rabble of able-bodied vagrants on the highways—hopeless and sullen victims of one of those "inevitable" economic metamorphoses before which the startled conscience of society stands helpless. Organised resistance had ended with the murderous defeat of Kett's rebellion in East Anglia in the reign of Edward VI, and the disappointing failure of the Catholic counter reformation under his successor Mary to remedy the condition had about ended hope as well. All that the Elizabethan statesmen could do was to accept the consequences and look for palliatives.

As yet, however, the system was still in its infancy, with over two hundred years more to run, and, except for the five per cent or so of the population already pauperised or immediately threatened, its worst consequences were concealed by the very conditions that had brought it about. For one thing the birthrate fell, to which the enclosers comfortably retorted, " we have too great store of people in England already." For another those who managed to hold on found themselves better off than English peasants had ever been before. If rents were rising they would in the nature of things rise less rapidly than the price of seasonal crops ; and the fortunate or thrifty farmer, if he had to put aside plenty of ready cash, six or seven years' rent in advance, to renew his lease when due lest he should lose it to some covetous outsider, might hope on the other hand to save enough money, with so incredibly much of it about, to buy his holding outright from a needy or extravagant lord. The demand for, coupled with the rising price of, manufactured goods favoured the artisan with savings, anxious to break away from the slow mediæval progress from journeyman to master, while the enclosures provided him with a constantly replenished supply of cheap labour off the land ; as the same causes favoured the merchants with wares to turn over quickly and ships to man. For the first time in the experience of ordinary folk money made money—not simply by the old device of straightforward usury but by the more complicated rules of capitalistic enterprise. And with money came what most men valued even more, power and social opportunity as the ancient frontiers between the classes began to yield to the pressure of the new economic forces.

Although these frontiers had never been so rigid as upon the continent, four such classes were nevertheless definitely recognised. First in order came the gentry, numbering " in effect any one who can live without manual labour and bear the port, charge and countenance of a gentleman." A man might be born into this rank or he might acquire it by eminence in the liberal professions, the armed services or " good counsell given at home " provided he had the money to buy a coat-of-arms from the college of heralds, " who in the charter of the same doe of custom pretend antiquity and service and many gaie things," in particular Norman descent, which was rated higher than Saxon. For the Crown it was a useful system of rewards, since it cost the Treasury nothing and the gentle-man paid taxes like anybody else. Included in this class were knights, all of them made and none born so, even the king ; the knights banneret, distinguished by the cutting off of the pointed end of their knights' pennants to make them resemble the banner of a baron ; and all the various grades of the nobility, hereditary and ecclesias-tical. Untitled members of this class were ordinarily addressed as " Master," the rest, except for a more punctilious formality, very much as to-day, including the courtesy title of " Lord " before the Christian names of the sons of dukes and marquesses and the eldest sons of earls, who had otherwise the same standing in law as common esquires. Ladies several times married—very frequent occurrences because of the killing masculine pace—retained the highest rank of their several husbands.

Next came the citizens or burgesses, merchants, lawyers, manu-facturers, bankers and the like, whose virtual monopoly of the kingdom's spreading commerce was fast obliterating the very precise legal status long affixed to them by the municipal charters. By definition " freemen within the cities and of likely substance to bear office in the same," their real powers had so expanded as to be practically indefinable. They were the lords of the towns with the same proud exclusiveness as the great land-owning families were the lords of the shires. In the management of their respective boroughs' affairs and the choice of their parliamentary representatives they maintained a close-packed resistance to interference from above or below, while in the high councils of state they managed to exercise a very effective if less direct influence. Not only did they frequently climb into the ranks of the gentry, but the gentry often gladly welcomed the opportunity of descending amongst them. Some, like Elizabeth's maternal family long before, even married into the higher nobility, or else, by purchasing from the Court of Wards the custody of a peer's orphaned son or daughter during minority, contrived that their children should do so. But mostly they were content to remain what they were, maintaining their corporate rule over the towns of the realm and of its trade " even unto New Spain, Cathaia, Turkey and Muscovia," and keeping when they chose a state equal to that of the greatest.

After them followed the yeomen, the class of the forty-shilling freeholder and the skilled craftsmen possessed of the franchise. They were the backbone of the kingdom, the chief producers of its wealth and its reliance in time of war ; and it was they more than any other class who were either swiftly made or abruptly ruined by the dizzy new pace of the times. Many were driven to the roads or the sea, but of the rest a good number managed " with grasping, frequenting of markets and keeping of servants (not idle servants as gentlemen do, but as both getting their own and their masters' living)" not only to " live wealthily, keep good houses and travel to get riches " themselves, but to amass enough " to buy land of unthrifty gentlemen, and after sending their sons to the schools, universities and inns of court ; or otherwise leaving them sufficient land so they may live without labour . . . make them by these means to become gentlemen. . . ." Not a few of the soldiers, sailors and statesmen to whose remembered names the touch of the Queen's sword added the prefix of knighthood owned in the background a father still addressed as " Goodman " or simply as John or Thomas.

The last class consisted of day-labourers, poor husbandmen, retailers without free land, copyholders and all artificers as tailors, shoemakers, carpenters, brickmakers, etc. Free only in the sense that the law knew no slaves or bondmen, but possessed of no voice in their own government, they might nevertheless in the cities or towns take the place of yeomen at inquests and serve in the villages as churchwardens, sidesmen, ale-conners and sometimes as constables. Little or no education was given them ; in the elementary matter of time they reckoned in no smaller denomination than half or at the best quarter-hours. Yet if unlettered and perhaps (like Shakespeare's yokels) occasionally turgid-witted, they were on the whole sharply drawn in character and sturdily independent of speech : " merrie without malice and plaine without inward . . . craft." Unfortunately also in this class, largely recruited from it and often relegated to it, was included the inevitable riff-raff of a swiftly-changing society—dispossessed yeomen turned into desperate vagrants, discharged soldiers unfit for or averse from other employment, and the great swarms of idle serving-men spoilt by expensive living when in work, hangers-on of whoever could keep them when out of it, inciting the rich, the young and the lawless above themselves ; the running sore of the Elizabethan social order and the insoluble problem of Elizabethan government.

Not that the rich, the young and lawless needed much incitement. The prevailing spirit of unrest and unruliness was by no means peculiar to the poor and unlettered ; in varying degree it infected all classes, and nowhere more than in the seats of learning where the youth of the three upper met and for a while mingled. There was " scarce a corporate town in the realm without a good Grammar School, liberally endowed for the relief of poor scholars " and in these the sons of the gentry, the burgesses and the yeomen alike, pursued their elementary studies in English grammar, Latin, scripture and mathematics. In addition there were the more specialised " collegiate churches " like Winchester, Eton and Windsor, which offered free board as well as education to particularly gifted students elected to them.

From these institutions it was presumed—the fundamental presumption of the whole system—that the cleverer students without other wordly prospects would proceed at sixteen or so to one of the universities or to London to prepare for the church, the law, medicine or teaching. But a university education had become the fashion ; in fact, more than a fashion, a rage ; in Oxford and Cambridge alone there were said to be 3000 students in residence. The scholarships intended for the sons of the poor were often snatched by the sons of the rich eager for a little fun or even in some cases a little more learning in pleasant surroundings before deciding what to do next ; and since they were not all sufficiently bright to win admission on merit, bribery and social pressure were freely used to assist them in the elections. Once entered, most of them studied " little other than histories (romances), tables, dice and trifles as men that make not their living by their study the end of their purpose," found plenty of time in consequence to " ruffle and riot it out," dressed with the gaudiness of their elders, and when called to task by the president or dean " thought it sufficient to say that they be gentlemen, which grieveth many not a little." From this scholastic orgy these young blades often passed on to the Inns of Court for a brief and hopeful fling at the law accompanied by a career " abroad in the streets of London where they were scarce able to be bridled by any good order at all." From this system somehow emerged a generation of men represented by Sir Walter Raleigh at one end and Oliver Cromwell at the other.

Of those that remained behind, many won fame as scholars. But an inordinate number simply hung on to " live like drone bees on the fat of the colleges "—and no wonder, when even the successful men of action, the Leicesters and the Raleighs, occasionally sighed for escape from the turbulence of the world outside. It was not a world for the meek, the contemplative and the poor in spirit. Passion was swift and envy keen ; and all the violence of a naturally unruly race (the masterful Elizabeth herself called them her " ungovernable beasts of English ") were played upon by every common motive of criminality—sudden wealth and equally sudden poverty, the too-accessible temptations of glittering display, a religious and social order still in upheaval.' Shrewdness, cunning and good luck might gain property, but it often took an alert eye and a strong arm to protect it when so much of it necessarily accompanied the owner's person, whether on his back or, if he were a man of substance out on business, in his saddle-bags. The professional thieves were legion, nor were they always by any means of lowly origin. No man ever went out without at least a dagger, while the nobility and their servants alike wore swords and rapiers, often of inordinate length, in the belief that this made them more effective. On the highways men carried not only dagger and pistol but staves twelve or thirteen feet long ending in twelve-inch iron pikes ; weapons not seldom brought into use after a night at an inn—and very good inns they were, as a rule, with a wide choice of victuals and clean bedding and napery at an extra cost of a penny—where the chamberlains, hostlers and tapsters, after estimating the value inside the guests' saddle-bags when lifting them off, sent a highwayman after them or along with them as a recommended companion. " Three hundred and upward," a German traveller reported, " are hanged annually in London " for thieving alone. In the towns, chiefly, of course, the capital, men went in danger not only of robbery with violence but of the sudden deadly brawls between serving-men in drunken heat over the feuds and jealousies of the houses whose liveries they wore. The children of the Earl of Shrewsbury, at the end of a letter describing a series of such frays on the same day in the winter of 1578-9, all of them involving grave injuries, apologised for writing of " these trifling matters " in the absence of any news of importance.

In vain the authorities attempted to put a stop to this thieving and rioting. The Lord Mayor issued a proclamation forbidding the use of the smooth-cudgel, commonly called the Bastinado, either with or without the iron pike, the Privy Council another prohibiting the wearing of swords beyond a certain length. They were obeyed like the similar edicts against excessive fashions. In the effort to relieve the dangerous and growing congestion in the towns, the government brought in a statute to limit the number of new houses in these areas ; the result was a still greater overcrowing and the more rapid dispersal of vagrants on the roads. Believing that the root of the evil might lie in the too early marriage of the poor whereby a race of paupers ripe for disorder was being bred, the authorities tried to discourage the practice until the young couple could afford a proper dwelling ; the young tended therefore to desist from matrimony but not from propagating their kind, to the worry of the parishes saddled with the subsequent crop of bastards. The ruling class were unable to diagnose an ill of which they were the chief beneficiaries, any more than they would have thought of attributing it to the example they themselves set a display-loving and sports-mad race in their amusements—their reckless blood-chases with half-savage hounds, the horses imported from far and near for the furious collisions of the tourney, their mastiffs, selected for natural fierceness and made fiercer in training by bull and bear baiting without a collar to protect the throat and by practice fights against men armed with shields, in order finally to be turned out to fight in threes against a bear or fours against a lion ; diversions highly gratifying to and in their degree imitated by the populace.

The machinery that governed this throbbing human organism was a curious blend of old and new, of feudal and modern. Two forces were constantly at work on it, the centralising tendency introduced by the despotic mood of the Tudors and the need of the times on the one hand, ingrained local custom, habit and rivalries on the other. Viewed in one aspect it was awe-inspiring and apparantly all-powerful, in the other cumbersome, diffuse and antiquated. Its authority was tremendous but not uniform ; it could crush political opposition with brutal efficiency but only with the greatest difficulty command the financial support to keep itself solvent. Some parts of the country reverenced it as semi-divine, others detested it as an infernal machine for destroying men's natural liberties. Henry VIII and Elizabeth had tried to reconcile the two tendencies through regional Councils under the presidency of royal deputies, but their success, judged by the sporadic outbreaks of discontent, especially in the North, had not been outstanding.

For, more and more, with the slow—and not really very slow for so considerable a happening—but sure transformation of a parochial and feudal into a consciously national and competitive society, the central power in London intruded itself upon the attention. In the previous generation that power had thrust its agents into the remotest parts of the land to obliterate with astonishing, almost unbelievable, irresistibility, living features of it like the abbeys that seemed to have been rooted in it for ever ; and to interpose between its people and their God, as Head of His church in place of a vague and distant Pope in Rome, a very near and formidably distinct Prince in London. In London also assembled the Parliament which, even while it passed increasingly under the mighty shadow of the Crown, represented so far as it represented anything the dominant movement of the time towards the concerns of trade. There too dwelt the master-traders whose silent and secret force radiated through every important deliberation of Parliament and Crown alike. And there, or very nearby according to the season, resided the Court upon which was becoming ever more concentrated the imagination and the material ambitions of the nation as a whole and of its younger and eagerer members in particular. For good or ill the destiny of the kingdom was bound up as never before with its capital.

It was not only incomparably the most important of the twenty-six cities of England, it was one of the great cities of Europe, with a population of perhaps 150,000 and growing, so rapidly that to feed, house and check disorder and plague among its swarms had become one of the most pressing of national anxieties.[1] To the east of the soaring Gothic pile of St. Paul's on Ludgate Hill—its chief landmark—lay the city proper, girt by its ancient walls and connected with the opposite bank of the river which was its vital artery by a bridge whose nineteen arches and avenue of buildings made it one of the most impressive sights in Europe. From the bridge one could look down-river and see coming up or going out on the tide the " vast concourse of ships " of all sizes and shapes which caused even the Venetian Ambassador, used enough to such spectacles if any man was, to exclaim with admiration and envy.

From amongst its citizens were annually chosen the twenty-four aldermen who governed the City almost like an independent

---

[1] The growth of London at this time was due almost entirely to the influx from the country. The epidemics of plague frequently brought the number of deaths up to the number of births—estimated at 4200 annually.

republic, neither the king (who might not even enter it without permission) nor his ministers interfering in any way. Sober in speech and dress, knowing their own collective worth and imbued with a profound corporate spirit—so much so that few individual figures emerge in the whole period—they gave the most complete and formidable expression to the strain in the national character known as Puritan. Nevertheless the same corporate pride spurred them to mount on appropriate occasions ceremonies as brilliant as a Veronese painting ; and their official head the Mayor, styled " lord " during his term of office and always knighted afterwards, dressed his wife like a duchess and kept such state " during his term of office as no public officer in Europe may compare in port and countenance."

On the other, the west side of St. Paul's, beyond the Temple, lay the capital city of Westminster. As one approached it from the City, making for its focal point at Whitehall, one passed along the muddy trickle of the Fleet through teeming human warrens from among which rose the massive stone and brick town houses of the higher nobility—Norfolk and Arundel and Essex House, Baynard's Castle, historic residence of the Earls of Sussex, and Durham Place, in the early part of the reign the Spanish Embassy, where Adelphi Terrace lately was, each with its water-gate and landing stairs on the Thames, and farther north and west the fine new mansions of William Cecil, Lord Burghley, and of Robert Dudley, Earl of Leicester, where Leicester Square now is. The streets, though from the architectural point of view considered remarkably handsome, were by all other standards narrow, crooked, ill-paved, noisome and at night dark and dangerous as well, so that the tenants of these houses and their suites whenever possible travelled by river.

The river was, in fact, the main boulevard of the capital, its fashionable thoroughfare, in a special sense its royal highway. On its banks stood nearly all the royal palaces—Greenwich, Whitehall, Hampton Court, Richmond and Windsor—as well as the royal arsenal at the Tower, the Mint nearby, the Houses of Parliament and the London residence of the Primate of England and permanent High Chaplain to the king ; and between these various points when the Court was in residence gaily painted and coloured barges moved up and down to the rhythmic propulsion of oars on the royal business. As well as the capital's chief highway, the river, with its thousands of swans, was also its most attractive playground, the scene in fair weather of water carnivals and once or twice in a famous frost of ice-carnivals, with all manner of sporting competitions, the most fantastically ingenious floats, fireworks and music. Beyond the bend in the river between the Abbey and Lambeth Palace it began to flow again through the northward-spreading fields and woods in which the followers of the Court practised their riding and shooting with the bow or gun and held their stately if not always decorous picnics—fashionable counterpart to the vigorous recreation of the populace in the fields to the east with the annual climax of St. Bartholomew's Fair at the end of August.

During most of the year Westminster, unlike the City with its perennial activity, presented the appearance of a placid backwater where the law-courts and lesser officialdom pursued their unhurried labours until the return of the Court caused it to burst into brilliant and bustling life. It is exceedingly difficult for later (as it would indeed have been for earlier) ages to recapture that transforming effect of the Court's presence because next to impossible fully to imagine what a Tudor Court signified. To do so it would be necessary to revive an emotion that has disappeared possibly for ever ; an emotion of which we perhaps catch a faint harmonic before the royal tombs in the Lady's Chapel at Westminster or at St. Denis or the Kapuzinergruft in Vienna, where for the moment religion and history seem to be part of one another. For the Tudor idea of royalty was of something definitely supernatural—a portion of divinity visibly surrounding a mortal. It can be traced over and over in Shakespeare and his contemporaries as a fundamental assumption, an unquestioning acceptance of an objective and unchangeable truth. Henry VII, round whom it first centred, symbolised it with an order for all mastiffs to be hanged for baiting lions, " their natural lords and sovereigns," and a fine falcon's neck wrung for daring to attack an eagle. One of Elizabeth's ministers formulated it with simple directness in rebuking opposition to her will with the reminder that, after all, " She is our God on earth."

But in addition to being the earthly household of this semi-divine being, the Court was also the centre of pretty nearly all the major activities of the State. The same officials who supervised its domestic concerns managed the affairs of the kingdom, both in their separate titular capacities and collectively as members of the Privy Council, the supreme advisory and executive body through whom the Queen determined and carried out her policies. The Lord Chamberlain, head of the household, and the Lord High Admiral, head of the Navy, the Vice-Chamberlain, who was also the Household Treasurer, and the Lord High Treasurer, who was the chief political minister, the Master of Horse in charge of the royal stables and the Master of the Ordnance, presumptive commander-in-chief in time of war, were alike members of the Council and of the court, much of the year resident in it. They were politicians and functionaries, administrators and—as members of the Courts of Request, High Commission and Star Chamber—judges all at the same time. It was very much as if the Cabinet, part of the judiciary, the Civil Service, the High Command of the Army and Navy, as well as the foreign embassies when the Court was on progress, lived and worked under one roof.

Yet even this did not exhaust the Court's significance. It not only enshrined the sovereign and housed her government, it summed up in itself the cultural aspirations of her subjects. Coming to court on business or out of curiosity, the provincial saw spread before him all the material splendour, all the physical objects of spiritual satisfaction, of which the local examples already presented to his vision had set it aflame. At the great stone entrance gate he would likely be passed at a jingling trot, or observe lolling in the green outer courtyard or against the walls of the long gleaming corridors through which he was conducted, " great trains and troops of serving men which attend upon the nobility of England in their several liveries, and with differences of cognisances upon their sleeves, whereby it is known to whom they pertain . . . much like to the show of the peacock's tail in full (spread) or some meadow garnished with infinite kinds and varieties of flowers." One thing that would at once have struck him was the comparative good order that these ordinarily unruly pests maintained, simply because the Queen would tolerate no nonsense in her immediate vicinity : a preference enforced at need by the removal, with the solemn panoply of a state execution, of an outstanding offender's right hand.

The visitor while waiting would observe about him in " the offices of the Court, Bibles, Acts and Monuments of the Church History, and lay Chronicles (as well as copies of the classics) lying about for the exercise of such as came into the same—whereby the strayer into the Court of England upon the sudden, shall rather imagine himself to come into some public school of the Universities, where many give ear to one that readeth, than into a Prince's palace." For the men who from these precincts ran the affairs of England, or merely hung about them by favour or in hope of preference, were one and all readers, with a taste kept pure by the practice of reprinting the choicest of the old for sheer lack of the indiscriminate new. Few of the courtiers did not speak at least one foreign language, and many knew several as well as Latin and Greek. Even the more boisterous sort of courtier was likely to be nearer the intellectual level of the patricians of the eighteenth century than the aristrocratic ruffians of the fourteenth, while if the visitor, his business concluded, took the opportunity to stroll into the surrounding fields, he might at a suitable hour have discovered the more scholarly of them, and not only the young but the middle-aged, indulging in quite astonishing feats of skill and strength.

Nor were these accomplishments exclusive to the men. Though the wives of the courtiers were not encouraged to reside within the establishment, it necessarily contained a large complement of women in attendance on the Queen ; and these contributed equally to make the Court a model for the country. They too read assiduously and with discrimination and knew their modern as well as the classic tongues. The able-bodied were expected to be as keen and capable in sports as the men, and all to be reasonably expert in needle-work and music, the younger in particular going in " much for lutes, cithernes, pricksong and all kinds of music when not in attendance on the Queen." Many wrote original works or translated from the lesser-known tongues into English or Latin ; many, in particular of the elder ones, were " skilful in surgery and distillation of waters, besides sundry artificial practices pertaining to the ornature and commendation of their bodies." And all were supposed to be skilled at a " number of delicate dishes of their own devising, mostly after the Portingale fashion."

Of their sisters of the middle-class apparently not so much was expected :

"With regard to the women," says the Dutch chronicler previously quoted, " they are entirely in the power of the men, except in matters of life and death, yet they are not kept so closely and strictly as in Spain and elsewhere. They are not locked up, but have free management of their household, like the Netherlanders and their other neighbours. They are gay in their clothing, taking well their ease, leaving house-work to the servant-maids, and are fond of sitting, finely dressed, before their doors to see the passers-by and to be seen of them. In all banquets and dinner-parties they have the most honour, sitting to the upper end of the board, and being served first. Their time is spent in riding, lounging, card-playing, and making merry with their gossips at child-bearings, christenings, churchings and buryings ; and all this conduct the men wink at, because such are the customs of the land. They much commend, however, the industry and careful habits of the German and Netherland women, who do the work which in England devolves upon the men. Hence, England is called the paradise of married women, for the unmarried girls are kept much more strictly. . ."

Ultimately the visitor would reach the royal apartments, comprising the Presence Chamber, where the Queen gave both her public audiences and frequent large-scale entertainments, the Privy Chamber where she transcated more informal business, and the galleried Bed Chamber where she pursued her recreations and entertained her familiars. Into the second two the visitor would be unlikely to penetrate unless he or his business were of exceptional consequence ; conversely, apart from such business, everybody and everything likely to interest him would towards late afternoon be found in the spacious Presence Chamber. There he would at last set eyes on the two individuals who personified the Court much as the Court summed up the current ideals of the nation. One of them, instantly recognisable by her flaming hair, pale face and strident voice, was the sovereign whose character and accomplishments made her the inspiration, the pride and the terror of Court and nation alike. The other, standing nearby—for they were never willingly far apart, even in the crowded Presence Chamber—was a tall, dark man, strikingly handsome, conspicuously well dressed even for that assembly, with features in which vivacity and haughtiness and a figure in which stateliness and grace were singularly blended : the Queen's reputed lover and undisputed favourite, Robert Dudley, Earl of Leicester.

For him the great majority of his countrymen cherished a hatred often as startling in its intensity as their love for her. In part the one emotion explained the other, the love expressing itself in a natural jealousy, distrust and resentment of the influence he wielded over her and the unparalleled power and wealth he had amassed through her favour. But there was another and profounder cause. It was an age of grandeur which spontaneously accorded him the nickname of *le Grand Esquire* or simply *Monsieur le Grand* : an age of adventure of which he was literally the arch-adventurer ; an age essentially enigmatic to which he contributed the most perplexing of riddles. It thus saw itself reflected in him, and not altogether liking what it saw, used him as a mirror against which it hurled back its dislike. The sinister designs it imputed to him, the thousand crimes and villanies of which it accused him (none of which it ever succeeded in proving), were less objective criticisms of his doings than projections of its own unacknowledged impulses. In short, its exaggerated hatred arose largely from the obscure recognition in him of the very qualities in itself that made him perhaps the most Elizabethan of Elizabethans.

Chapter Two

TUDOR AND DUDLEY

FOR THIRTY YEARS, from shortly after Elizabeth's accession in the autumn of 1558 until his death, Robert Dudley held first place in her heart without serious rival or interruption. To her subjects there seemed something supernatural if not positively unholy in this feat of fidelity. Constancy was a virtue as little expected in a woman, a creature " painted forth by nature to be weak, frail, impatient, feeble and foolish," as it was in a Renaissance prince, a species of which her father, whose fancy had roamed dissatisfied from woman to woman and whose trust from minister to minister, provided a standing example. To this infirmity of her sex and station Elizabeth was in general no exception. Her heart could be a possession scarcely less precarious than Henry VIII's. She loved men easily and loved to be loved by them ; and her love being one of the world's chief prizes, " many and great ones did strive for it," often to their chagrin and in the case of Seymour, the first excitement of her adolescence, and of Essex, the fond foible of her old age, to the loss of their presumptuous heads. Only Robert Dudley, of all those who at one time or another gained that wayward and coveted prize, seemed to have the secret of retaining it.

On the nature of that secret the speculation of the age managed to reach a substantial measure of agreement. Was there, asks Camden in Book I of his *Historie of the most Renowned and Victorious Princesse Elizabeth; late Queen of England;* was there " a Vertue of his, wherefor he gave some shadowed tokens " to her alone ? Or did he owe his success to " their common condition of imprisonment under Queen Mary," when they faced death together at twenty ? Or should the explanation rather be looked for in " nativity and the hidden consent of the stars at the hour of his birth, and therefore a straight conjunction of their minds ? "

Between these three hypotheses the father of Elizabethan historians hesitated to pronounce judgment : " A man cannot easily say." His contemporaries, however, failed to see why not and plumped for the third by a resounding majority. As early as the third year of the reign the authorities found occasion to punish, among others, " five or six clergymen . . . as wizards and necromancers in whose possession were found calculations of the nativity of the Queen and Lord Robert," but without any apparent effect save to stimulate further research in this direction. Camden himself apparently came in the end to the same conclusion, for reverting to the topic of Leicester in Book III of his *Historie*; he speaks of Elizabeth simply as " one to whom by reason of a certain conjunction of their minds and that haply through a hidden conjunction of the stars (which the Greek astrologers term Synastria) he was most dear."

Synastria was not the only influence at work at the hour of their birth, however, to create a pre-natal affinity between them. The social unit known as the House, larger than the family but smaller than the Roman *gens* or Scottish clan, constituted a powerful working bond between blood relations of the ruling classes ; a similar tie of sentiment and interest often united more or less permanently two or more of such houses in an alliance of almost dynastic force ; and of these ties none was more potent than that between the houses of Tudor and Dudley, which coincided almost exactly with the duration of the Tudor monarchy. The curious fascination which three generations of Dudleys exercised upon three generations of Tudors, who thrice made and twice ruined them— and were twice almost ruined by them—is one of the fateful facts of English history.

It began with the return of Henry Tudor, third in descent from a Welsh steward, from exile in France to claim the throne of England. At that time, 1485, an inconspicuous freeholder named Dudley farmed the not very important manor of Atherington in Sussex, concerted marriages for his children with those of the neighbouring land-owners, and sent his eldest son Edmund to read law at Gray's Inn. He claimed to be sprung from the baronial family of Sutton, Lords Dudley, a mixed Norman-Saxon stock so decayed that the present holder of the title was popularly known as Lord Quondam ; but the connection, though ably argued by his descendants, was contested with equal heat and ability by their enemies, whose genealogists grafted them upon an itinerant carpenter from the town of Dudley in Worcestershire. The evidence is confused, and his real origins impartial opinion leaves uncertain. Equally obscure are the reasons that prompted Henry Tudor, shortly after the victory at Bosworth Field which gave him the throne as Henry VII, to select Edmund Dudley, then a young lawyer of twenty-two, for a career in the royal service.

It proved a prosperous connection for both. The new king needed money, and since in those simple days the virtues of taxation were still largely undiscovered, Dudley, a genius at putting " hateful business into good language," perfected the only alternative method of getting it, namely, stealing it for him. With the collaboration of another lawyer, Richard Empson, son of a Towcester sieve-maker, he exhumed obsolete crimes and antique flaws in land titles, packed juries and bribed or browbeat judges, and so by the end of the reign contrived to transfer an impressive quantity of private property into the coffers of the Crown. In recognition of these services he received not only a share in the takings but a special prize in the form of a ward, Elizabeth Grey, daughter of Edward late Viscount de Lisle, through whom he gained, when in due course he married her, control of an extensive estate and for his three sons by her the right to display in their arms the historic quarterings of Beauchamps and Nevilles, Earls of Warwick, and of Talbots, Earls of Shrewsbury.

Then, in 1509, Henry VII died and a youth of eighteen succeeded him as Henry VIII. The new king, a lover of popularity, invited all who had suffered any wrong in his father's time to come to him for redress ; almost as one man the English people rose and shouted for the blood of Empson and Dudley. With the treasure they had amassed for his father now comfortably in his possession Henry had no further use for the pair's talents and graciously consented. On August 28th, 1510, Edmund's head fell on Tower Hill despite much tearful ingenuity on his part to save it. His wife and children, stripped of their patrimony and even in sort of legal existence by Act of Attainder, descended upon the charity of relatives and friends. Thus ended the first Dudley cycle.

The second was even more spectacular. Though off to a slower start, before it was over it all but whirled the Dudleys alongside the Tudors on to the throne. Edmund's eldest son John, then a boy of nine, was adopted by Sir Richard Guildford, his father's partner in many a profitable outrage. If the Dudley blood were cleansed John would be eligible to recover a tidy inheritance, and Sir Richard, with the future of a small daughter Jane to provide for, set to work. It took time ; to be greedy and an upstart were the two conjoint crimes the age found it hardest to forgive ; in fact, it never did forgive them in the Dudleys. Nevertheless after two years Sir Richard extracted the King's permission to bring a bill into Parliament for the repeal of the attainder. Nine years later, in 1523, as Jane entered on her task of replenishing the Dudley stock, John began on his of refurbishing the Dudley name. From his first venture, a campaign in France under the King's brother-in-law, Charles Brandon, Duke of Suffolk, he won a knighthood on the field for gallantry. Nine years more elapsed, however, during which Jane bore him four sons and a daughter or two, before Henry VIII signified, through John's appointment to be Master of the Armoury in the Tower, that he had at last forgiven him for cutting his father's head off.

It was at this favourable tide in the Dudley fortunes that Jane was delivered of her fifth son, Robert, and the King's new wife, Anne Boleyn, of a daughter, his second, Elizabeth. Of the circumstances surrounding the infant Robert's birth, where it happened and when, nothing definite is known. It may have taken place in the Tower but more probably in his parents' small manorhouse on the river out towards Chelsea. As to the date, tradition places it in 1532 or 1533, with 1533 able to adduce in support of its claim the planetary collusion, later detected and exposed by the astrologers, to link his nativity with Elizabeth's ; though what precise conjunction existed between the motion of the planets in the early morning of September 7th, 1533, her birthday, and an unknown hour on an unspecified June 24th, which he once lightly alleged to be his, is now perhaps beyond the power of astrological science to determine.

Another nine years passed, each of them marked by John

Dudley's further advance in the royal favour. His feats in the tilt-yard, where he unfailingly tumbled opposition from the saddle with the magic in the tip of his painted lance, would alone have recommended his " very comely person " to the fat monarch who had in his youth fancied himself the peerless champion at this sport ; but he also happened to be the ablest commander both by land and sea that had yet served the Tudors. His family was installed at court and the younger members, including Robert, who was considered both in looks and character most nearly to resemble him, brought up to share the play and studies of the Princess Elizabeth and, later, the heir-apparent Prince Edward, born in 1537. In 1542 he was raised to the peerage with the title, derived from his mother, of Viscount de Lisle, and made Warden of the Scottish Marches and Lord Admiral for life. A year later he became a knight of the Garter for sweeping the French out of the Channel and storming Boulogne, the following year a member of the Privy Council, and shortly before Henry's death in January, 1547, Lieutenant-General of all His Majesty's armed forces.

The transition from one reign to the next, which had ruined Edmund, did not halt his son's rise even momentarily. Henry had designated him by will one of the sixteen regents to govern the kingdom during Edward VI's minority ; and though the new King's maternal uncle, Edward Seymour, Duke of Somerset, over-rode the will and made himself sole Protector, Dudley was able to name virtually his own terms for agreeing. They were not modest. Soon the Bear and the Ragged Staff,[1] distinctive badge of the Earls of Warwick, proclaimed on his servants' liveries the revival of the historic title borne by no subject since the passing of the King-Maker. Other good things followed, rich sinecures, and castles galore—Warwick Castle, " the seat of my ancestors " on his mother's side, and Dudley Castle from his somewhat hypothetical ancestors on the other side, together with the revenues needful for his new dignity.

And even all this was merely by the way. After the long and brutal despotism of Henry VIII the country fell into a disorder which the well-meaning Protector found it impossible to control. In the spring of 1549 his own brother planned a rebellion with intent to marry the Princess Elizabeth and seize the government ; though he was suppressed and beheaded, the affair shook Somerset's credit besides saddling him with the shameful responsibility for his brother's death. A few months later the peasants of East Anglia, maddened by the enclosure of the common lands, broke loose against the whole existing order and started for London under the leadership of Jack Kett. Terrified out of their wits, the owning classes shrieked for the new Earl of Warwick, " the best man of warre in the realm," to save them from the oncoming hordes. He did so, at Dussindale in Norfolk, in a battle which only his theatrical chivalry redeemed from simple massacre, and returned to find the country at his feet. A bloodless revolution in October ended with Somerset in the Tower and Warwick dictator of England.

His arrogance grew uncontrollable, his taste for magnificence insatiable. As an example of the power of sheer unscrupulous genius to get on without popularity he stands alone in English history. By way of following he had only the extreme Protestants, the " hot Puritans " of a later date, who out of impatience with Somerset's limping advance towards root-and-branch Reform, had adopted him as their " Moses and Joshua " rolled into one. The rest of his countrymen loathed him for his greed and his overbearing temper ; particularly the great, whom he treated as if they had been forward menials and he the son of a Duke instead of a crooked financier. He made the Lords of the Council " wait upon him daily at his house to learn his pleasure " ; from under their noses he snatched the estates and perquisites for which their mouths watered. When he had himself created Duke of Northumberland —the first subject unconnected with the royal blood ever to hold ducal rank—their fingers itched to knife him for his presumption. But his headsmen struck quicker than his enemies' assassins, and with the young King in fascinated subjection to him, he had little to fear in the way of a general rising of the people.

Only the inscrutable future—that ever-present terror of the adventurer—appeared to need guarding against, and it he did his best to secure by means of his children. His younger sons he made the inseperable companions of the King's study and Bed-Chamber, so that it became practically impossible to see him day or night without a Dudley present. His eldest daughter Mary he married to Edward's most intimate friend, young Henry Sidney of Penshurst, and betrothed his second, Catherine, to the eldest son of the Earl of Huntingdon, a descendant of the House of York with a contingent claim to the throne. For his heir, named like him John, he negotiated, as a sort of counter-insurance, an alliance with a daughter of his late rival, the Protector Somerset, shortly before finally making up his mind to send the ex-Protector to the block on the charge " of practising the death of the King's Councillors."

Of his remaining children of marriageable age there remained only Robert to dispose of, and for him he was apparently content with a more modest connection. On May 24th, 1550, he signed a contract for the young man's marriage with the only daughter and heiress of Sir John Robsart, a substantial Norfolk landowner, both the principals being then about seventeen. Whether he actively contrived the match in the belief that it was the best he could reasonably expect for a son so far down on the list of seniority, or whether Robert independently met and fell in love with Amy Robsart and persuaded his ambitious parent to bless the union there is no means of knowing. A stipulation in the contract that it should be carried into effect only " if the said Robert and Amye will thereunto condescend and agree " suggests the ordinary conventional arrangement initiated by the two elders and passively endorsed by the two younger parties to it. But it is also possible to conjecture that William Cecil, reviewing Robert's fitness to marry Elizabeth in an exceedingly important memorandum drawn up a few years later, may have had the marriage with Amy in mind when he noted in reflecting upon Robert's history, " *Nuptiae carnales a laetitia incipiunt et in luctu terminantur.*"

In either event it started out under the brightest of auspices. The two fathers made comfortable settlements, and the King not only offered his palace at Sheen for the wedding but honoured it with his presence, afterwards recording in his diary that amongst the festivities " there were several gentlemen who did strive which should first take away a goose's head which hanged alive on two cross-posts." The couple then settled in Norfolk, where for three years Robert played the part of a young married squire. Probably even then he had no intention of keeping it up for ever—no Dudley after his great-grandfather was long able to endure the quiet life—though in later years he often looked back on it with a sort of poetic nostalgia, or thought he did, like so many other successful worldlings of that hard-driven time. In point of fact it must have been pleasant enough while it lasted, with his father's reflected glory and his father-in-law's local influence to bolster his youthful importance in the eyes of his tenants and neighbours, and plenty of society for the athletic pastimes at which he was to remain a notable performer well into middle-age. There were also plenty of more serious employments to occupy him, not only the management of fairly extensive and somewhat scattered estates, but the office, jointly bestowed upon him and his father-in-law by the King, of Steward of Manor Rising and Constable of its famous castle, and attendance upon various great magnates like the Earl of Sussex in the impressive duties of Lord Justice and Lord Lieutenant of the county. An occasional journey to Court, at his father's prompting and without Amy as a rule, provided a stimulating change and an opportunity to renew useful contacts.

Suddenly from this pleasant and promising routine he was whirled into the adventure that for the second time laid the Dudleys low. Round the beginning of May, 1553, the Duke of Northumberland learned from the King's doctors that the fifteen-year-old consumptive had only a few weeks more to live. After him loomed in the legitimate order of succession his elder sister Mary, daughter of Henry VIII's first wife Katharine of Aragon, and behind the Duke's expectant enemies—the Catholics on whose faith he had trampled, the old nobility whose aristocratic appetites he had thwarted. There remained no alternative but to overthrow legitimacy or wait supinely for it to overthrow him.

With superb energy he rose to the challenge. Nearly twenty years before Henry VIII had disinherited both his daughters as bastards. Ten years later he restored them with the provision, subsequently ratified by Parliament, that if all three of his children died childless the throne should pass to the issue of his younger sister Mary, wife of Charles Brandon, Duke of Suffolk. What had been done by one royal will and undone by another might be redone by a third. Northumberland drew up a "devise" which simply lifted the King's sisters out of the order of succession and declared his rightful heir to be his cousin Lady Jane Grey, Mary Brandon's eldest granddaughter. At the same time he hurried forward a marriage between Lady Jane and his eldest unmarried son Guildford with the idea of making them joint sovereigns. On June 21st the King, who had feverishly collaborated in brow-beating his ministers and judges into submission, signed the devise, and two days later died.

Northumberland threw a double cordon of guards round Greenwich Palace to keep the news from leaking into the country and stealthily seized the Tower with its store of treasure and munitions. At the same time he sent orders to close the ports, after which he needed only to gain possession of Mary, who was on her way south from Norfolk to attend her brother in his illness, for his revolution to be complete. This crucial task he entrusted to Robert, whom he sent with a detachment of horse to meet and hurry her quietly into the capital on the pretext that the King had taken a turn for the worse. It was the first military experience of England's Commander-in-Chief and Viceroy upon the continent in her struggle with Spain.

By some secret conduit word reached Mary at Hunsdon in Hertfordshire ahead of Robert's searching cavalry. She turned and fled to Kenninghall, a seat of the Dukes of Norfolk, those blue-blooded Howards whom her father had so merrily decimated but who nursed an even more passionate grudge against the upstart house of Dudley. There she issued a proclamation asserting her right to her people's love and loyalty and fled on a step ahead of Robert's swift pursuit. He followed, picking up reinforcements on the way under his eldest brother Warwick, but she continued out of his reach to the Howard fastness of Framlingham. Robert gave up the chase at King's Lynn, where he had his sister-in-law Lady Jane proclaimed for the first time and paused to await his father's further orders.

They never came. News trickled through instead that the country was rising for Mary ; that Northumberland, urged by his accomplices, had reluctantly left London, much doubting the fidelity of those same accomplices, to undertake her capture in person ; that London had in fact revolted and his confederates either turned against him or been imprisoned ; and finally that the Duke himself had been arrested in Cambridge and brought back to the capital a prisoner. Presently a detachment of the royal forces appeared at King's Lynn to claim Robert's own surrender and lead him by way of Framlingham to join the others of his family in the Tower.

On August 18th Northumberland appeared with his eldest son before a jury composed largely of his late confederates to plead guilty to high treason. Nothing in his life became him less than the leaving of it. He wrote grovelling letters to the Queen, cringed before the colleagues who had been prudent enough to abandon him in time. It all availed him nothing. In the early morning of August 22nd he left the Gate House for the fatal patch of greensward his father had had to tread forty-three years before almost to the day. A few minutes later, supporting himself against the east rail of the scaffold, he delivered his valedictory to the curious crowd below. It was the kind of occasion from which many a lesser man snatched a radiant shred of immortality ; he utilised it for a last orgy of cant and self-pity : " But not I alone the original doer thereof, I assure you, for there were some others procured the same, but I will not name them, for I will hurt no man now. . . ." Like two incurable flaws in the brilliant Dudley metal ran the parallel impulses to evoke hatred in prosperity and to blame adversity on other people.

They buried him alongside his victim the Protector, between two Queens of England, Anne Boleyn and Catherine Howard, by the high altar of St. Peter's Church in the Tower. In another wing of the same institution his widow and five sons[1] meanwhile waited to learn how far offended Majesty intended to visit on the third generation of their shattered house the sins of the second.

[1] Jane Dudley bore thirteen children in all, eight sons and five daughters, but only seven were alive at their father's death—John Earl of Warwick, Ambrose, Robert, Guildford, Henry, Mary Lady Sidney and Catherine Countess of Huntingdon

Chapter Three

Months elapsed before the new government resolved what to do with them. It had more pressing matters to occupy its attention that autumn of 1553—a resettlement of religion, the Queen's marriage and, not least, the distribution of Northumberland's property amongst its members and friends. The bailiffs not only entered into possession of castles and manors but stripped them of their contents down to the Duchess's very " stuff, apparel and silks " ; the fruits of twenty-five years of public service and unappeasable rapacity changed hands in less than as many weeks. By the time the strong, the noisy and the deserving had satisfied their claim on the late dictator's estate, it had shrunk to little if any more than his widow's original marriage portion.

She herself was soon released, in part to assist the authorities in the melancholy business of completing the inventory of her belongings before carting them off; her youngest son Henry followed soon afterwards because of his youth. The rest remained behind in varying states of suspense. John, the eldest, condemned at the same time as his father, lived on at the Queen's pleasure. So presently, after four months awaiting trial, did Ambrose, the next in age, Guildford and Lady Jane, who all three on a dark November morning left the Tower for the Guildhall in company with Archbishop Cranmer, and returned to it a few hours later likewise under sentence of death. Robert's case for some reason was kept for separate consideration.

Had nothing further occurred it is probable that the whole of the little company would have escaped with their lives. Tudor justice may have been harsh, but its mysterious workings left room for a large and capricious play of mercy ; and Mary Tudor was by nature a merciful woman. But the country was already brewing up for another crisis. It had not yet made up its mind whether it wanted to be Catholic or Protestant, and definitely objected to what looked like a determination on Mary's part to hustle it into a decision by engaging herself to her cousin Philip, the heir of Spain. When the Count of Egmont came over at the New Year to begin arrangements for the marriage the Londoners, never very affectionate to foreigners, hurled insults and their small sons hard-packed snowballs after the plumed caps of the gentlemen in his train—forerunners of the more deadly missiles to follow whose significance seems to have escaped the unhappy Queen peering short-sightedly through her faded blue eyes at her fiancé's portrait, oblivious of the knowing mirth of those about her or apparently of anything but the hunger stored up in her wizened body by thirty-seven affection-starved years.

It was in this atmosphere that Robert Dudley took his place behind Bishop Ridley in a little procession that wound through the City's crooked snow-covered streets to the Guildhall, the axe with its edge turned away from them gleaming ahead. The tribunal under the presidency of the Earl of Sussex, whom he had not long since attended as honoured junior in similar ceremonies, made short work of the business. Robert pleaded guilty to complicity in his father's treason, heard Sussex sentence him to be hanged, cut down alive and quartered, and returned (in the historic phraseology of the death sentence) whence he came, the axe this time pointing its sharp edge towards him.

Scarcely had the door of his prison clanged behind him than the bursting storm almost wrenched it open again. Sir Thomas Wyatt led an army from Kent across the Thames down on London as Lady Jane's father, the Duke of Suffolk, whom Mary had pardoned for his part in the Northumberland affair, stirred up simultaneous risings amongst the Protestants of the West Country and the Midlands. So far as they had a common purpose it was to depose Mary, marry her half-sister Elizabeth to Edward Courtenay, Earl of Devon and heir of the White Rose, and set the young couple on the throne in the Protestant interest. Only the Queen's superb courage defeated them. As Wyatt's men sent her guards flying down Knightsbridge to Hyde Park Corner, as Norfolk's own train-bands deserted to them and her panic-stricken ministers urged her to save herself by flight, she met the emergency with a typical Tudor demand on the loyalty of her people : "What I am ye right well know—I am your Queen . . . like true men stand fast against these rebels, both your enemies and ours ; and fear them not, for I assure you I fear them nothing at all." Against the power in that appeal Wyatt hurled himself in vain. At Ludgate Circus he stuck, bogged in the hostility of a people who might grumble at the dynasty but took it as one of the more precious if not quite perfect gifts of God. Three days later Guildford and his wife were executed for their part in Northumberland's conspiracy as a reprisal for her father's participation in Wyatt's.

The three remaining Dudleys shuddered but survived. Though often in the days, and especially the nights, that followed they must have started at every sight or sound of their gaolers, expecting to learn that their room had been preferred to their company. For the Tower could no longer begin to meet the demands on its space. They saw it filled, evacuated by the headsman, refilled overnight. The lesser prisons, teeming with its overflow, disgorged their own surpluses into the churches, where " the poorest sort lay eighty in a heep " until the gallows, which sprouted in ones, twos and threes all over London and the country round, began to relieve the congestion at the rate of as many as four hundred a day.

On a cold rainy morning towards the end of March a barge shot down the tide from Westminster to the Tower with a fresh prisoner, a tall, white-faced, red-haired young woman of nineteen. As she stepped on the landing stairs her legs crumpled under her and she sank weeping on the wet stones. She was the Queen's half-sister, the Lady Elizabeth, lately arrested on the suspicion of having encouraged Wyatt to strike on her behalf. For a moment she sat there under the pelting downpour, empty of hope for almost the first and last time in her life . . . remembering beyond a doubt her mother who had also passed through that gate and failed to come out alive : her father's saucy harlot, Anne Boleyn, on whose account Mary so bitterly hated her for the wrong done her own unhappy mother. Her poise partly restored, the girl stood up, said to her sceptical escort, " I come no traitor, but as true a woman to the Queen's Majesty as any now living," and ascended with her usual proud gait to the Keeper's house.

After that she recovered quickly. The Crown's lawyers, as sceptical as her escort, worked over her mercilessly to prove her statement false ; then gave it up with the verdict whose substance the Queen herself expressed in an exasperated sigh of " God knows ! " In May Elizabeth departed to a less perilous confinement in one of her own country houses.

But not before Robert Dudley, according to a tradition already full grown in his lifetime, had taken better advantage of her stay than had the lawyers. For it was during those two months that he contrived to meet his distinguished fellow-prisoner and make her fall in love with him. Certainly a better setting for the purpose would be hard to imagine. A young woman with a complicated emotional history, a young man notably handsome and with a bold gay tongue to take her out of herself after long hours of deadly fencing with thin-lipped curiosity . . . both of them at each encounter excitingly aware that one or the other might no longer be alive to keep the tryst on the morrow. The fact that the young man happened to be married would have created no awkwardness, quite the opposite in fact, in the eyes of a young woman most unlikely ever to be allowed a husband of her own choosing ; indeed, in the circumstances, ever to have a husband at all.

Unluckily tradition, as so often with romantics, discredits its own story by trying to improve on it. Wherever the two first met it was not in the Tower. John Dudley had made a point of his offspring mingling with the royal children as often and freely as possible, so that Robert's first presentation to Elizabeth must have occurred when both were still at the stage of declining *amo* in shrill treble for Master Roger Ascham. It is not even easy to understand how an acquaintance formed in the grim old fortress should have found occasion to ripen under the cold vigilance that surrounded Elizabeth during her confinement. That part of it cannot be dismissed, however, as altogether improbable. Love now and then circumvented the Tower's locksmiths like any other ; and sometimes it even happened that a young couple confined in different parts of it for the crime of having fallen in love contrary to public

policy, managed to disconcert public policy still further by convert-
ing their prison into a maternity hospital.[1]

By the time Elizabeth departed for Woodstock the country had
shaken down into a state of sullen resignation and Mary was able
to put away her gallows in favour of other decorations more appropriate to the welcome of a bridegroom. The Dudleys, now fairly
certain of their lives unless something turned up, settled back to
calculate the chances of an act of royal grace that should throw
them out into the world to begin life again on practically nothing.

So far as practicable the government generally spared its
prisoners of state the meaner miseries of confinement. The three
Dudleys received £2 3s. 4d. a week each for " diet " (Warwick, as
the eldest, being granted an extra 4d.), 13s. 4d. for two servants
apiece and the same amount for wood, coal and candles—or at least
these sums were allotted to the Lieutenant of the Tower for their
keep. The airy " leades " of the Bell Tower were thrown open to
them for exercise, and their wives permitted to visit them bringing
additional comforts and news from the outside.

Yet the boredom, particularly when evening came, must often
have been excruciating. The walls of their cells still exhibit their
testimonials to it in the form of various patient carvings . . . a
ROBART DUDLEY executed by the owner of that name in the
room he originally occupied alone on the ground floor of the
Beauchamp Tower ; a JANE pathetically incised by the husband
for whom she had such little use in the large octagonal chamber he
shared with Warwick on the floor above ; Warwick's own name
surmounted by two bears and ragged staves in high relief encircled
with roses, acorns, gillyflowers and honeysuckle representing the
initials of his four brothers—R. A. G. H.—as the sculptor states in
a bit of verse beneath. A sprig of oak, the personal device of
" R. D.," later blossomed stonily in the same apartment after
Guildford's death and Robert's removal upstairs to join Warwick.

The anniversary of their commitment came round and with it
the hot weather, harbinger of the Tower's dreaded annual guest.

---

[1] Among the better known examples are Somerset's son, the Earl of Hertford,
who there had two children by Lady Jane Grey's sister Catherine, and Sir Walter
Raleigh, whose second son was born during an imprisonment imposed upon him
by Elizabeth for having secretly married one of her maids of honour.

Nearly every summer transformed London into a stinking pest-house, especially the low-lying parts of it stretching dankly along the river. It was apparently these successive waves of plague in their chief current form of " sweating sickness " which had already carried off Robert's five small brothers and sisters. The thought of what the crowded old prison might have been like at that season nauseates the imagination ; even at the best of times spacious country houses had to be vacated after several months in order to be rendered " sweet " again for human occupancy. Warwick sickened first ; Robert, his cell-mate, and Ambrose, alone in the Nun's Bower after Henry's release, fearfully awaited their turn.

Meanwhile their mother floated on the fringes of the Court like some sorrowing, tenacious ghost, to plead with any one who would listen to her for her son's freedom. But her voice failed to be heard in the excitement of the Court's departure for Winchester, where it converged on another procession equally brilliant coming up from Southampton to attend the Prince of Spain at his marriage on July 25th. Undiscouraged, she attached herself on its return to the Spanish ladies whose husbands were now such a power in the land that they scarcely dared venture out for fear of being assaulted by the populace. From her little store she courted one with a bit of lace or embroidery, another with a rare trinket, a third with an exotic pet . . . and all of them unconsciously with pity for her own indomitable self. On October 18th, 1554, their intercession won a free pardon for her sons. Three days later Warwick died at his brother-in-law Sir Henry Sidney's castle of Penshurst.

One task more Jane Dudley set herself, to remove the attainder from the sons remaining to her, but she did not live to accomplish it. By the New Year of 1555 she knew that she was dying, so she called for pen and ink and with her own hand distilled her maternal anguish into a long and remarkable will : " my verie Harte and Mynde in the bestowing of my goodes and landes, as I would have it, myn own self hath done it." To " those that did my sonnes good " went the rest of her sad little chattels—her " book clock that hath the sun and the moon on it " to a Spanish lord, " that is beyond the seas," to the Duchess of Alba her green parrot, " having nothing worthy of her else," with a prayer " to continue a good

ladye to all my children, as she has begun." Ambrose, now his
father's heir, inherited the manor of Hales Owen, the only one of
any importance left her, " by God's law and man's my very own
land, by my lord my dear husband's gift." Robert and Henry
received an income of fifty marks (£33) a year charged on other
land, Robert's wife a gown of wrought velvet, Henry's another of
" black pinkt velvet."

Then the fact of her sons standing " presently attainted of high
treason " apparently struck her in all its terrible significance : the
law might intervene to deny them any right of inheritance whatever, so in a final clause she made everything over to her four
executors, " trusting in their fidelity " not to betray the true heirs.
And after that there was nothing more she could do but implore
Philip and Mary, her executors, her friends, everybody, over and
over to be befriend her children and protect their interests under
the will " although it be not in such due form and order as it should
have been." She died on January 22, 1555, and was buried in the
parish church of Chelsea, with "little solemnity," as she had directed,
" for I had liefer a thousandfold my debts to be paid and the poor
to be given unto than any pompe to be showed upon my wretched
carcass, that hath had at times too much in this world." A monument
in coloured brass affixed to the wall of the church told with wifely
pride of the thirteen sons and daughters she had borne to " the high
and mighty prince, John Dudley, Duke of Northumberland, K.G.,
etc., etc.," until church and monument alike were shattered to
fragments on a winter's night nearly four hundred years later.

Only a few hints, most of them of a later time, indicate how
Robert lived and on what during the next two and a half years.
Probably his wife and his father-in-law saw more of him then than
they ever had before or ever would again. Though his mother's
will was admitted to probate, the Crown had sequestered practically
everything he owned, as well as Amy's dowry, but John Robsart
had plenty more, and there could have been no question of keeping
the wolf from the door. Nevertheless the routine of sheep-shearing
and fold-mending, of planting and selling, must have been an
excessively dull one for a young man used to the pace and glitter

of courts and conscious of the need for a far more exacting call on his abilities.

The domestic side of his life cannot have done much to brighten the rest of it. His wife had grown up in a position not altogether good for her character, that of her father's recognised heiress though the youngest child in a household full of other children ; for her mother, who died the year before her marriage to Robert, had already had four by a previous husband, Roger Appleyard, another Norfolk squire, when John Robsart, a bachelor with an illegitimate son, married her rather late in life. Otherwise not much is known of Amy—extraordinarily little considering she died the heroine of a scandal that rocked the world—but that little suggests that their straitened existence was no more to her taste than her husband's. He at least could satisfy in the commercial side of farming a certain natural aptitude for business and in his leisure hours he had his sports and books ; virtual necessities of life to any one educated at the court of Henry VIII. Amy could scarcely read or write (in her two extant letters she was responsible only for the initial of her signature), disliked housekeeping so sincerely that she gave it up the first chance she got, and doted on all the feminine extravagances they could neither afford nor have found much occasion to display. A docile, luxurious creature, on the evidence of those two letters, kind-hearted and uncertain of herself, as readily frightened by good fortune as depressed by bad.[1]

Whatever physical attraction originally existed between the two had soon dwindled, at least on Robert's side, to indifference ; even before his committal to the Tower he was in the habit of leaving her for long periods and the walls of his cell record no longing for her, though she apparently visited him there once or twice. Very early, certainly no later than the dreary interval after his release, he must have realised that his marriage would never satisfy the four ruling passions of his nature—power and possessions unbounded, with children to inherit them and women of the kind to which he

[1] Both letters were written several years later, though their exact dates are uncertain. One, to a steward of her husband's named Flowerdew, relates to the sale of some wool, the other adds to an impressive list of purchases from a London tailor an order for a velvet gown "with such a collar as you make my rosse taffyta gown."

would gravitate to the end of his days : high-born, subtle, worldly. Amy would not only never help him to succeed, she was sterile and clinging and commonplace.

What she felt about it is harder to know. Her letter to the steward Flowerdew, written after the great change in their fortunes, indicates a timorous affection if little remaining joy ; and Robert's whole subsequent career exists to prove how hard it was for any woman who fell in love with him ever to get over it. In part, perhaps, because of his natural mastery of those little courtesies and attentions which he continued to show Amy even after they had begun to live apart.

He would not have remained buried in Norfolk two and a half years, he would not have remained there a month, if anything else had been open to him. But there was nothing. His small military experience offered no outlet, since England was still at peace despite the reiterated prophecies of the Queen's critics that her marriage must sooner or later involve her in Spain's interminable quarrel with France. He had been trained for none of the professions, like so many of his contemporaries with a career to make ; he and his brothers had not even followed the new fashion of going to Oxford or Cambridge for a few terms. He could read Latin and Italian with ease, had a natural taste for mathematics (to the detriment of his classics, mourned Roger Ascham, who admired his intellect), and a specialised knowledge of " good and sound writers," according to a scholarly Secretary of State who knew him from boyhood, " on the best used governments and chief laws that have been made in all ages." Useful accomplishments for a courtier and public servant but not of much use for anything else.

The court allured him as the flame the moth, just as brightly and as dangerously. The burning of the Protestants had begun in February of 1555, many of the new religion had fled abroad, many of the rest stayed to plot at home. For an attainted person the capital was a good place to keep away from, nevertheless Robert made at least one journey there in the early summer of that year Apparently he and his brothers lent their presence to some furtive gatherings in Saint Paul's—common headquarters for money-changers, prostitutes and political agitators—for in July they received a stern warning from the authorities to withdraw to the country and stay there. The odds became still greater that none of them would ever set foot inside Court so long as Mary had anything to say in the matter. And Mary was just turned forty.

But she was in love, with a jealous desperation that alternated between tearing Philip's portrait to strips with her fingernails when she heard tales of his infidelities and sending relays of couriers to Brussels, whither he had returned not long after their marriage, with agonised prayers for his return. By and by he did return, briefly, to wheedle the wife who could deny him nothing into the war with France, as the wise had long ago predicted he would. To the Dudleys the long-awaited chance had come. Robert tried to raise his own company of forty gentlemen to go out under his command and for their equipment sold lands to the annual value of a hundred marks, twice the amount of his mother's legacy.[1] But only five of the forty made good their promise—continental wars were never popular with Englishmen and this one least of all —so he had to be satisfied with an appointment as Master of the Ordnance to the Earl of Pembroke, leader of the expeditionary force and an old associate of his father's. All three of the brothers distinguished themselves at the battle of Saint Quentin, where on August 10th, 1557, Spain and her English ally routed the French army sent to the relief of the Admiral Coligny, besieged within the town . . . and where Henry was killed, reducing the original thirteen of Jane Dudley's children to four, at which number they remained until it came to Robert's turn thirty-one years later. As a reward for his conspicuous gallantry in the action Philip sent him to Greenwich with special despatches for Mary—and perhaps a covering letter as well, for on March 7th, 1558, Parliament lifted the attainder.

So far Spanish gratitude could carry him, but apparently no farther. Or perhaps he no longer cared to exploit it further. The whole cause that Philip and Mary represented was plainly near

[1] Various parcels of his and Amy's inheritance had apparently been allowed to pass to them, including Hemesby Manor, near Yarmouth, in 1556, originally settled on him and Amy in 1553 by his father, and some of John Robsart's property on his death early in 1557. The motives and legal machinery involved are obscure and complicated.

collapse. In January the French had revenged their defeat at St. Quentin by the capture of Calais, England's last continental possession, a loss that so infuriated Mary's subjects that men began to doubt whether she could long keep her throne. But her life was already ebbing . . . for the second time she tried to delude herself, as she had done in 1555, that her illness was due to pregnancy, but the people merely mocked her with sardonic unbelief. The young, the unattached, the prudent hurried to Hatfield to kneel to the rising sun, Elizabeth. Robert sold some more land and sent her the proceeds, in case she should have to fight for her rights as Mary had had to fight for hers against his father. By the end of July he had taken up his station conveniently near at Hays in Kent.

Mary died in the early morning of November 17th. Immediately afterward Robert Dudley, "mounted on a snow-white steed, being well-skilled in managing a mounted horse," set off for Hatfield to lay his homage also at the new Queen's slender feet. The old chronicler does no more than justice to the outcome of that ride when he adds, "His beauty, stature and florrid youth recommended him."

Chapter Four

" THE KING THAT IS TO BE "

CLEARLY the one right way for a Queen to reward a young man come to proffer his services with so fine an equestrian flourish was to make him Master of her Horse. So Elizabeth thought—and did. And despite everything the gossips later said, the appointment probably represented her exact sentiments towards him at the time. The post happened to be about the most decorative at her disposal and he the candidate best qualified to fill it. Some sort of place he would have been entitled to merely on the strength of past affiliations, some vacancy created by the departure on political grounds of one of the functionaries inherited from Mary ; just as his brother Ambrose became Master of the Ordnance, an appointment that had as little to do with the new Queen's personal feelings as that of William Cecil, middle-aged and thoroughly domesticated, to be her Principal Secretary.

As for Robert, whether or not he secretly aspired as yet to be master of her heart, he was well satisfied for the present with being master of her stables. The pay was excellent, a thousand marks a year, with perquisites which brought it up to a round £1500. He had his own table at Court, of the quality " furnished for lords," gratis, of course, like the other high officers of the household, and a vast establishment under his orders : from a Chief Avenor at £40 a year down to four yeomen bit-makers at fourpence a day each, with a regiment of squires, riders, footmen, coachmen, littermen, saddlers and farriers in between.

In return he owed the by no means negligible duty of keeping the Court at all times provided with adequate land transport. That meant horses and mules to buy, both at home and abroad, for strength and for show ; to have them fit to drag the gorgeous painted carriages and heavy provision wagons over dusty, rutted hill and dale, and to bring them to the end of the day's journey looking reasonably representative of a royal " progress." And, amongst a host of other jobs, that of providing mounts for Elizabeth, one of the most enthusiastic horsewomen in Europe.

He loved the work. A born horseman, he loved his beasts and did as much as any man alive to improve the then inferior English breeds. Even more he loved the show ; the great public processions when he followed directly behind the Queen on his black charger and heard the cheers for her turn into gasps of admiration for himself. Nearly every Elizabethan of note had that sense of a crowd in relation to himself as a spectacle, but none of them ever seriously disputed Robert Dudley's supremacy in the art of dazzling by personal splendour. Years later, when Elizabeth had loaded him with honours and responsibilities enough to satisfy half a dozen men, he still refused to give up his Mastership of the Horse.

His first taste of this delight came on November 28th, when the Queen, after a five days' sojourn at the Charterhouse, made her official entrance by way of the Barbican and Cripplegate into the City. The Mayor rode first with the Garter King-at-Arms, who carried the sceptre ; after them followed the gentlemen pensioners in red damask bearing their gilded axes, the heralds in the colours of their respective orders, the tall footmen in crimson and silver stamped front and back with the cipher E. R. . . . " my lord of Pembroke bare the Queen's sword ; then came her Grace on horseback, in purple velvet with a scarf about her neck, and the sergeants of arms about her Grace ; and next after rode Lord Robert Dudley, the master of her horse." Guns and voices roared in unison, " the Wayts (wights) of the City sounded loud music " on their trumpets as the cavalcade passed through streets giddy with flags and tapestries, coloured cloths and silks, by way of the walls to Bishopsgate and thence to Mark Lane. There the Tower stood in sight, where Elizabeth was to remain for several weeks, its artillery chanting a welcome that lasted half an hour ; and its new mistress, remembering another, less joyous entry, said to those round her :

> " Some have fallen from being princes of this land to be prisoners in this place ; I am raised from being a prisoner in this place to be a Prince of this land. That dejection was a work of God's justice ; this advancement is a work of his mercy. . . ."

No one within the sound of her voice had a better right to a hearty " Amen " than the son of the " high and mighty prince " lying headless within.

The procession to Whitehall followed on December 23rd, the Coronation—grandest spectacle of all, when Robert rode behind Elizabeth's litter leading her white hackney draped in cloth of gold that hung to the ground—on January 15th, the opening of Parliament ten days later. And after that he receded for a while into the background as Elizabeth became absorbed in the more serious business of a reign.

There was no lack of it to keep her occupied that winter. An empty treasury, a mountain of debt, a currency hopelessly debased . . . a foreign war to liquidate, with the painful loss of prestige involved in signing away Calais, "jewel of England's crown," . . . a national Church to reconstruct which the Reformers, determined since their late troubles to blast forthwith a foundation for the New Jerusalem, and the Catholics, ready to be goaded into revolt if the old Roman edifice were materially altered, should both equally recognise as the House of God. Nevertheless by April things had somehow got pulled round. While Elizabeth pinched and hoarded, her financial wizard in Antwerp, Sir Thomas Gresham, conjured up loans on her non-existent credit. At Cateau-Cambrésis in Flanders her delegates hatched out by sheer obstinancy a treaty better than might have been expected ; in London her ministers pushed through Parliament a religious settlement from which almost everybody might hope for almost anything. With the coming of spring the tone of the country had so far improved that for the first time for years its inhabitants found themselves in agreement on what they wanted next. And Elizabeth, who knew only too well what that was and had been dodging it all winter, found herself facing a united demand that she get married as quickly as possible.

Her attitude towards the subject sometimes came close to impairing her wonderful popularity in which she took such joy. She repeatedly declared that she did not want to marry and would not do so unless she absolutely had to. . . . " It shall be a full satisfaction both for my name and my glory also, if when I shall let my last breath, it may be ingraven upon my marble tomb, Here lyeth Elizabeth, which reigned a Virgin and died a virgin." True, no one imagined that she meant the statement to be taken literaly : " Being a Maid, she must marry." How could a woman, a creature " painted forth by nature to be weak, frail, impatient, feeble and foolish "[1] possibly expect to keep the unruliest people in Europe, not to mention an imperfectly tamed aristocracy, in order ? Or enforce their rights and defend them against other princes' subjects ? Her sister's unfortunate choice in no way invalidated the argument ; it emphasised her need to make a wiser one, but otherwise did nothing to absolve her from the duty of finding someone " to relieve her of those labours which are fit only for men." While reserving to herself, naturally, those other labours possible only to women. For she was the last of her line, and if any accident befell her before she presented the realm with a small red-headed Tudor the only successor on whom it might positively count would be anarchy.

There was more to it even than that. For a country like England, surrounded by neighbours immensely stronger than herself, a powerful friend abroad constituted a basic necessity of life. The cost ordinarily ran high, sometimes to virtual loss of independence, but in this instance, with a Crown Matrimonial to offer for which nearly every reigning house in Europe had already entered into spirited bidding on behalf of its most eligible unmarried male, there appeared to be an excellent chance of obtaining one on favourable terms. Who knew but that in the looming struggle between the two great systems of thought, Catholic and Protestant, the ruler of England might not reassert its classic right to decide the continental balance ? " Everything depends on the husband this woman chooses," wrote the Spaniard de Feria, far and away the most important ambassador at Elizabeth's court, " for the King's will is paramount here in all things." It was a fair summary of the universal opinion . . . of everybody's, that is, except Elizabeth's own, who, with ten or a dozen suitors competing for her answer, encouraged,

---

[1] A note from John Knox's *First Blast of the Trumpet Against the Monstrous Regiment of Women*, recently sounded amidst general applause.

retreated, laughed at their pretensions or rebuked them to their faces for unmannerly rivalry, as if incredulous of her advisers' warning that unless she chose one before she succeeded in discouraging the lot, they could not be answerable for the consequence to herself or to England.

Officially, of course, Robert Dudley had no part in these high matters of policy. He was not a member of the Privy Council, and so far as one could tell held no views of his own on diplomacy, finance or religion. In fact, William Cecil, principal director of affairs under the Queen, thought he could be spared from the country altogether, for in November he put him down on the list of ambassadors to be sent to Elizabeth's fellow-sovereigns with the official announcement of her accession ; but something, or someone, intervened and when the rest scattered on their errands, Robert stayed behind. It may have been from this incident that Feria—to whose king in Brussels Cecil had intended Robert to go—gleaned the impression, which he transmitted to Philip in December, that the Queen was keeping her Master of the Horse in closer attendance than the nature of his departmental duties strictly required ; at any rate he held it strongly enough to include Robert amongst the four of Elizabeth's servants best worth bribing. Nothing came of this either, however. Robert thought it best to refuse the bribe and Feria, apparently soon convinced that gossip had exaggerated his influence, did not press him further. After that he incurred no further ambassadorial notice until spring.

By then the Queen of England's marriage had become the absorbing topic from Stockholm to Constantinople and her current residence a humming factory of rumours to account for the difficulties she was making about it. She had decided to marry, now, later ; to please her subjects, to please herself. " She spoke like a woman who will only accept a great prince " . . . " she would have no one she did not love." The odds on the various candidates in the City's betting books lengthened and contracted like mercury in a fever. She would never marry, since she knew herself to be incapable : " for certain reasons my spies have given me, I understand she will not bear children." The whisper disturbed men's ears a while, then trickled underground, though never to disappear completely. She would not marry, according to another rumour put out on the 18th April, because—

The new rumour mingled briefly with the rest, then developed swiftly into a roar of conviction so stunning as to drown them out. She would not marry because she had already set her heart on a man she could not have : "They say she is in love with Lord Robert Dudley and never lets him leave her."

This time rumour neither lied nor exaggerated. If anything it understated, since in duration and intensity, the only terms in which emotion may be measured, the truth was to surpass all possible expectation. Elizabeth's love for Robert outlasted his lifetime and ended only with hers : the final and unanswerable witness to it was found locked in a little chest by her bedside after her death. For nearly thirty years, while he grew bald, red-faced and paunchy, she continued never to let him out of her sight except with pain and under strong compulsion. Her flirtations, her half-calculated indiscretions with Alençon, her quasi-maternal passion for Robert's stepson Essex in her old age, were in quite other categories of feeling. As for him, her love was so much the most important thing in his life as to be utterly inseparable from it, its transcendant external reality.

Upon Elizabeth's subjects the immediate effect of the news was very much as if worshippers come to lay their prayers before an adored if somewhat inscrutable idol suddenly beheld on its face an expression of mocking indifference. Dismay, grief, anger, fear, every emotion of which a shocked and cheated people were capable, swirled round her throne. Though it was not against her, sheltered by the almost sacred reverence accorded Tudor majesty, that the fury chiefly raged, but against Robert. The world knew little of him yet, but that little was quite enough. His lineage obscure, his house founded upon corruption and twice dishonoured within living memory, himself a traitor but recently restored, a parasite upon the royal bounty, an adventurer with everything to take and nothing to give—the very last sort of man in every respect with whom Elizabeth's subjects would have chosen to see her name coupled.

And though she could not marry him, since he already had a

wife, the scandal of the connection might make it impossible for her to marry elsewhere with advantage. Unless even worse happened. . . . "She is more feared than her sister was, and gives her orders and has her way as absolutely as her father did." No one had to be reminded of her father's way when he was in love. The imperious will of Henry VIII, which had stopped at nothing, bound by the strongest of human ties to the insatiable ambition of John Dudley which had also stopped at nothing . . . a poor outlook altogether for the happiness of England—or of Amy Dudley.

Far from agreeing that her lover was a national misfortune, Elizabeth openly gloried in him. The phrase " during the last few days " in Feria's announcement of April 18th not only reveals how fresh the affair still was, but how little trouble she could have taken to keep it dark.[1] No one ever accused her of being unable to baffle curiosity for longer than that when she wanted to. She did not want to, for one thing because she would not deprive herself, any more than any other woman head over heels about a man for the first time in her life, of the sensation of talking about him. She even incited his critics to abuse him in her presence for the sheer pleasure of flinging " his many perfections " in their faces. There, she triumphantly informed them, went the only sort of man she could gladly be induced to marry : " not one "—in scornful allusion to some hapless suitor they pressed upon her—" who would sit home all day among the cinders." And she would turn her eyes to follow him, " comely in all the lineaments of his body," moving through the congestion of the Presence Chamber with the effortless grace to which even his enemies were obliged to concede their caste's superlative adjective of " princely," or go out to watch him bring down a running stag with one deft stroke of the lance at the full gallop or a flying bird with a single sure arrow. " Like her father King Harry," as one commentator by no means friendly to Robert remarked, " she loved a *man*."

But slander she would not have, however much she gave

[1] Had it been going on much longer it seems inconceivable that Feria's and the other ambassadors' paid ferrets would not have found it out sooner. This would seem to dispose of the antiquaries' later tale of a love affair in the Tower.

occasion for it. She rebuked it, punished it, laughed at it ; the one thing she would not do was let it force her into discretion. Once when she was engaged in a shooting match for a wager she stole into the staked enclosure dressed as a serving-maid to one of her own ladies to watch him, and when he had finished startled the onlookers by revealing herself to him with the smiling claim that " he was beholden to her for that she had passed the pikes for his sake." Like her father, who had been ready to take on the whole of Christendom rather than give up her mother, she reserved the right to judge her own actions : what was the use of being a Queen by divine right if she could not exercise her ordinary human right to love " the most perfect and virtuous man she knew."? If people could not see in him what she saw, they could take her royal word for it that she showed him no more grace than " his honourable nature and dealing deserved." If they chose to put an improper construction on her favour, they could take the chance of expiating their lewdness in her prisons.

The deterrent naturally proved ineffective. Those who did not disbelieve her outright continued, to her almost equal displeasure, to speculate on what, if she were telling the truth, might be the cause of so bizarre a truth. For though her subjects came in time to share her somewhat blatant pride in her virginity, they were seldom, even when they believed in it, inclined to put it down to a native, nun-like purity. Yet despite the most searching and persistent curiosity—a curiosity not altogether prurient, since many vital concerns hung on it—the precise character of her relationship with Robert soon became and to the end remained enveloped in a seemingly impenetrable mystery.

Was she his mistress in the ordinary sense ? If not, was it by her own choice or because she was incapable of such relations with any man ? She herself swore several years later on what she believed to be her deathbed " that though she loved, and always had loved, Lord Robert, as God was her witness, nothing improper had ever passed between them." Not long afterwards the French Ambassador on the word of his Spanish colleague, " swore to me . . . that he had been assured by a person who was in a position to know that

Lord Robert had slept with the Queen on New Year's night." Her contemporary Camden, who had access to much secret history, records that "men cursed Huic, the Queen's physician, for dissuading her from marriage for I know not what female infirmity." The intimate correspondence between the statesmen who spent the best part of their lives persuading her to marry (including Cecil, Camden's principal source of information on such matters) testifies to her freedom from any female infirmity more serious than a chronic inability to make up her mind. Each item of evidence cancels out another and the whole mass seems to add up to nothing.

It is an answer that Elizabeth might have approved but not one that logic can accept. The only conceivable condition under which she could have been neither chaste nor unchaste, capable nor incapable, was never to have existed at all. If she was capable and yet, despite her admittedly strong inclination for Robert, elected to remain chaste, she was presumably constrained either by moral scruples or external circumstances. Moral scruples, whether hers or Robert's, do not somehow sound conclusive ; while external circumstances would have applied to her, the Queen, alone. That she should because of them have remained chaste and at the same time insisted on his remaining faithful would not be strange, but everything points to her having actually counted on his doing so and to his never having once disappointed her during the whole clamorous decade between twenty-five and thirty-five—facts which would almost warrant, if the hypothesis of her chastity be true, her revision into a prodigy of innocence and his into a monument of marble constancy ; guises not easily reconcilable with their known natures. The same reasoning holds if she was chaste because incapable, even more strongly, because for obstacles from without that might in time have been overcome is substituted an impediment in her that never could be. The combination of capable and unchaste at once raises the spectre of consequences ; a pregnancy would have been a disaster of the very first order, current contraceptive methods were more of a snare than a precaution, and a belief in her own sterility would have had to be remarkably firm to tempt her into confirming it by repeated experiment. All three hypotheses seem improbable, while the fourth, the association of unchaste and incapable, is on the face of it a contradiction in terms.

As Elizabeth demurely said of herself after eluding her sister's examiners in the Tower :

> *Much suspected of me,*
> *Nothing proved can be.*

And yet, though the known facts seem to prove nothing, the suspicion still remains that the long and—on one side at least passionate intimacy between the two was not purely platonic. The notion somehow offends intuition and common sense ; it was simply not in character. Perhaps the reason that each hypothesis breaks down is that there was no single and straightforward truth exclusive to any one of them, but a sythesis of half truths distributed amongst all of them ; curiosity may have been misled into attaching too literal and technically exact a meaning to the terms " capable " and " chaste." Elizabeth and Robert, two people who, when serious conflict threatened between desire and circumstances, made it a rule of life to seek an accommodation with both, may have carried this policy into their private relationship : conceding, whether out of expedience or the necessity imposed by some physical flaw in her, just enough to continence to avoid the varied dangers of incontinence. Having regard to the well-known fact that physical flaws are often the outcome of irreconcilable psychological compulsions, it may not be irrelevant to conjecture, moreover, how much any sexual disability from which she suffered owed to the impossible need of reconciling the compliance of a mistress with Majesty's abhorrence of final submission to a lover.

Nothing she had was too good for him—though every estate, honour, perquisite, jewel that he could flaunt compromised her still further. When her confidential lady, Katherine Ashley, begged her on her knees to consider her reputation, Elizabeth pointed at the functionaries on duty in her apartments and demanded, how with that faithful regiment surveying her day and night, she could possibly be expected to misbehave herself . . . though " if she ever had the will, or found pleasure in such a dishonourable life—

from which God preserve her—she did not know of any one who could forbid her." Not could any one forbid her, when Robert complained that his quarters on the ground floor of the palace were too damp, to give him another set on the next floor adjoining her own . . . in defiance of those who took pains to remark on the convenience of the change for escaping the faithful regiment. To the best of her ability she insisted on eating her cake and having it and making it do for Robert as well.

It did exceedingly well, at least to begin with. Even for a man whose measure of himself was that of son to a dictator and brother to a nine-days' King of England. On June 6th he stood in St. George's Chapel at Windsor with Norfolk, Northampton and Rutland, the only Duke, the only Marquess and one of the first Earls of the realm, to receive the Garter, highest badge of honour at an English sovereign's disposal. In the same year, 1559, Elizabeth bestowed upon him " a capital mansion, called the Dairy House " at Kew—once the property of Sir John Gates who had perished with his father—and other lands carved out of the old monastery sites ; the lieutenancy of the forest and castle of Windsor and a licence to export woollen cloths free of duty, one an office, the other a privilege rich with potential profit ; and sums of ready cash besides for current needs.

Whether in return he gave her an affection that in any way matched hers it would have been impossible for him or any one else to have said. The question simply did not arise. One cannot love a Fairy Godmother with a purely mortal passion ; no more could a man entertain for his sovereign, " our God on earth," the same sentiments as for a common everyday mistress. He *had* to love her by every law human and divine ; if she commanded him into bed with her, it was his part as a good subject loyally to obey. The prerogative of Majesty comprised its own protocols of sex.

Nevertheless if Robert's pulses had not paid tribute to Majesty's earthly properties he would not have got where he did. Elizabeth was scarcely the woman to go on loving a man the best part of her life unless she felt satisfied that she was getting some adequate response. She was, after all, his sort of woman, spirited, wayward, vigorous of body, regal of address, cultivated to the finger-tips—

twice in after years he pursued and succumbed to blood relatives of hers, one of whom at least resembled her down to the pale olive skin and bright tawny hair. Just the sort of woman to provoke in him a sense of dreary contrast with the other to whom he had bound himself at seventeen—the wife whose future the world now tried to read with such fascinated expectancy.

She was then living at Denchworth in Berkshire, as a sort of highly paying guest with her own retinue in the house of a Mr. Hyde. Occasionally Robert journeyed down to see her there, often enough and staying long enough to lose, on the evidence of his account books, various small sums at play in the Hyde family circle and run so short of cash as to require hasty remittances from his steward for tips to the servants. Sometimes she came to see him in London, with a great splash of twelve horses expressly hired for the purpose at a cost of sixty shillings. Otherwise she put in her time visiting about the country, whither her husband's servants followed her with messages and somewhat lavish sums of money.

The separation between courtiers and their wives was imposed by custom, since the Court, organised for centuries on a masculine foundation, held no place for women except those selected for personal attendance on the Queen. Ordinarily, however, the wife of a man in Robert's position kept up an establishment in which her husband at the proper season held open house as became his rank. Probably Amy would have done so had he insisted ; since it appeared to be a matter of indifference to him she might well have shrunk from it out of fear of the burden or of lonesomeness. At the Hydes' she had plenty of company, for the family was a notably large one, and diversions to her taste.

It was " from Mr. Hyde's this VII of August "[1] that she wrote the one revealing letter of her life. Flowerdew, the steward in charge of a property in Norfolk she had brought to Robert by marriage, had sent to inquire about the sale of a shearing of wool to meet a debt to some farmers, of which Robert had already spoken to her. She had meant to see to it, she replied, but

[1] Probably 1559. The atmosphere of the letter strongly suggests a date after Robert's appointment to court, in November, 1558; by August, 1560, Amy had in all probability left the Hydes for Cumnor.

" I forgot to move my lord thereof, before his departing, he being sore troubled with weighty affairs, and I not being altogether in quiet for his sudden departing. . . . Of my own authority . . . (now) desiring that you will make the sale of the wool so soon as is possible . . for my lord so justly required me at his departing, to see those poor men satisfied, as though it had been a matter depending upon life ; whereby I force not to sustain a little loss thereby to satisfy my lord's desire. . . ."

" Of my own authority "—if the marriage had degenerated into a mere convenient wordly arrangement, at least the wife possessed the dignity of an equal partnership in it, so far as it went. And was far from happy with her condition. For an awkward correspondent Amy managed to pack into those few lines of a business letter an extraordinary amount of information about herself and her lord. Her awe of him and her anxiety to please him ; the mixture of solicitude and dread aroused in her by the " weighty affairs " drawing him from her ; her perception of the best trait in his nature, the quick generosity that could not bear " those poor men " to suffer through any fault of his. While from between the lines there peeps a relationship already poisoned by unspoken reproach on one side exasperating an uneasy conscience on the other.

With the echoes of a universal clamour to assist her, she would not have had much trouble piecing together the cause of his preoccupation. He meant to marry Elizabeth if a way could be found ; as the months rolled by it became increasingly dangerous for a way not to be found. Everything for which he lived hung by the thread of her favour : if any changing mood of hers frayed it, if his enemies with the aid of overwhelming public opinion succeeded in cutting it, he was done for. He had embarked on a venture as perilous in its way as his father's, one for which there seemed to be no issue between complete triumph and utter ruin.

He did not dare, of course, avow his ambition openly—any more than Elizabeth would have dared to encourage it openly so long as the problem of Amy remained unsolved. He set to work, discreetly and adroitly, to build up a following. The fierce Dudley temper retired for a space " into his pocket " ; with " mild and submissive behaviour " he turned the charm that had captivated Elizabeth upon his colleagues at court. Various of them, old adherents of his father chiefly, and others drawn together by unwillingness to accept another foreign marriage, began to look on him as a leader. Then, changing his tactics to disarm suspicion, he became in September, 1559, a partisan of Elizabeth's marriage with the Archduke Charles, son of the Holy Roman Emperor and Spain's official candidate. Through his sister Mary, Lady Sidney, he approached Feria's successor, the Bishop de Quadra, with the assurance that if the Archduke came in person Elizabeth would accept him.

Robert's sworn enemies, the feudal potentates whose aristo-cratic conservatism inclined them to the Catholic and Imperial Charles, let out a whoop of joy. Who should know the Queen's mind better than her favourite and his sister, now recognised as one of the Queen's most confidential ladies ? But the Bishop, though impressed, would not risk sending for his august candidate until he extracted a forthright yes or no from Elizabeth herself. With the result that Elizabeth, who had connived at the manœuvre to keep everybody's hopes in play, found herself obliged when cornered in November to disavow the Dudleys' mind-reading with a somewhat embarrassed laugh. The great nobles turned with venom on their deceiver. The Duke of Norfolk, the chief of them, " spoke out so plainly " to him that they came within an inch of crossing rapiers : for Robert, unabashed at his exposure, boldly counter-attacked by telling the Duke that " he was neither a good Englishman nor a loyal subject for wishing the Queen to marry outside the realm."

The implication was too obvious. If not outside then inside, and inside by now meant one man only. His enemies began to hanker for his blood. Their foreign sympathisers egged them on with openly expressed wonder that the country should be so poor as to contain no man of sufficient spirit to poignard him for his presumption. Plots took shape, dissolved, re-formed, round some of the most illustrious names in the land. One, involving a plan by some servants of the Earl of Arundel, Norfolk's father-in-law and a late pretender to the Queen's hand, "to shoot him with a dag from out a shop," was serious enough to engross the judicial attention of the Privy Council itself. It was lucky for Robert that political assassination had become an obsolete art in England.

Yet if he were not to die someone had to . . . it was inconceivable that the triangle could endure indefinitely. At the first outbreak of the scandal the previous April Amy had been reported as likely to settle the difficulty by succumbing to " a malady in one of her breasts " from which she " has been ailing for some time." Over seven months had elapsed and the cancer, if cancer there was, had apparently made no progress. Then after his deception in November the new Spanish Ambassador de Quadra wrote straight out to Philip II :

" I have heard from a personwho is accustomed to giving me veracious news that Lord Robert has sent to poison his wife. Certainly all that the Queen will do with us in the matter of her marriage is only keeping the country engaged with words until this wicked deed is consummated."

Apparently superfluous wives were as hard to kill in England as mischievous upstarts. At the end of March, 1560, Amy still lived. Yet Robert, " who is assuming every day a more masterful part in affairs " had just as surely not abated his designs : it even got about that he " told somebody, who has not kept silent, that he will be in a very different position a year from now, if he lived. . . ." He may have meant no more than that Elizabeth had promised him the earldom he craved, but in the circumstances the unguarded remark naturally set all hearers to exploring for some possible middle road between abject resignation and outright murder. And to finding it in the precedent twice set by Henry VIII. " They say he is thinking of divorcing his wife."

If he was he soon thought better of it ; though it is unlikely that he could for a moment have so utterly deceived himself as to what the people and the Church of England would stand for. There matters stood for a few months while affairs in Scotland claimed the general attention. On March 29th an English force crossed the border to help the Protestant Scot rebels to expel their French masters. It was an enterprise of which Philip II could not approve, for though he did not love the French, he loved Protestants still less. He threatened—and to mollify him Elizabeth had publicly to promise in so many words to marry his cousin the Archduke. By June her army had taken Edinburgh, in July a treaty concluded in the same city permanently removed the threat of a French invasion by way of England's " postern gate " and established a durable peace between the two halves of Britain for the first time in their homicidal annals.

Not for years had the country had such cause for rejoicing. The treaty's principal author, William Cecil, journeyed down from Edinburgh to Hampton Court in eager expectation of everything a grateful sovereign could bestow—a further increment of power, honours and even more substantial tokens of favour to be invested in the future greatness of his large and growing family. But when he reached the Queen's presence he received instead of compliments a torrent of blame . . . unreasonable blame, for the most part, from a woman who looked ill from a plain disorder of the nerves. Dazed and depressed Cecil looked about him for an explanation.

He had no trouble in finding it. Some mysterious crisis had come in her relations with Robert Dudley. No one could tell the Secretary how it had arisen, but nearly every one felt sure now what it portended. In fact, she herself let slip to the Duke of Norfolk the pregnant hint that " she would be married ere six months were up "—and by that few imagined that she meant the Archduke. Persons close to her testified that the haughty Tudor will was already submitted to her lover's as to a masterful consort's. And not only the Court but the country seethed with expectation of imminent happenings. On the 13th of this same August old Annie " Mother " Dowe of Brentford appeared before the magistrates to receive sentence for repeating to her neighbours that the Queen was with child by Lord Robert. Elsewhere, too, men murmured sullenly of a bastard Dudley in the offing who might one day be palmed off on them as God's anointed. The

QUEEN ELIZABETH
From the National Portrait Gallery.   Painter unknown.

ambassadors representing the princely foreign suitors were ready to throw in their hands ; the chief of them saluted Robert in one of his letters home as " the King that is to be."

On August 30th the Court moved to Windsor. There, at the end of the following week occurred one of the strangest interviews recorded in history. William Cecil, Prime Minister of England in effect if not in title, the arch-heretic whom Spain stood committed to destroy together with his Reformation, admitted His Catholic Majesty's ambassador into secret conference for the purpose of pouring out his fears for his country's future and confessing that he was at the end of his tether.

Neither of the parties to the conversation is altogether to be trusted. De Quadra was working underhand, unbeknown even to his King, to bring about an alliance between Spain and France for the overthrow of Elizabeth in the Catholic interest. Cecil had been made by Somerset and deserted him ; he had been raised by Northumberland and deserted him too ; and managed to serve under Mary without losing eligibility for service under Elizabeth. He was a cat always lighting on his feet on the winning side, a master in the art he so vividly described as " throwing the stone without that the hand be seen." But he stood nearer the ascertainable truth in most matters than any other man in the kingdom ; nor, from what he had recently intimated to his friends Randolph and Throckmorton, the English ambassadors in Edinburgh and Paris respectively, is there any reason to suppose that the Spaniard misrepresented him.

" After many protestations and entreaties that I would keep it secret (wrote de Quadra to his King's half-sister, the Regent of the Netherlands) he told me that the Queen was conducting herself in such a fashion that for his part he thought it best to retire. For he was too bad a sailor, when he saw a storm coming, not to make port when he had power to do so. . . . He begged me for the love of God to warn the Queen as to her irregular conduct and to persuade her not to abandon her business as she did. . . . Then he repeated to me twice over Lord Robert were better in Paradise. . . .

" And finally he said they were scheming to put Lord Robert's wife to death, and that now she was publicly reported to be ill, but she was not so, on the contrary was quite well and taking good care not to be poisoned. . . ."

That same week-end Amy was found with her neck broken at the bottom of a flight of stairs.

Chapter Five

MURDER, ACCIDENT OR SUICIDE?

CUMNOR HALL lay three or four miles to the north of the market town of Abingdon, about half-way between it and Oxford. The house, once the property of the abbots of Abingdon, had been leased a few years earlier by Anthony Forster, " treasurer " to Lord Robert Dudley, from William Owen, who had inherited it from his father George Owen, Henry VIII's physician. It was a large, rectangular building in monastic style, surrounded by terraced walks, trees and ponds, with a view over the downs and the spire of a church rising immediately behind. Exactly when and why Amy transferred her residence there is unknown ; trustworthy information as to how much the move owed to her own restlessness and how much to her husband's promptings would throw an interesting light on what followed. Besides Forster and his wife there were living in the house at the time Mrs. William Owen, for some reason apart from her husband, and Mrs. John Odingsells, the widowed sister of Amy's former host, Mr. Hyde of Denchworth, whom Amy seems to have brought along as a sort of companion.

Round noon of Sunday, September 8th, 1560, Thomas Blount, confidential servant and distant kinsman to Robert Dudley, left Windsor for Cumnor on his master's private business. A few hours later he met another, lesser, servant speeding in the opposite direction, who at sight of him pulled up and gasped out that their lady was dead. Blount, a man professionally incapable of surprise, swiftly extracted such details as the other could supply. There were not many. " By a fall from a pair of stairs " . . . how and at what hour Bowes did not know . . . he and his fellow-servants had all been sent that morning to Abingdon Fair . . . their mistress had tried to send " her own sort " as well and quarrelled with Mrs. Odingsells for declining to go . . . who had found the body and when he could not say.

He galloped on towards his destination. Blount, instead of doing the same, as one would have expected, or else turning back for fresh orders in view of this sudden development, adopted the somewhat curious alternative of proceeding only as far as Abingdon, where he put up for the night at an inn. " Because I was desirious to hear what news went abroad," he explained to Robert by letter, " at my supper I called for mine host and asked him what news was thereabout, taking upon me I was going into Gloucestershire."[1]

The explanation is perfectly plausible. Blount realised—as any intelligent man must have done in his place—that the ultimate verdict in this affair rested with public opinion, and he wanted the earliest available sample of it. For whatever the technical truth might turn out to be, no tribunal lower than the whole body of the English people was competent to pronounce sentence : especially if the end of the cause should find Majesty herself standing alongside her lover in the dock. It was not unnatural, therefore, for Robert's exceedingly capable agent to be less concerned with how Amy died than with how people thought she had died.

There is, of course, another possible explanation. If Blount was expecting Bowes' announcement there would have been no particular reason for his rushing on to Cumnor to learn what he already knew or going back to Windsor for orders he already had. On that possibility, however, the first word belonged to the Bishop de Quadra, who did not speak it till three days later.

The landlord, like many of his profession, was very glad to talk but very cautious about committing himself to anything that might later be held against him. " What is your judgment and that of the people ? " asked Blount, after expressing proper interest in the landlord's repetition of the tale he had already had from Bowes.

" Some were disposed to say well and some evil."

" What is your own judgment ? "

" By my troth, I judge it a very misfortune because it chanced

---

[1] The quotations in this chapter, unless otherwise attributed, are from five letters exchanged between Robert and Blount in the course of the following week or so. Together they contain the only direct surviving account of the circumstances immediately surrounding Amy's death. Their validity will be discussed later.

in that honest gentleman's house ; his great honesty doth much curb the thoughts of the people."

Plainly Forster's name had already come up in the popular gossip, coupled with the possibility of foul play. Shrewdly surmising that the humble publican's testimonial to a stranger might not be the last word on the character borne by the magnate of Cumnor amongst his neighbours, Blount laid the topic aside for further investigation and took up another. " Methinks that some of her people that waited on her should somewhat say to this ? "

" No, sir, but little ; for it was said they were all here at the fair and none left with her."

" How might that chance ? " asked Blount, who of course already knew from Bowes.

" It is said she rose very early and commanded all her sort to go to the fair, and would suffer none to tarry at home ; and thereof is much judged."

With the arrow of suspicion thus momentarily fixed at suicide, Blount broke off contact with public opinion for the night. He must have done some further listening in and around the tap-room next morning, however, for the day was well advanced before he turned up at Cumnor.

Meantime Bowes had arrived at Windsor with his story. If the bereaved husband felt any grief, pain or horror, he put them aside for a more convenient season. His first thought, like Blount's, was of the world, his second of Blount, whom he naturally imagined to be already on the scene. " The greatness and suddenness of the misfortune doth so perplex me, until I hear from you how the matter standeth, or how this evil should light upon me, considering what the malicious world will say, as I can take no rest."

Certainly if he was innocent few men have ever been caught in such a fearful web of circumstance. One misstep, one move capable of a sinister interpretation when the facts came to light, and Amy dead might prove an even more effective obstacle to his ambition than Amy alive. Yet something had to be done, for of all tokens of guilt the worst was to seem to do nothing. Swiftly he racked his brain, " considering my case in many ways," in the briefest possible time decided that only complete openness could save him. By evening he had sent a courier to Amy's family in Norfolk with an urgent summons to be present at the inques "that they be privy and see how all things do proceed," and anothe to Blount with his instructions :

> "And, because I have no way to purge myself of the maliciou talk but one which is the very plain truth to be known, I pray you . . . that you will use all the devises and means that you can possible for the learning of the truth ; wherein have no respect to any living person. And, as by your own travail and diligence, as likewise by order and law, I mean by calling of the Coroner and charging him to the uttermost from me . . . to make choice of no light or slight persons, but the discreetest and most substantial men for the juries, such as for their knowledge may be able to search thoroughly . . . the bottom of the matter, and for their uprightness will deal sincerely therein. . . ."

What did he suspect ? Almost anything. "For as the cause and manner thereof does marvelleous trouble me . . . send me your true conceit and opinion whether it happened by evil chance or by villainy." Curiously he made no reference to the one tangible fact so far, Amy's strange conduct of the previous morning, which Bowes must surely have reported to him.

Another thing he did in the course of the day was to see Elizabeth. When he left her it was with orders to retire to his house at Kew and stay there under arrest until further notice. If only some eavesdropper had noted down what passed at that interview. . . .

Before the messenger "riding for life" could deliver Robert's letter at Cumnor on the Tuesday, Blount anticipated some of its contents. At his coming he found most of the jury chosen and part of them already in the house. His impression, after a close individual survey, was favourable : "I judge them, and especially some of them, to be as wise and able men to be chosen upon such a matter, being but countrymen, as ever I saw. . . . I have good hope they will conceal no fault, if any be . . ."

By " fault " he intentionally took up Robert's cue of " villainy " and with his very next word squarely yoked it to the question of who the villain, if any, might be : " for, as they are wise, so are they, as I hear, part of them very enemies to Anthony Forster." Blount had not listened to the local gossip for nothing. Having learned that the master of Cumnor enjoyed no such unanimous esteem amongst his neighbours as the landlord had reported, he perceived that " his great honesty " could not be counted on in itself to curb the thoughts of the people—therefore the best jury from the point of view of Robert's interests was one unlikely to show him any indulgence. For if a crime had really been committed, who was more likely, after all, to incur the law's fundamental tests of opportunity and motive than the only male in authority over the fatal household, the retainer who by one shrewd stroke might inseverably attach his fortunes to those of a King of England ? So reasoned Blount, and pretty plainly assumed, by his unceremonious introduction of the subject, that Robert must be thinking along the same lines.

We know very little of the shadowy figure thus projected into the tragedy. Blount, who mentions him in no other connection, seems to have had only the barest acquaintance with him, while Robert, who must have had great confidence in him to put him in charge of his financial affairs, never mentions him by name at all. That he was well connected is attested by his marriage to a niece of Lord Williams of Thame, Keeper of the Tower during Robert's imprisonment and later Lord High Chamberlain under Philip and Mary. The Latin epitaph on his tombstone warrants him to have been " a very amiable man, very learned, a great musician, builder and planter." So that such moderate evidence of later prosperity as his purchase of the freehold of Cumnor and his entry into Parliament do not in themselves imply an adequate prior motive on his part for murder.

Having taken stock of the jury, to whom he delivered Robert's charge when it arrived next day, Blount turned to investigate on his own account. The first witness he selected to examine was Amy's maid Pirto " who doth dearly love her."

Pirto was able to amplify out of her own knowledge Bowes' and the landlord's hearsay tale of the events of the Sunday morning.

Her mistress had arisen unusually early and ordered the whole household, "her own sort" and their servants included, to Abingdon Fair for the morning. Her friends demurred, especially Mrs. Odingsells, who "said it was no day for a gentlewoman to go in, the morrow was much better." Amy, "very angry," retorted "that she might choose at her own pleasure, but that all hers should go." One of the others, presumably Mr. or Mrs. Forster, asked who would keep her company if all went. Mrs. Owen, she replied, would keep her company at dinner. Whether she was making an exception of Mrs. Owen, or whether in a huff she meant that she would dine with Mrs. Owen after the latter's return but with nobody else is not clear ; nor who apart from Amy stayed in the end and who went.[1]

But one thing was absolutely clear, that Amy, the same Amy who could never bear to be alone, had done her best to rid the house of every human being in it. The incongruity struck Blount at once, but in his characteristic fashion he led the other person to dot the i's and cross the t's. What did she make of it all, he asked Pirto with misleading casualness, "chance or villainy ? "

The maid fell into the trap. "By my faith," she cried, "I do judge very chance, and neither done by man nor by herself."

He said nothing. There was no need for him to. The impulsive addition of the last three words revealed her thought as clear as daylight. She did not believe for a moment that there had been a murder, but in her heart she feared suicide ; therefore it would be better that all inquiry should be dropped and everybody charitably subscribe to a verdict of accident—anything rather than the mistress she had so dearly loved should be branded through eternity with the crime of self-slaughter.

Some look of his, however, or else her own instinct warned Pirto that she had let out the dreadful thought her mind shunned by the very violence of her denial. Hoping to retrieve her mistake, she blundered in more deeply. Her mistress, she earnestly declared, had been a good, virtuous gentlewoman, and daily would pray

[1] Abingdon's annual fair was always held in February (Holinshed, I, 411) so the event here referred to was probably some local festival, on the occasion of the Nativity of the Virgin. The Sabbath was the usual day for the vulgar, hence Mrs. Odingsell's objection.

pon her knees. The very last person, indeed, to have contemplated
o sinful an act. . . . Why, continued the artless serving-maid to
linch her argument, " I myself have heard her pray to God to
deliver her from desperation."

" Then," intimated the bland voice of her inquisitor, " she
might have (had) some evil toy in her mind."

" No, good Master Blount," wildly protested his victim, " do
not judge so of my words ; if you should so gather, I am sorry I
said so much."

But Master Blount was already off on the trail. The result of
his further researches into Amy's mental state appeared, repeated
twice over for emphasis, in the report he sent off to Robert on the
Wednesday : " Truly the tales I do hear of her maketh me to
think she had a strange mind in her ; as I will tell you at my
coming."

The report reached Kew on Thursday. To Robert, looking
frantically for an early delivery from his suspense, it brought
only disappointment. " Until I hear from you again," began the
answer he despatched later on the same day, " how the matter
falleth out in very truth, I cannot be quiet." With " the discreet
jury you say you are already chosen," he professed himself satisfied,
and prayed Blount to convey again his desire that " as ever I shall
think good of them, that they will . . . truly deal in this matter."
But of the possibility of Amy's suicide, which filled over half the
report, again not a word. In fact, the only part of it on which he
made any direct comment was the end, concerning the jurors and
their attitude towards Forster—as though his mind had impatiently
rejected in the reading every other hypothesis except that of foul
play.

His answer to Blount was brief and the gist of it ran, " God
willing, I have never fear (of) the due prosecution accordingly,
what person soever it may appear to touch, as well for the just
punishment of the act as for mine own true justification ; for "—
and here it seems impossible to doubt that the solution he preferred
was murder, since by assisting in the murderer's prosecution he
would have the chance to clear himself—" for, as I would be sorry

in my heart any such evil should be committed, so should it well appear to the world my innocency by my dealing in the matter."

In that respect he was quite right. The country, in the throes of one of its periodic moral eruptions, smelt a crime and demanded a criminal. From Coventry a popular preacher named Lever warned Cecil and Sir Francis Knollys, another of the Privy Council, of the " grievous and dangerous suspicion and muttering " thereabout " of the death of her who was the wife of Lord Robert Dudley " and boldly insisted on " due inquiry, and justice openly known." Others were even more specific. The Queen of France, Mary Stuart—one day to lose her own kingdom of Scotland through a curiously similar happening—remarked with ironic innuendo on the lucky chance that her cousin of England was now free to marry " her horse keeper." To shift the terrible presumption resting on his shoulders before public opinion finally hardened against him, more was required of Robert than mere proof of his innocence ; it was imperative for him to fasten guilt speedily and unmistakably on someone else's.

But neither Blount nor the jury proved capable of producing a felon to order, as the former admitted in his next letter dated Friday the 13th ; otherwise his news was encouraging. The jury " kept very secret ; and yet I do hear a whispering that they can find no presumption of evil. . . . And I think," added the writer with pious asperity, " some of them be sorry for it, God forgive me." His own opinion was " much quieted ; the more I search of it, the more free it doth appear to me." The only reason he gave for his sudden tranquillity was that he could not conceive of any one killing a lady in Amy's social position or of any lady in that position killing herself. He would leave Cumnor on the morrow, he concluded, with a pause for breakfast at Abingdon to see one of the jury again, and wait upon his Lordship with whatever further intelligence he might pick up later the same day.

Presumably he did and returned again to Cumnor, but without leaving any trace of his passage or the confidential matters he had saved to divulge in person. Apparently he failed to impart his own " quiet " to his employer, for Robert not only sent him back to

Cumnor but unbeknown to him obeyed the dangerous impulse to get into direct touch with the jury.[1]

It was an irregularity he would have ample leisure to regret. Nor did it procure him anything beyond the respectful assurance from " one Smith, that seemeth to be the foreman " of what he already knew ; so far as Smith and his colleagues could now foresee, their judgment would be one of death by misadventure.

There in abruptness and confusion the available record of the inquest ends. From subsequent references we know that the foreman correctly anticipated the final verdict. Exactly when and why the jury reached it we cannot know, since the official transcript of the proceedings which once existed has disappeared. Virtually the whole of our meagre knowledge of the circumstances surrounding Amy's death thus rests upon the five letters between Robert and Blount—an unsatisfactory group of exhibits in that they also serve as the only direct testimony to Robert's innocence and might therefore have been compiled for that purpose.

On Wednesday, September 11th, the day that Blount sent off his first report from Cumnor, another agent completed an even longer report for his own superior. The agent was Alvarez de Quadra, Bishop of Aquila in the Kingdom of Naples and Spanish Ambassador to the Court of St. James, his correspondent Margaret of Parma, Regent of the Netherlands for Philip II, the report part of the same letter from which the account of the writer's interview with Cecil has already been drawn.

The letter begins with the statement that the writer arrived at Windsor " *cinco dios ha*," that is Friday the 6th, describes an audience of some duration with the Queen, then " after these conversations " his meeting with Cecil, and goes on immediately to add, " The day

[1] Robert finally confessed this to Blount in the last of the five letters exchanged between them. It is a somewhat perplexing document. Unlike the others, it bears no date, merely its place of origin "from Windsor." The date of Robert's release from arrest at Kew is unknown. The letter must have been written after that of Thursday, September 12th, else the contents of the two could have been combined. If it was not written on the 13th, there would have been no reason to write on the 14th, since by then Robert knew that Blount was on his way to him. The probable date seems the 16th or 17th rather than the 13th or 15th.

after this took place the Queen told me, on her return from hunting
that Lord Robert's wife was dead, or nearly so, and begged me to
say nothing about it."

The most important diplomat in England, come to discuss
essential business with the Queen, would not have been kept
waiting long for his audience ; he may even have arranged it
beforehand. It is therefore possible that de Quadra saw Elizabeth
not later than Saturday the 7th ; and though he does not say so
the tone of his letter distinctly implies that he spoke with Cecil
shortly afterwards on the same day, when he heard from the
Secretary that Amy was about to die. In that event " the day
after " on which Elizabeth informed him that Amy was already
" dead, or nearly so " refers to the fatal Sunday itself, and the
phrase " on her return from hunting " to some time before eleven
in the morning[1] . . . with Bowes still many hours' hard riding
away.

It seems to follow, then, that Elizabeth, informed by Robert in
advance that he had sent to kill his wife, precisely as Cecil had
foretold, through some misunderstanding of the day on which the
crime was to be perpetrated, gave it away *before it happened*, or at
least before the news could have arrived at Windsor. And that
Robert and Blount separated that same morning with the rough
notes for their subsequent correspondence already agreed between
them.

In comparing the two sets of evidence it is important to
remember the purpose for which each was composed. De Quadra
had all along been trying to persuade his superiors into an invasion
of England with the argument that Elizabeth's hold on her people's
affection was too feeble for her to put up any serious resistance ;
the scandal of Amy's death fell to his hand so opportunely that he
felt justified in urging the enterprise on Madame de Parma at once
without even waiting for the consent of their master Philip II, who
was by then back in Spain. On Robert's side the question of

[1] Since hunting was ordinarily concluded before dinner. If de Quadra's
audience with Elizabeth took place on the Friday and his interview with Cecil
later that same day, the conclusion is even more striking. If he saw
Elizabeth on the Friday and Cecil on the Saturday, the argument remains
unaffected.

urpose is, of course, everything. If his and Blount's letters are
what they purport to be, confidential communications written
impromptu under stress, there is something wrong with de Quadra's
chronology. If de Quadra's chronology, and the conclusion based
upon it, are sound, Robert and Blount could only have been
writing for effect.

But effect on whom? There is not the faintest indication that
anybody, including Robert's staunchest defenders, so much as
knew of the existence of the letters during the debate that raged
over Amy's death for months and years. Nor is it easy to understand why, if the letters were written to impress the public, Blount
should allude to secrets he could divulge only to Robert, or why
Robert should give away his shady correspondence with the foreman of the jury—an indiscretion for which he himself is the sole
authority and which he humbly promised Blount not to repeat.
Matters like these could easily have been omitted from documents
intended for hostile scrutiny.

And in their place might have been inserted some decent show
of grief. A man hearing of the demise of a pet dog could not have
displayed a more callous indifference than Robert to the sudden,
violent death of the woman to whom he had been married for ten
years. Not the slightest curiosity about her extraordinary conduct
on the fatal morning, not the most languid interest in her " desperation." . . . He seems to have been so absorbed in his own innocence
that he overlooked the obvious device of bolstering it by an emotion
he did not feel.[1]

De Quadra, no less intent on convicting him of guilt, also had
an end in view ; the suspicion is therefore permitted whether in
his zeal to reach it he did not overreach it. He remembered to
note his arrival on the 6th ; why did he leave his interviews with
Elizabeth and Cecil in a timeless void, then drive in like a hammer-
blow that seemingly specific and damning " the day after ? " And

[1] The original letters have disappeared, and their content is only known
through copies preserved at the Pepysian Library at Cambridge. The copies
appear (according to experts) to be in Blount's hand, and may have been made by
him to submit in answer to an accusation brought against Robert in 1567 by
John Appleyard, Amy's half-brother (see p. 125). A strong argument for their
fidelity is the fact that the suspicious passages were not deleted in the copying.

why did he wait till the 11th before sealing his despatch ? He ha
seen Elizabeth, the chief purpose of his coming. He had als
received a confession from Cecil, her chief minister, of a kind
can rarely have been an ambassador's privilege to write home abou
Next day came the staggering intelligence that her lover's wife wa
dead and she free to marry. If he had all that budget of news o
Sunday and dawled till Wednesday before sending it off, he wa
no more fit for his post than the Queen who fatuously confesse
to being a murderess before she was sure of it. In fact, he foun
nothing to add on the 11th except a postscript to the effect tha
Elizabeth had said in Italian " *Si ha rotto il collo*," (her neck wa
broken) a detail that must have been common property at Windso
by Monday morning.

There is something just a bit too artful about his artless neglec
of those all-important dates. It conjures up a picture of an elderl
gentleman in sober episcopal garments sitting down to read th
notes he had made of his experiences between Friday and Monday
of being struck by the virtue of compression for obtaining a desire
artistic effect ; and then taking up his quill to draft a narrative un
blemished by too pedantic a regard for dates. That " dead, o
nearly so " in his report of Elizabeth's original announcement
though utterly meaningless coming from her, would from hin
have served as a first-class excuse to his correspondent for no
concluding his despatch before he had made sure.

Incidentally his star witness let him down. The one man who
could have corroborated him was Cecil and about this time Ceci
rode over to Kew by way of demonstrating to the world that he
would be no party to the popular hue and cry. As souveni
of his visit he preserved an affecting letter of gratitude for hi
" great, great friendship " written him by Robert a few day
later. . . .

" I thank you for being here—I am very loath to wish you
here again, but I would be very glad to be with you there. . .
I pray you let me hear from you what you think best for me
to do . . . methinks I am here all this while as it were in a
dream, and too far from the place where I ought to be. (P.S.)

beseech you, sir, forget not to offer up the humble sacrifice you promised me."

The postscript may refer to some gift delivered by Cecil on Robert's behalf to their common earthly deity. It may not be relevant to note that the Secretary, who later in an important private memorandum wrote of Robert as "infamed" by his wife's death, nowhere ever suggested that he was guilty of it. In fact he served on the committee of the Privy Council which even years later punished John Appleyard for putting that suggestion forward.

How did Amy die? It seems almost incredible that on the very day after Cecil prophesied her imminent removal she should have suffered a violent death without the operation of guilt. It would be equally astounding if, on the very morning she apparently elected to kill herself, her design should have been forestalled by a push or a stumble down the fatal stairs. Each coincidence denies the other but both, separately or jointly, challenge the jury's verdict of accident. Yet what imaginable kind of stairs would serve the purpose either of suicide or murder?

Cumnor Hall was long ago demolished; we do not know whether its staircase was circular, steep and narrow or straight and broad with the usual landings. Whichever it was, it is hardly conceivable that a murderer would dare select that method of homicide for the very good reason that his victims might live to tell the tale.[1]

Nor is it easier to imagine a woman bent on her own destruction taking a way more likely to end in painful injury than in swift

---

[1] Robert's enemies later recognised this difficulty and invented various ingenious explanations to overcome it. The most popular of them declared that Amy had been killed elsewhere, either by strangling or a dagger thrust in the head, then had her neck broken to cover the bruises, before her body was arranged at the foot of the stairs. Another version, the product of a heated Italian brain, is that Robert's minions drove five six-inch nails into her head, covered them with tar to prevent bleeding and painted them to resemble life. All these yarns presuppose the absence of an inquest, a secret burial, and other reckless contradictions of known fact. The best known of them, in Sir Walter Scott's *Kenilworth*, seems to be a blend of various of these fantasies.

A staircase preserved in a nearby farmhouse is said to be the original from Cumnor Hall, but is not generally accepted by the antiquarians.

release. A staircase well would, of course, answer both the objections and correspondingly impair the theory of accident, though here again the murderer or murderers would have been running the risk of a tell-tale scream (unless Amy obligingly cleared the house to make things as easy as possible for them) before they could lift and throw an able-bodied woman over the balustrade.

On the whole the limited evidence that we have would seem to accord best with suicide. Amy's urgent anxiety to be left alone, the mental state vividly described by her maid Pirto, furnish between them the only consistent clues in the whole business. Perhaps there was something more to the story of a cancer in the breast than mere gossip ; perhaps she had brooded over Robert's neglect until it affected her mind . . . particularly if she had heard the ghastly rumours that she was to be destroyed because she stood in his way.[1]

The charitable formula of " suicide while of unsound mind " appears not yet to have been invented. Might not the jury, satisfied that Amy had not been murdered, have felt that no good would be done to anybody by proceeding to a verdict that immortally (the phrase is Elizabeth's) touched her honour ? They had eliminated the only name ever mentioned in connection with foul play, Forster's, knowing for certain that he could not count on Robert's protection, and that in fact, as Elizabeth publicly stated a few weeks later, he was not even in the house at the time. Having paid their tribute to duty, the jurors might well have allowed themselves one to human pity.

On Sunday, September 22nd, Amy was buried in the Church of St. Mary the Virgin at Oxford. Eighty poor men and women marched in the procession, followed by the members of the University walking two by two, the choir in surplices singing, Rouge Cross and the Lancaster herald in long gowns with hoods, Amy's half-brother Appleyard carrying a banner, and the Clarenceux King-at-Arms. Then came the coffin borne by eight tall yeomen with four alternates (" for the way was far ") then the

[1] According to modern psychology a person of Amy's type and condition—a woman, that is, suffering from a frustrated love of splendour and in a state of hysterical depression—would if bent on self-destruction be most likely to choose the method of throwing herself from a height.

chief mourner, Mrs. Norris, daughter of Mrs. Forster's uncle, Lord Williams of Thame, assisted by other ladies, including Mrs. Blount. Robert, forbidden by custom to be present, spent the day at Court, which had gone into mourning. The funeral is estimated to have cost him " better than £2000 "

Chapter Six

ELIZABETH DISPOSES

As little persuaded by the jury's verdict of Robert's innocence as by Amy's handsome obsequies of his grief, public opinion rejected it instantly and outright. Too many circumstances remained unexplained, too much suspicion undispersed ; and the popular judgment ended where it had begun, in the conviction that a man so universally disliked with so strong a motive for committing a murder must in fact have committed it. In vain Robert, foreseeing how it would be, on receipt of the foreman's letter anticipating the verdict, wrote to Blount the anxious wish that " another substantial company of honest men might try again for the more knowledge of the truth." The law was satisfied of the cause of Amy's death and the only more knowledge of any real interest to him or any one else was its consequences.

Few doubted what they would be or that they would follow swiftly. " She is in a fair way," predicted de Quadra, reporting the universal expectation that the nuptials would be announced as soon as the decencies of mourning permitted, " to lie down one evening the Queen and wake next morning plain Madame Elizabeth, she and her paramour with her." It seemed the only reasonable estimate of the situation—a situation to be twice repeated in her reign, once in real life and laid in Scotland, and once in a play, the most famous of all plays, laid in Denmark. There was on the face of it no good reason why the tangle of the ambitious lover, the superfluous spouse and the opportune death should, in the present instance as in the later ones, lead to any other dénouement than the re-marriage in haste and the bloody retribution.

The preachers raved against the marriage from their pulpits, her ambassadors in foreign capitals sent frenzied messages to the Council that it be stopped by any means. The news of it, wrote Randolph from Edinburgh, " so passioneth my heart that no grief

I ever felt was like unto it." Throckmorton in Paris wished that he might crawl away somewhere and die. "If the matter be not already determined," he wrote to Cecil on October 28th, "*in visceribus Jesu Christi* I conjure you to do all your endeavour to hinder it." The expectation of it, he added, was undoing the triumph of the Scottish campaign in the spring : the French Crown was refusing to ratify the Treaty of Edinburgh in the belief that internal "discontentation" and "the loss of all foreign countenance" would soon deprive England of the means of enforcing it. "The bruits be so brim and maliciously reported here I know not where to turn. . . . One laugheth at us, another revileth us, another threateneth the Queen. Some let not to say What religion is this, that a subject shall kill his wife and the Prince not only bear withal but marry him ? "

For she was head not only of the state but of the church, the personal symbol of the spiritual revolution on which her subjects' lives and fortunes, the national existence even, had been staked. What hope was there of its succeeding if she herself discredited it by blatant immorality ? Of the English people confiding their souls to the government of an adulteress and murderess practically self-confessed ?

Yet on the other side was Robert pleading to her sense of justice as well as her love. If to marry him might be taken as the reward of his guilt, not to marry him would in the circumstances be practically as good as publishing her disbelief in his innocence. Nor were all the important personages and powerful reasons of state against him. The Lord Deputy of Ireland, for instance, Thomas Ratcliffe, Earl of Sussex, whose father had sentenced Robert to death and who for his own part was many times to regret that the sentence had not been carried out, in October wrote to Cecil with soldierly forthrightness that the important thing was not whom her Majesty chose, but that she should " choose speedily, and therein follow so much her own affection as by the looking upon him she would choose *omnes eius sensus titillarentur* (her whole being may be moved to desire) which shall be the readiest way with the help of God to bring us a blessed prince. . . .

" If I knew (he continued) that England had other rightful

inheritors I would then advise otherwise . . . but, seeing that . . . no riches, friendship, foreign alliance or other present commodity that can come by a husband can serve her turn without issue of her body—if the Queen will love anybody, let her love where and whom she list, and him . . . will I love, serve and honour to the uttermost."

That was Robert's, and if she cared to play it, Elizabeth's trump card. There *were* no other rightful inheritors ; nothing but remote pretenders like the Queen of Scots and Catherine Gray, Lady Jane's sister, whose partisans even now were plotting against the present and future peace of England. The dangers of an open succession might yet reconcile the country to Robert as an alternative to nobody.

Only too alert to this possibility, the enemies of the marriage took feverish counsel with one another on how to forestall it. In November Throckmorton, privately coached by Cecil, sent his secretary, an able young man named Jones, to lay before her in person the disastrous effect upon the people's affections and the welfare of the state unless she got rid of Robert altogether. " In as vehement language as the case required," Jones, adroitly fitting the argument that Robert's character rendered him unfit for her to marry into the conclusion that it likewise rendered him unfit for her to associate with, charged the whole Dudley tribe collectively with incorrigible disloyalty and Robert specifically with his wife's death. At one point, amused at the lavish tarring of her lover's family, " she laughed and forthwith turned herself to one side and then the other " ; but with regard to Amy's death explained " very patiently " and in some detail " how it had been tried in the country and found contrary to that which had been reported." Nevertheless Jones noticed that, despite her laughter and quiet conviction of Robert's innocence, the strain was telling : " she looketh not so well as she did by a great deal ; surely the matter of my Lord Robert doth much perplex her." Not dissatisfied with his own eloquence he concluded, after taking the opinion of the leading men at court, that " it (the marriage) is never likely to take place and the talk thereof is somewhat slack."

Within a month the opinion had been completely reversed. The court observed—what Jones himself had earlier reported—that Robert continued to display the bearing of the king-to-be. He was uncannily familiar with the secret content of the State despatches ; he sent for their bearers to interrogate them in private as by natural right ; and he continued to enjoy his privilege of access to the Queen's intimate presence where his entreaties would sound louder in her ears than all the clamour of the world outside. One by one, in a contagious fright lest she give them Robert for a master after all, the opposition began to come round : Randolph —Cecil, who advised Throckmorton that there was no longer any use in " swimming against the stream "—Throckmorton, whom the advice pricked into sending home eulogies of Robert and apologies for having maligned him. By Christmas it was circumstantially reported that the wedding had already taken place in secret at the London residence of Robert's friend the Earl of Pembroke.

And so it went. And so, while the weeks lengthened into months and the months into decades, it was to go on with many variations but no substantial alteration. The crisis was never passed because it was never reached ; Elizabeth's yes or no was always about to be but never spoken and the end found her and Robert in almost precisely the same relative position as the beginning. That is the extraordinary, and disconcerting, peculiarity of the story. Without changing course it quietly and completely changes character. From the first muted rumour of Elizabeth's partiality for Robert to the stunning climax of Amy's death it moved forward with the headlong momentum of tragedy. Then, having carried the action to the appointed brink of disaster in less than seventeen months, it wobbled to a standstill and there remained wobbling for approximately as many years. What had been a drama petered out into a problem. The spectator, seeing nothing further happening, relaxes into frowning speculation on what it was that stopped things from happening.

Something in Elizabeth certainly, since it was always for her to speak the decisive word. It is even—given the advantage of looking back and seeing her and her ways all in a piece—possible roughly to surmise what that something was. Unlike her subjects, doomed to look forward in chronically frustrated expectancy, she took no delight whatever in dramatic occasions. Again and again she made it her business to blight them by every means in her power. From the impassioned inquiry into Mary Stuart's guilt of the authorship of the Casket letters she deliberately procured " a verdict that was no verdict." Against the oppressive menace of Spain she continued for years to fight a war that was no war. To that extent it was quite in character for her to keep Robert in play, like many less-favoured suitors, with an answer that was no answer.

But that was not the whole of it. There was a profound and striking difference between Robert's courtship and her other major predicaments. Those she intended to follow the course they did until events overruled her, compelling her in the end to execute Mary Stuart and openly challenge Spain in arms. But events failed to overrule her intention with regard to Robert because she had no intention. All the probabilities point to her having really and ardently wanted his wooing to succeed, somehow, sometime. If only circumstances would permit . . . over and over she said that, blaming them when they did not. Yet at times they did, even encouraged her—just as at other times they bade her put him out of her mind for good. Had events been the moving factor in her hesitation, they would assuredly have ended it one way or the other : have forced her to decide something instead of leaving her with the obvious incapacity to decide anything. Something else must have been at work to account for that inflexible irresolution, some instinct deep in the recesses of her being, powerful enough both to paralyse will and to reduce events to a series of conflicting and meaningless futilities.

She herself early gave an inkling of what it might be. It had been expected as the Christmas season approached that she would grant Robert his coveted earldom, as well as restoring that of Warwick to his elder brother Ambrose—a mark of favour which from a sovereign notoriously slow to grant titles might serve to test public opinion and prepare it for the greater distinction in store. The bills were presented to her on the day appointed ; when, instead of signing them she slashed them through with a knife, remarking caustically that " the Dudleys have been traitors for three generations." Protests and reproaches from Robert. She smiled, seemed to relent. . . . " No, no," she soothed him with an affectionate clap on the cheek, " the Bear and Ragged Staff are not so soon overthrown." It looked as though she had provoked a lovers' quarrel for the mere fun of making it up. His friends, thinking the occasion propitious, eagerly pressed her to marry him at once. But no—" She pupped with her lips : she would not marry a subject . . . men would come to ask for my lord's grace." Then, they urged, she might make him a king, as Mary had made Philip. " That," however, " she would in no wise agree to."

How could she agree to it ? Her father might love as he chose without sacrificing power because he was a man and that sort of man ; her sister willingly sacrificed more power than was wise because she was that sort of woman. But for Elizabeth, a female Henry in sexual susceptibility as in autocratic temper, no peaceful adjustment between the two forces was possible. Woman and Queen could not both be satisfied. " I know your stately stomach, Madame," the shrewd young Scottish diplomat James Melville observed to her with the freedom of a privileged familiar, " Ye think gene ye married ye would be but Queen of England, and now ye are King and Queen baith ; ye may not suffer a commander." That was the crux of the matter. There was no way of permitting a husband to exercise the authority over herself which all law and custom required and her own deepest feminine instinct approved, without at the same time according him the jealously-cherished authority which pertained to the sovereign alone.

The lesson that her heart could only be indulged at the expense of the stately stomach had been the first unforgettable experience of her adolescence. The instructor was Lord Thomas Seymour, second husband to her father's widow Catherine Parr, in whose house she was then living : a handsome schemer with a magnificent conceit better justified by the quality of his body than of his brains. Philanderings disguised as the playful affection of a man in middle age for a precocious girl of fifteen . . . ticklings in bed, smackings boisterously administered on the seat of correction . . . none of it apparently to Elizabeth's distaste until it turned out after his wife's death to be Seymour's preface to a scheme for marrying her and using her both to overturn his brother the Protector and superseding Mary in the succession. Then the government had taken notice, and Elizabeth, enlightened and terrified simultaneously, repudiated him in order to save her skin and as much of her reputation as would keep her from being disqualified of her place in the dynastic order outright. It was a sufficiently rude awakening to induce her to fight shy of lovers and suitors for ten years, until she was safely Queen and Robert Dudley came along.

It was certainly not of her royal will that she fell in love with him. Could she have helped herself she would have preferred to avoid all serious masculine entanglements whatever. The measure of her feeling for him is that she could not help herself. At least the woman could not . . . the Queen often considered him on the whole more of a trial than those problems of state, her ten or fifteen other suitors, lumped together.

The very elements in his character that fascinated the mistress roused in the sovereign a fear and distrust that at times amounted very nearly to downright hatred. The overbearing Dudley temper, his pride and his exuberant masculinity no whit inferior to Henry VIII's own—to the woman they were irresistible, with their promise of mastery decently veiled under a courtier's deference, a lover's humility, blandishments soaring not infrequently to the level of poetry. The Queen could not, would not, stomach them at any price.

Over and over, furiously, publicly, vainly, she tried to put him in his place. " My lord," she snapped, ' with her wonted oath ' when he tried to take a high hand with one of her servants, " my favour is not so locked up for you that others shall not partake thereof . . . if you think to rule here, I will take a course to see you forthcoming ! I will have here but one mistress and no master." It was she herself who repeated to him with glee Mary Stuart's quip about her marrying her " horse master." Again and again she reminded him that he was her creature, whom she had raised and could degrade at her pleasure ; that his ancestry was not of the best, his blood not long since attainted. She struck him, threatened him with banishment from her presence and other unspeakable punishments. . . .

None of which ever came near to execution. In fact if, as happened now and then when she squelched him with particular ferocity, he sued for permission to leave Court, she publicly commanded and privately coaxed him to get the notion out of his head. Only once did she vary the procedure. She told him—it was nine months or so after Amy's death—that she had decided to invite the King of Sweden over with a view to matrimony. He told her that the King of Sweden was an imbecile—which happened to be true. She ordered him to mind his own business : who was he to disparage royalty ? He suggested that her marriage was very much his business. Let him understand here and now, she retorted, that she would never dream of dishonouring herself by marrying him or anybody like him. In that case, he announced, he would be grateful for her permission to go away to sea. Go and welcome, she rejoined. Nevertheless the King of Sweden was put off with an excuse and Robert changed his mind about going to sea.

Enthusiastically as her subjects wished him at the bottom of it, often as her own exasperation consigned him lower than that, she knew that she could never bear to part with him. He was her physical ideal, her intellectual complement, her masculine other self. However often their temperaments clashed and their opinions differed, they looked on life in very much the same way, a fact to which she gave instinctive recognition in the nickname she bestowed on him of her " two eyes " ; and it was under this symbol (written ◉ ◉), instead of the nickname of Robin which she retained for conversational purposes, that she invariably referred to him and he to himself in their letters to one another. They had the same realistic humour, the same contempt for the cant they were ready enough to profess outwardly when it served their ends. Writing to Sussex in Ireland Robert described the Treaty of Edinburgh as " a perfect peace concluded forever, if it last so long." The remark was on a par with Elizabeth's jibes at Cecil's Presbyterian allies in Scotland as his " brother saints " or her outburst to the monks who would have symbolically lit her way to her coronation with their tapers in broad daylight, "Away with those torches ! We can see well enough ! " Amidst the strained vigilance and grimacing postures imposed on her by the routine of state he was her point of rest, the one human being with whom she could sometimes relax and be herself.

Even to the Queen he was an asset of inestimable value. Like every other monarch of her time she would have died of shame had her Court not done her credit, and on the unimpeachable word of roving Italians who had drunk their Castiglione pure she possessed in Robert as brilliant an ornament as could be found in any court in Europe. He could dress, he could talk, he had manner. His compliments set the tone for polish, his conversation for point. His " wit, capable at once of entertaining agreeably and of designing deeply . . . together with a Delivery and Presence, commanded instant attention and respect." Whether as Master of the Festivities or of Ceremonies, no one pretended to equal his flair for spectacular invention or ritual splendour. As for his clothes, no such choice, exotic, diverse, costly and dazzling array of silks, satins, perfumed Spanish leathers and gold and silver Flemish laces—not to mention the gems of every cut and colour strewn all over them and the plumes to top them off—took turns emerging from any wardrobe in England except Elizabeth's own.

If only she could have taken the chance of making him Consort without the risk that he would aspire to be king. But she knew him too well ; she would not have loved him as she did, or at all, had he been the sort meekly to accept petticoat government in his own house. And once married to her, he would have no lack of facilities for asserting himself. Every intriguer and flatterer with a grievance in the kingdom " would come to ask for my lord's grace," every form of discontent sue for his leadership in opposing her will. If she had a child (the secret longing of her heart which blazed into speech on one memorable occasion) he as its natural guardian would exercise the incalculable influence of trustee to the future. After having, just to avoid such difficulties, so stoutly resisted her people's clamour that she marry, could anything be more incongruous than to provoke a really dangerous conflict with them for the sake of marrying a man whose character and insight into her weaknesses promised a life-long struggle in which she would be lucky to more than hold her own ?

Yet if she refused him ? Her alert Tudor jealousy—that torment of possessiveness to assuage which her mother and dainty, wayward Catherine Howard had had to die—permitted her no illusion as to her ability to hold him for the woman once he was assured he would never possess the Queen. And then ? She had no need to search far for the answer. She had but to shift her glance unexpectedly from Robert to surprise it peeping out nearby from under the cluster of jewelled caps demurely bent over a book or bit of embroidery. She could have named them at any given given moment in the order of his preference, those other ladies waiting for the moment when Majesty should leave the competition open. In that conflict she could hope for no better than even terms . . . which the passing of the years must remorselessly transform into prohibitive odds against her.

All the more reason, therefore, to overlook no present advantage. The magic wand tapped in steady cadence, and at each beat a new estate or office, a licence to levy a tax on this or a percentage on that, gushed forth its golden stream for his refreshment. Less directly she put him in the way of much other profit as well, for the post of favourite, though unofficial, was far from merely honorary. To its holder came such as were anxious for the royal notice and ready to pay for it, in tribute ranging from oxen of legendary proportions to silver plate engraved with his arms, from barrels of mackerel of the season's choicest catch to purses bulging with the Mint's choicest products.

The title of Favourite represented one of Majesty's most important attributes, the right to confer upon a subject by act of will a place in the hierarchic scheme which in the ordinary way only those born of the blood would have been eligible to fill : a very necessary right to sovereigns unwilling to be monopolised by a closed corporation of relatives. But Elizabeth could go further. Having no near relatives, at least none nearer than female cousins in the second degree, it was open to her to set Robert up in their stead as a kind of vicarious Prince of the Blood. Precisely as she charged Cecil as the beginning of her reign with the duties of Chief

Minister, so she gradually vested Robert with those of " my brother and best friend." He entertained visiting royalty on her behalf ; when she appeared to be dying in the autumn of 1562 she solemnly bound the Council to make him Protector until the succession could be settled ; reigning houses with princesses to dispose of and an eye on English friendship began to take note of him in case Elizabeth decided not to have him herself. It was an expedient dictated by tenderness, a compromise designed both to raise him above the seduction of rivals and establish him in the world's eye as fit, if she could bring herself to it, to mate with herself.

How soon she knew in her heart that she would never so bring herself it is impossible to say. She did not envisage ultimates. Instinct and policy, working with her in smooth combination, counselled her in this, as in all the major problems of her life, to keep her attention on the matter in hand, to take her time, to strike the best possible working balance between conflicting demands. Blind infatuation, the clamour for all heaven in a moment, was not for her : the tragedy of Mary Stuart or of Hamlet's mother, which so very nearly threatened her on the morrow of Amy's death, failed to materialise because she utterly lacked their tragic potentiality. For the characteristics of tragedy are waste and speed, whereas hers were outstandingly thrift and delay. By delay she kept the worst from happening. By thrift she added the valuable result of making the lover do useful work for the Queen in return for the favours he obtained from the woman.

Chapter Seven

ROBERT PROPOSES

SHE HAD her way, if it was her way—one can never be quite sure—but not without a long and often bitter struggle.. She expected and prepared for it ; and so, after it dawned on him that his courtship was to be no swift and easy progress to its natural culmination in marriage, did he. Had she been able to bribe him into complaisance she would not have thought him worth the bribing, any more than it would have occurred to him to look upon himself as a glorified kept man. Her gifts, primarily rewards due from a just sovereign to a worthy subject, were also, as between themselves, an indispensable compensation, a kind of regulatory mechanism in a struggle in which he laboured under the unfair advantage of her royal birthright.

That advantage apart, they were exceedingly well-matched antagonists. It was the recognition of this fact that as much as anything brought them together in the first place and kept them together after the issue of the courtship was determined. Familiarity never bred contempt between them. She might storm at him but she never despised him for suffering what he could not avoid ; nor did he ever despise himself for the necessity of submitting to and serving a mistress for whom his veneration in her sovereign capacity could not but affect her fascination for him in her feminine capacity. His pride in her Majesty corresponded to hers in his masculinity. The varieties of her character—her tempers (so like summer storms, he once described them to Cecil), her sudden transitions from the goddess to the guttersnipe, the astonishing felicities of human insight and caustic honesty in her direct contacts with her humbler subjects—all aroused in him the same delighted appreciation that his silky and dangerous graces excited in her. He knew what he was up against and respected what he knew. Better than any one he could understand her absolute need of self-preservation and self-assertion, the vanity in her so immense as to be almost impersonal, and so address himself with supreme self-confidence to the task of subduing them to his purpose, because they were the very motives operating in him on the same grand scale.

It was this even matching of personalities that made the struggle so long and hard. But it was Elizabeth's initial advantage of position that determined its conduct and finally its outcome. As woman she could say no, effectually and without even meaning to, simply by saying nothing. As queen she could compel him to accept that for her answer. He could not withdraw from the courtship without provoking a resentment in her which would cost him about everything he valued in the world. He could not get on with it because every step only plunged him deeper into its essential paradox.

How did one set about reversing an indecision? Or inducing omnipotence to furnish the necessary means of successfully combating itself? In the search for an answer to these conundrums he floundered from one contradiction to another, out of one vicious circle into another, without any consistent policy or any consecutive progress towards his goal. For against an immovable lack of purpose it proved impossible to apply any steady and cumulative pressure, or to explore a labyrinthine system of evasions except by groping in and out of blind alleys. All he could do was to try this and then that in the hope of somehow hitting upon the right solution. Most of these experiments are inevitably unrecorded, since they were applied directly to Elizabeth's mind, the invisible field of action with which he maintained his own secret communications. But occasionally he had need to enlist the outside world and then for a moment, through some disconnected expedient, some tentative effort at adaptation, he offers a glimpse into the character of his relations with his mistress during the years while he still hoped to bring his courtship to a successful conclusion.

The first of these incidents occurred almost at the beginning, just after that Christmas season when she had refused him his earldom. Away off on the other side of Europe, at Trent in Tyrolean Austria, the great Council of the Church, convoked two decades earlier, was to resume its deliberations after a long adjournment in a supreme effort to restore the old unity of Christendom. To it Pope Pius IV had announced his intention of inviting representatives from all Christian states, and England by her answer to the invitation would disclose whether she regarded her breach with Rome as beyond repair. The Queen's ministers, chosen largely for the work of Reform, naturally advised her to refuse, a large part of her people and the larger part of her ancient nobility earnestly pressed her to accept ; what the Queen, a Protestant by necessity but deeply traditionalist in her sympathies, would decide she herself seemed to be far from knowing. Whichever way she decided it seemed certain that an outbreak of religious strife must follow.

At this juncture the Spanish Ambassador received a startling communication. Sir Henry Sidney, one of the most respected of the Queen's servants, called on him at his residence off the Strand to lay before him the following information. Elizabeth longed to shake herself free of " the tyranny of Cecil " and his fellow-heretics, " put religion right " and marry his—Sidney's—brother-in-law Robert so as to avail herself of his help in that undertaking. If Philip would adopt him as Spain's official candidate for her hand, thus assuring him of the support of the conservative elements in England, Robert would engage as King-Consort to lead an English delegation to Trent in person and " thereafter serve your Majesty as one of your own vassals."

A handsome offer, certainly ; from the viewpoint of the zealous Catholic who received it no less than the promise of an answer to prayer . . . were he but certain who was making it. If Elizabeth, as Sidney, later corroborated by Robert, assured him, then Heaven had indeed seen fit to crown his labours since coming to England. But if the offer emanated from no higher than Robert himself, merely to entertain it was to expose his august master to a resounding snub. Torn between eagerness and suspicion de Quadra told the brother-in-law that, though he could not of course enter into so momentous a transaction without his master's instructions—indeed even write for them unless Elizabeth expressly asked him to—he would nevertheless, in order to aid in eliciting such a request from her, seize the first occasion to recommend her to marry the young man—with whom he had recently associated her in a peculiarly revolting murder—" as warmly as he could desire."

Two days later he fulfilled his promise Elizabeth called him to her during a public audience and " and after many circumlocutions " said she would like to make him her confessor and tell him her secret. " She was no angel ; she did not deny she had some affection for Lord Robert . . . but——" Then followed a whole string, a very tangled string, of buts. While she had not definitely decided to marry . . . nevertheless she saw more clearly every day the need for marrying . . . but to satisfy the English humour it was desirable that she marry an Englishman. In short, how would Philip take it if she married one of her own servitors ?

The opening seemed made to order. Not only had Elizabeth broached the delicate subject herself, she had done it in such a way as to underline the inference that Robert's offer had been made with her knowledge and approval. Still wary, however, the Ambassador responded that he could not, of course, answer her question officially until it had been put down in black and white for reference to Madrid in proper form : but true to, even exceeding his promise to Robert, added that, speaking for himself, he had no doubt that Philip " would be delighted to hear of the advancement of Lord Robert, whom he had always held in great affection and esteem."

This cordial encouragement somehow failed to speed her to the next and decisive step. De Quadra, unable on the one hand to do more until he had heard from Madrid in answer to an informal request for instructions sent the day of his first interview with Sidney, on the other alarmed at the effect on his English friends of his sudden intimacy with the Queen and her detested favourite, tried for the time being to be seen as little in their company as possible. Robert assisted him by falling ill with chagrin and taking to his bed when Elizabeth delayed to act on his plea for the dispatch of an envoy empowered to open formal negotiations in Madrid. The Papal messenger bearing the invitation to Trent meanwhile set off for England via Brussels ; and at about the same time Philip II, ordinarily the most dilatory of correspondents, answered de Quadra's request for instructions by return of courier with a letter

completely endorsing the sentiments attributed to him and author-
ising his ambassador to close with Robert's offer once Elizabeth,
" whose words are little to be depended on," had made herself a
party to it in writing. That proviso fulfilled, she might count on
the Spanish Empire's blessing on her nuptials. As further evidence
of his cordiality he wrote the same day to his Chancellor in the
Netherlands ordering him not to allow the papal messenger to sail
until the marriage was settled so as not to embarrass or irritate
Elizabeth meantime.

While Philip's letter travelled northward, de Quadra made
application to the Privy Council for the messenger's admission.
Before the application could be acted upon—or Philip's letter
arrive—Elizabeth suddenly took the initiative. She sent Cecil—
of all people ! the intended sacrificial victim of the whole transaction
—to explain to the ambassador how painful it would be for the
Queen, " who was a modest maiden, and not inclined to marry,"
to be forced " to promise these means and expedients herself, like
a woman who sought to gratify her desires and went round asking
people to help her." To spare her this shame could not de Quadra
prevail upon his King to write her a letter pressing her to choose
" a gentleman of her realm " immediately with the promise to
befriend whomever she selected ? If Philip would do this for her,
she on her part would engage to lay his letter before a select
committee of the Lords and Commons to justify the matrimonial
decision she would place before them at the same time.

To this preposterous suggestion the Bishop replied by changing
the subject. For to suppose that Elizabeth and Cecil really expected
to jockey the King of Spain into the position of publicly imploring
her to marry her most unpopular subject argued a mental simplicity
on their part of which he entirely acquitted them. He could only
suppose that they had chosen this somewhat tortuous method to
notify him that the discussions were off, and congratulated himself
on having at no time " given them a chance to say that your Majesty
wished to sell them your countenance in exchange for a restitution
of religion ": a bargain which, " however just and holy in our
eyes " would not only " scandalise the heretics " but entail grave
" risk of offending the Catholics."

The congratulation turned out to be premature. The story, despite his care, had got round—how, he could not guess, though Elizabeth, when he taxed her, surmised that his English friends must have had it from the men of his household : a not implausible conjecture, seeing how many of them drew little extras from Cecil's secret funds. So that when the application for the Papal messenger to deliver the pontiff's invitation to " his dearest daughter in Christ " was refused, and de Quadra looked round to the English Catholic leaders to carry out their threats, or at the least to speak out their indignation, he found them coldly looking the other way, less annoyed at the moment with Elizabeth for rebuffing the Pope than with Philip for embracing Robert Dudley . . . while from the Protestants there arose a pæan of thanks to the Queen who had resisted the blandishments of Rome even with her lover annexed to them. She, meanwhile, satisfied that the brewing religious crisis had been averted, took his illness in hand and by assiduous nursing, together with the award of a more salubrious apartment upstairs next her own, soon succeeded in restoring his health and spirits.

Nothing could have been more characteristic of her than to seize upon whatever device lay handy to keep the threatened peace of her realm—the first duty to which she had sworn, after all, in the solemn articles of her coronation oath. But in this instance the device consisted of the opportunity to exploit her lover's unpopularity ; and the incident throws a light upon their relationship as revealing for Robert as it must have been disconcerting. Whether she deliberately fooled him, as he bitterly protested, or made him a conscious party to the fooling of de Quadra, as the latter at one moment suspected (though if so Robert gave a remarkably life-like performance of a man utterly deceived), there is no certain means of knowing since there were naturally no witnesses to what passed between them. But fooling or fooled from his point of view made little difference, since it could hardly have been more agreeable to be the knowing agent than the ignorant decoy of a stratagem which in either case rested on the derision of his dearest hope. The blunt and inescapable fact stood out that he had been made to serve her purpose rather than his own ; like any other seeker after her bounty, she expected him to earn it if he was to receive it, love or no love and at whatever sacrifice of his feelings where her notion of the good of her state was concerned. She was prepared to do no less herself.

It says nothing against Robert that he was willing to accept such an arrangement; other men, of rarer fibre and abilities, accepted it as an understood condition of her service. But for him there was a special complication. He owed his position neither to recognised merit nor the sacred prerogative of birth; he was simply a Favourite, a creature whose undeserved fortune other men regarded as an affront to be wiped out only by his spectacular downfall. Majesty alone, who had made him, could protect him, and although it was his supreme luck that Majesty happened to wear a female form, it also entailed the possibility of her casting him off any time he ceased to please. Far as he had gone he must always go further if only to secure himself against falling back; become so strong through her help that even she could not overthrow him, attain such power in the state that she might dare to marry him. Like Lucifer he could not rest content with mere bounty, but must partake of the very nature of the being who had made him. Then, with things more nearly equal between them, one would see who was master. For although the advantage of regality would still be hers, there was also in such a contest an advantage in being more loved than loving.

In brief the task to which Robert perforce dedicated himself was to become a statesman while remaining the Favourite. The approach to Philip II was his first effort in that direction, his earliest effort at a political combination. It is one of the paradoxes of his career that, having started out to become a statesman primarily in order to marry Elizabeth, he became an exceedingly important one despite—indeed because of—not marrying her.

Not, however, as a champion of the lost cause of English Catholicism, though it was some while yet before he recognised that it was a profitless cause for him. The motives that attracted him to it were mixed, in part a sense that its large but disorganised forces offered the most promising scope for the political leadership he was anxious to exert, in part the comparative upstart's desire for affinity with the blue blood and proud tradition of the old nobility, to his share in which, through the slender grand-maternal link with Beauchamps, Talbots and Greys, he never neglected the slightest occasion for calling attention. When Cecil started a mild persecution " of certain Mass-mongers " that Spring " for the rebating of the Papist's humours," he took their part with the Queen so earnestly that de Quadra was moved to write " things would be much worse if Lord Robert were not on our side." In this practice he was to continue even after the evolution of his interests and ideas had carried him to the extreme opposite side.

His Spanish overture concludes with an epilogue in good Elizabethan vein. The following St. John's Day, while waiting with the Queen and de Quadra in her galley for the midsummer water festival to begin, he and Elizabeth sat " joking as usual," when the Bishop's wandering attention was arrested by the abrupt suggestion from Robert that he might marry them then and there. The Spaniard gravely agreed, with a homily on how they might thus " extricate themselves from the tyranny of the Councillors who had possession of the Queen and her affairs." Only Elizabeth seemed doubtful : she was not sure the Bishop knew English enough for the purpose. Since neither of the others apparently dared to suggest that Latin would do for the nuptials of the head of the Church of England, the conversation again lapsed into joking, " which (de Quadra ended gloomily) she likes to do much better than talking business."

The second incident is in the nature of an interlude. Courtship was suspended in favour of war. The massacre of a Huguenot congregation by the retainers of the Duke of Guise, the French Catholic leader, in the spring of 1562, had plunged France into the orgy of blood and fire that was to last the rest of the century. The Catholics seized the young King, Charles IX and the Queen-Regent his mother, Catherine de Medici, who promptly made common cause with their captors and appealed to the King of Spain for help. The Huguenots under the Prince of Condé fortified themselves in Normandy and sent out a similar appeal to their fellow-Protestant Elizabeth. English ruling opinion was confused and divided. It was plainly to English interest that militant papistry should not dominate the government of France ; there was grave objection on the other hand, not least on Elizabeth's part, to intervening in a struggle on the side of rebels against the royal authority. But popular feeling, whipped up by tales of Catholic atrocities brought by refugees from across the Channel, proved irresistible. It was decided to send an expeditionary force to help defend Rouen and another and larger under Robert's brother Ambrose, now Earl of Warwick, to take possession of Havre under a treaty concluded with Condé.

" Thanks be to God," exulted the King of Spain's late would-be vassal, " her Majesty doth not so much measure common policy as she doth weigh the prosperity of true religion." There is no reason to doubt his sincerity ; even his contemporaries did not doubt it. Already there was noted in England the tendency in time of foreign troubles to resolve differences of opinion, even over " true religion," into elementary patriotism " as musicians do make melody of discord."

Only Elizabeth could not see it in quite that way. For she hated war, revolted by its senseless waste as passionately as her lover was attracted by its pomp and its straightforward masculine dramatisation of energy and will. Barely had she gone in than she wished she were out ; and having no feasible way of getting out, vented her irritation upon the servants who had induced her to go in until their sanity and the efficiency of her arms threatened to break down together.

Upon Robert devolved the task of buttressing both. His tactful handling of her amounted almost to a separate function of government. As the Council was the agency for instructing and communicating her mind, he became the agent for regulating and imparting her moods. Did a minister totter from her presence babbling the rough draft of a letter of resignation, an hour's *tête-à-tête* between the Queen and her favourite ordinarily ended with the former pensive at her virginals and a scrawl " in haste " from the latter to the afflicted statesman delicately inviting attention to the transitory character of the female tantrum : and so another crisis was averted. When Rouen fell in October (a disaster owing in part to her refusal to bear the cost of reinforcement) the

Councillors, scarcely less terrified of what she would say than of what she might do when she heard the news, delegated to Robert the duty of breaking it to her : with the result that instead of washing her hands of the war on the spot, she gave way to " a marvellous remorse that she hath not dealt more frankly for it . . . but she will be willing enough to the maintenance of that (which) is bygone : which doth much rejoice me ; for I had feared she had rather blamed the advisers than to proceed further." In fact the only person she blamed at all was her commander in the field, Poynings, " that would venture to send 200 men (to relieve Rouen) and would not send 1000, saying his blame would have been as much for 200 as for 1000."

So Robert was drafted into keeping her up to the mark when the Principal Secretary himself (for the letter was addressed to Cecil) dared not even approach her . . . perhaps because Cecil, who believed " matter of weight too much for a woman's knowledge " habitually told her what she ought to do, whereas Robert could not conceal from her his rapture at what she was capable of doing once a matter had been properly presented to her intelligence. *Mutatis mutandis*, Queen Victoria, Gladstone and Disraeli.

Other such emergencies fell to him. He became indispensable, even made friends : amongst them his old antagonist Throckmorton, who invited him to become godfather to a new-born son and remained his devoted follower till death. By his exertions for the troops he won the first loyalty of young officers who would follow him many years later to the Netherlands : and in the form of a criticism of his brother by one of the latter's lieutenants received perhaps the sincerest compliment of his life—" His Lordship (Warwick) hath some of Lord Robert's faults, that is, loath to punish, glad to give, and loath to deny anything demanded."

It was during this autumn that Elizabeth fell ill of smallpox and extracted (so it was reported) a promise from her ministers to make him Protector of the Realm in the event of her death. A few days later she raised him to the Privy Council, amongst whose most diligent and influential members he was to remain for over a quarter of a century. And a few months later she gave him Kenilworth, to become his favourite residence as long as he lived and associated with his name forever. For England, thanks to a reconciliation between Catholic and Huguenot in France and a terrible plague at Havre, the war was an unredeemed failure, but for Robert it was, apart from that, an unqualified success.

In September of the following year, 1564, he was made Earl of Leicester. The honour came to him not for any duty well done, not out of a sudden overflow of Elizabeth's affection, but to decorate him for a service he had neither the will nor the ability to render. It consisted of offering himself in marriage to the young, lovely and celebrated widow, Mary Stuart, Queen of Scots.

Next to Elizabeth herself she was the best catch in Europe—a reigning Queen conspicuously in need of a husband to help her govern a most ungovernable people with whom she was out of sympathy. Succeeding to her throne at the age of eleven days, on her father's death after a battle with the English, she had been driven out at five by an English army to seek refuge in her mother's country of France. There she had been brought up, married at sixteen to the invalid prince, a year her junior, who was shortly to become King as Francis II, and widowed at eighteen after a married life of twenty months. Still but twenty-one, an almost friendless orphan whose obvious need of protection aroused in her fellow-monarchs an interest not dissimilar to and no more disinterested than the emotion which her femininity inspired in the other sex, both her political difficulties and her own desires had from the moment of her return made her early re-marriage inevitable, though the delicate problem of choice had imposed a reluctant delay.

Two general alternatives lay open to her. She could either take a husband favoured by the Calvinist clique she had found in control at Edinburgh and by their patroness the Queen of England, or she could ally herself to one of the great continental dynasties. Devoutly Catholic, very French and superbly conscious of the royalty in her blood, the thought of taking a husband at the dictation of her subject politicians or the cousin she honestly regarded as a bastard and usurper—a usurper, moreover, of her own rights to the English throne—filled her with the profoundest distaste. Rather than that she had preferred to remain unmarried while her diplomats tested the possibilities of procuring for her a Valois or a Hapsburg—her thirteen year old brother-in-law Charles IX of France, Philip II's son and heir Don Carlos or Elizabeth's perennial suitor the Archduke Charles of Austria.

But barring the way in all three directions stood the obstinate hostility of Elizabeth. Having gone to war the year before Mary's return to expel a French garrison from Scotland, she was not prepared to see it or any similar foreign influence return in the train of a King-Consort. Nor was she particularly disposed to gratify Mary. Apart from being transparently jealous of her youth and the provoking unanimity of her rhapsodists, she had good reason to be suspicious of her intentions. As Queen of France she had openly, in Elizabeth's view flagrantly, flaunted the arms of England with her own ; and though the Treaty of Edinburgh had stipulated that she cease doing so, Mary had contemptuously snubbed the treaty. For Elizabeth to allow a woman who claimed her crown to secure the backing of a great continental power would plainly not do : how to stop her was, however, another matter. Elizabeth might hold things up a while by making matrimonial passes of her own in competition with Mary's. She might threaten the Scots with her wrath if their Queen's husband turned out to be named Charles whether in its French, Spanish or Germanic form. But both devices were too familiar to be taken altogether seriously. Should Mary's pride, self-will and impulsiveness happen at any moment to coincide with the current policy of the guardians of any one of the three princes, the resulting combination would be beyond Elizabeth's power to intimidate. She had to think of something better. Her thought issued in an offer to Mary of the subject whom she could guarantee from personal experience to be " the most perfect and virtuous man she knew."

On the face of it it was an insult to stop the breath. Merely to associate the name of her paramour, the odious parvenu with blood twice attained, with that of the daughter of the royal Stuarts and widow in her own oft-repeated phrase of " the greatest King in Christendom," could only be regarded as a wanton lack of taste. In fact the suave Scottish statesman to whom Elizabeth first uttered the suggestion did so regard it and tried to turn it aside with embarrassed laugh and a joke of his own. When Mary herself heard of it the walls of Holyrood quivered with her resentment. But, like Elizabeth, she had to act like a queen even if she felt like a woman. To retort that she was not prepared to take to her bed and throne her cousin's discarded fancy man would, as one woman to another, have been agreeable, but to a stronger neighbour hardly prudent : particularly in view of the fact that to obtain the one thing after the Crown of England she most wanted in the world, her recognition as successor to that Crown, she would require Elizabeth's assent and co-operation.

For though the next heir by legitimate descent, the widespread English prejudice against being ruled by a foreigner or a papist so told against her that they had already led to her being disqualified under Henry VIII's will as ratified by Act of Parliament. She would need Elizabeth's active connivance to have the Act repealed and her title officially recognised : and meanwhile, in the hope of appeasing English prejudice, she was privately meditating, as an alternative to her other plans, a marriage to her cousin Lord Darnley who, though a Stuart with a claim only second to hers, as an Englishman suffered from neither of her disqualifications. But again she could not dispense with Elizabeth's help, since the young man could not leave England without Elizabeth's passport. So her anger remained unuttered and instead of a scornful refusal she answered Elizabeth with a grateful expression of readiness to have Robert if the solemn proclamation of her title went with him.

How Robert felt—whether Elizabeth even consulted his feelings —one cannot know or expect to know. Whatever arguments, whatever heartburning, the situation entailed, they thrashed it out, as was their custom, in private. Such slight evidence as exists suggests that he was not at all eager to marry a lady who, all things taken together, passed for the most desirable bride in Christendom ; and even if he had been, he would scarcely have dared to let Elizabeth think so. Dutifully, in response to promptings from the English ambassador in Edinburgh, he sent Mary a present of three or four geldings. From the same source he received a most inflammatory description of the domestic bliss awaiting the young Queen

of Scots' husband. From various other quarters was he pushed to
exhibit a warmer interest in a proposal destined to make him, after
all, father to a new race of British kings. It may have been to
stimulate his zeal as well as to enhance his eligibility that Elizabeth
in the course of the protracted negotiations created him Earl of
Leicester, a title last borne by Henry V and hitherto reserved for
the sons of kings alone.

The scene of his investment, as reported by James Melville,
whom Mary had recently sent to London as a sort of special
matrimonial envoy, is as curious as it is familiar. " And to causes
the Queen my mistress to think more of him, I was required to
stay till I had seen him made Earl of Leicester, with great solemnity
at Westminster ; herself (Elizabeth) helping to put on his ceremonial, himself sitting on his knees before her, keeping a great
gravity and discreet behaviour ; but she could not refrain from
putting her hand in his neck to kittle him smilingly, the French
Ambassador and I standing beside her."

The ceremony finished, Elizabeth, with a fond look at the new
earl, asked Melville how he liked him. " As he was a worthy
subject," replied the canny Scot, " he was happy that he had
encountered a worthy princess that could discern and reward good
service." Her glance turned " towards my Lord Darnley, who as
nearest Prince of the Blood bore the sword of honour that day
before her "—and with whom Melville was in secret touch on
Mary's behalf to render ridiculous all the purpose of the day's
ceremony. " Yet," remarked Elizabeth with disconcerting shrewdness, " ye like better of yonder long lad." Smoothly Melville
parried the thrust with a private assurance that " no woman of
spirit would make choice of such a man—for he was very lusty,
beardless and lady-faced."

The sequel was to show that Elizabeth had observed and
weighed the significance of those traits as well as Melville. Did
she also, one wonders, have regard to the effect on Mary when
Melville reported how she had fondled the neck of his rival, her
fabricated prince of the blood ? She may have ; she was not much
given to uncalculated impulses in public. And yet there may have
been something else as well, a gesture to soothe, or to reassure the

young man kneeling with such " great gravity " before her, decked out like a sacrificial bull for delivery into Scotland. It is hard to resist the suspicion that the apparently mischievous straying of her fingers was meant to convey more than appeared to the spectators : either the wordless reminder that if he went her love would go with him, or the renewal of a secret promise that he would not, despite the solemn and brilliant evidence just offered to the contrary, have to go at all.

Or again, as in other emergencies, she may not have known herself how it would work out in the end. The solemn and irrevocable deed of the succession to Mary she would not grant for the reason she stated over and over, in one form or another : never more vividly than when she rejected the demand of her Parliament two years later that she name an heir with the stormy refusal " in her lifetime to lay her own winding sheet before her eyes, yea, make her own grave while she liveth and looketh on." For in the turbulent state of England, and the common experience of sixteenth century monarchy, a recognised alternative to the reigning sovereign implied an untouchable rival round whom all present discontent and potential rebellion would assuredly gather. And if this was true of any known successor, how much truer of Mary with her belief in her right to Elizabeth's crown here and now. What Elizabeth intended, so far as she intended anything beyond confusing and distracting the younger Queen, was to persuade her to accept Robert without condition : and if she did that, perhaps let her have him in the certainty that she, Elizabeth, could place absolute trust in the husband she had chosen for her. While conversely Mary might well have had him if her year of hard and patient bargaining had convinced her that there was no other way to establish her claim.

What followed certainly neither Queen could have foreseen from the beginning. How Elizabeth, to the consternation of her ministers, allowed Darnley to go into Scotland . . . how Mary, at first attracted to him, nursed him through an illness and fell wildly in love with him . . . how Elizabeth, ably supported by Robert, intimated that neither of them was any longer much interested in a Scottish marriage for him . . . and how Mary, hysterical with fury at being rejected by the man she had degraded herself to encourage, flung herself into Darnley's arms and published their banns forthwith.

In vain Elizabeth sternly demanded that she take them down again and sent Throckmorton, who knew her well from his Paris days, to repeat her demand with an offer to recognise her after all if she would have Robert instead. It was too late. She knew it was too late and Mary knew that she knew it. So did Throckmorton, deliberately kept waiting in London for weeks when he should have been hurried north at once if Elizabeth had really meant to break off the match with Darnley. The world in general believed that she had been outwitted by Mary into granting Darnley permission to go to Scotland. But a few of the better-placed spectators, like Throckmorton, Randolph and others, including later Mary herself, shrewdly guessed otherwise : that Elizabeth, after offering Robert, had the diabolic inspiration of withdrawing him in order to goad Mary into the alternative she foresaw would prove her ruin. As in fact it did.

That the success of the scheme depended at every stage on Elizabeth's ability to place absolute trust in Robert however things went was apparent throughout. But what seems to have struck no one was the oddity of the underlying assumption that the post of suitor to Elizabeth imposed upon him the obligation, if need arose, to marry Mary.

They had worked well together. In each emergency her love and his ambition had been subordinated to and even artfully utilized for the benefit of the state. But now for a time their ways parted as in each rose the suspicion that the other was no longer completely content with this static and too serviceable relationship of theirs. In each this led to the normal human desire for replacement of what was missing, to jealousy of the other for acting on that desire and then, through the discovery of their ability to hurt each other, to a slow and wary search for reconciliation. The incident which encloses the process was spread over several years, for it was not a specific act of collaboration on a purpose, but a process of transition. And not being a collaboration but a separation t at last reflects something of their different points of view instead of, like the others, little more than their dual point of view.

It arose indirectly out of the Queen of Scots' marriage with Lord Darnley. For with this union of the two most serious claims upon the succession, it looked to the ruling class in England as if they had suffered a dangerous reverse ; for if Elizabeth died unmarried while Mary had an heir, the outlook for the Protestant faith and the vast property rights now attached to it were bleak indeed. A clamour arose such as Elizabeth had not heard since the first days of her reign that she take a husband without further delay. Not only militant Anglicans joined in but ordinary people frightened of a foreign successor or no successor at all other than the survivor of a bloody elimination by civil war. To make matters worse Elizabeth had, with the country in this mood, to summon Parliament to help her out of an acute financial distress she had brought on herself by her unlucky venture in France.

That a sullen House of Commons would demand a marriage in return for its money went without saying. Elizabeth tried to forestall it by a brisk revival of interest in the Archduke Charles, most plausible and patient of her regular suitors. As a token of her sincerity she agreed, contrary to her usual practice of insisting that any man who thought her worth marrying must consider her worth visiting, to send a distinguished embassy to Vienna—a really compromising gesture, since it exposed her to the risk of a rebuff. Even so she provoked little but scepticism. She had played, if not this particular trick, some variation of it too often ; her present need to play it once more was too plain ; and in addition, more important than all the rest, there was still Robert Dudley. How could the Archduke or his Imperial father consider forming a connection with a woman compromised by so glaring a scandal ? How could any one believe in the sincerity of her desire to marry another so long as she refused to be separated from him an unnecessary minute ? Indeed he himself openly believed, and Cecil's papers seem strongly to support him, that if Elizabeth were really being driven to marry, he stood a better chance than at any time since Amy's death.

And then it was noticed that their intimacy was no longer what it had been. From various quarters came the astonished report that he had fallen into disfavour ; that he " seems lately to be more alone than usual and the Queen appears to display a certain coolness towards him." The rupture became so pronounced that one of the Emperor's informants pledged his credit in studious Latin that their relations were strictly chaste. Nevertheless the responsible statesmen declined to be impressed. She had used Robert before to score a political point : why not again ? But this time there was a difference. She had not only withdrawn her smiles from Robert but transferred them to somebody else—a newcomer to the court fresh from his Master of Arts degree at Cambridge. " She has begun to smile on a gentleman of her bed-chamber named Heneage, which has attracted a good deal of attention. He is married to a servant of the Queen's and is a young man of pleasant wit and bearing, and a good courtier."

And also, until now, " a great intimate of Lord Robert's," his protégé and one of his small band of sympathisers. So much so that " many people " thought, according to the new Spanish Ambassador de Silva, that the Heneage affair was " all make-believe simply devised to avoid jealousy." He was not an unfriendly witness ; unlike his predecessor de Quadra, who had died of the plague brought back from Havre, he was on most amiable terms with Elizabeth. Nevertheless he was wrong and the gossips right. Elizabeth had succumbed to the first though by no means the last of her fancies for new and attractive young men. The omniscient Cecil at about this time drew up two private memoranda carefully comparing the Austrian Archduke and the Earl of Leicester in respect of the advantages each could bring the Queen upon marriage —in " birth, degree, beauty and constitution, wealth, friendship, knowledge, likelihood to bear children, likelihood to love his wife, reputation," etc.—and under the heading of " friendship " the name of Thomas Heneage was significantly omitted from the Leicester column. To that omission Robert was shortly to add more positive proof.

He himself knew well enough that she was not merely using Heneage to throw dust into people's eyes. She was doing that too, no doubt ; why not, when she could serve her other, more

mpersonal needs in the very act of indulging her new affection ?
Was he himself not an outstanding example of the extraordinary
psychological economy which enabled her to combine at the same
time in the same person emotional satisfaction with political
calculation ? It was the sort of chance she never missed. She did
not even miss it with the distant Archduke, waiting gawky and
tractable amongst his horses, dogs and hawks, outside Vienna. One
morning in this same late summer of 1565, Robert invited de Silva
and the Imperial Ambassador to inspect the park of Richmond
Palace with him. As the three with their respective trains " were
riding to the riverside through the woods where the Queen lodges
. . . Leicester's fool made so much noise calling her that she came
undressed to the window." Seeing who it was, she announced her
intention of joining them as soon as she was dressed. An hour and
a half later she did so and walked apart with the two ambassadors.
The subject of the Archduke arose and the Austrian asked her for
a ruby ring she wore to send him by way of encouragement. She
refused, displaying a certain hurt that he had not seen fit to come
and pay his court in person. De Silva thereupon asked her whether
she had not noticed in their train someone " she had not seen before,
as perhaps she was entertaining more than she thought." Quickly
Elizabeth scanned the faces of the attendant gentlemen . . . " turned
white and was so agitated that I (the narrator is de Silva) could not
help laugh seeing her." The laugh gave it away : she collected
herself and smilingly remarked that that would not be a " bad way
for the Archduke to come if his dignity would permit, and I promise
you plenty of princes have come to see me in that manner." She
might have feigned the agitation but she could hardly have turned
white at the prospect of being confronted by her wooer in the flesh
unless the emotion it excited was genuine.

Robert debated with himself what to do. If the loss of her
favour were final, then to pursue his courtship further was dangerous
as well as idle. Not only would he be unsuccessful, he would be
accused of trying to spoil the most promising chance yet of the
Queen's marriage—with the result that his countrymen, and in
particular the Archduke's supporters amongst the colleagues whose
opinion he most valued, would hold him in greater dislike than

ever ; not to mention the Archduke himself if and when he came. Yet if he turned round and supported the Archduke, whether successfully or otherwise, he would, knowing his Elizabeth, give her " to think (as he pleaded to the Duke of Norfolk) he had relinquished his suit out of distaste for her—and so turn her regard into anger and enmity against him, which might cause her, woman-like, to undo him." And what if he still had a chance ? If despite appearances she still really loved him ? And if she did, how was he to find it out before taking any next and decisive step whatever ?

He sought counsel of his old adversary, now his devoted friend, Nicholas Throckmorton. From him he received the constructive, if unoriginal, suggestion " to make love to another lady and see how the Queen took it," and meanwhile " to ask leave to stay at his own house, as other noblemen do." Robert accepted the advice with almost suspicious alacrity ; and the readiness with which the lady received his advances argues an equal lack of unpreparedness on her part. She was Lettice Viscountess Hereford, " one of the best-looking ladies of the court," a favourite of the Queen's—at least till then—and daughter of her cousin and valued servant Sir Francis Knollys. Having duly followed the first part of Throck-morton's prescription Robert prepared to take the second and asked permission to leave court. Elizabeth would not hear of it : " In a great temper and very bitter words " she upbraided him at one and the same time for rudeness to Heneage and flirting with Lady Hereford. Robert withdrew to the privacy of his apartments until Cecil and the Earl of Sussex, for the sake of appearances and perhaps in hope of his support of the Imperial marriage, persuaded Elizabeth to summon him back. Philip of Spain, scanning with interest his ambassador's account of these proceedings, sagely noted that " the whole affair and its sequel clearly show that the Queen is in love with Robert."

But what the King of Spain took to be the sequel turned out to be merely the preface to many more recriminations and partings. Robert had to drop Lettice but Elizabeth made no motion to drop Heneage. The following January, on the day of the Epiphany, " a game of questions and answers was proposed, as usual among the merrymakers of the court at that season." But most unusually the post of King of the Festivities fell not to Robert but to Heneage. He commanded Robert to ask the Queen " which was the most difficult to erase from the mind, an evil opinion created by a wicked informer or jealousy ? " It was a piquant situation. With aplomb that deceived no one Robert put the question ; with demure enjoyment Elizabeth replied " courteously " that both were hard to get rid of, but that in her opinion jealousy was the harder. The game ended, Robert sent a friend to convey to Heneage his compliments and the threat of a beating. Heneage retorted that if Robert appeared with his stick he would have to deal with a sword that could cut and thrust. Knowing Elizabeth's sentiments about duelling at court, Robert had loftily if somewhat lamely " to postpone chastising him till he thought it time to do so." Nevertheless Elizabeth, when she heard of his message, angrily banished his friend from Court and drove Robert himself from her presence with the reminder that " if by her favour he became impudent, she would soon reform him, and that she could lower him just as she had raised him."

Altogether it was his purgatory of humiliation. A few months later Elizabeth again intervened with a scolding to stop him demanding satisfaction of the Earl of Sussex after a quarrelsome outbreak of nerves in Council. It was less than a year since he had dared, before a gallery of outraged spectators, to help himself casually to her handkerchief in order to wipe his face during a tennis match with no fear of reproach when he exchanged blows with the Duke of Norfolk for calling him " saucy." Now an even larger audience watched with fascination the signs of his descent into the outer darkness of Elizabeth's disfavour. A relative whom he left in charge of his interests while he rusticated at Kenilworth " to bring her back to her senses " wrote him with regard to some lands for which he was dealing with the Exchequer that the Chancellor, Sir Walter Mildmay, " would gladly do your bidding but is loath to offend her Majesty, ' who is in no wise disposed to hear anything that may do you good.' " It was even reported, according to the same correspondent, that she had said to her cousin Lord Hunsdon, " My lord, it hath often been said that you should be my Master of the Horse, but it is now likely to come true."

Robert did not wait supinely for his overthrow. If he was not to be her husband, if he was to cease being her favourite, he would at least, he seems to have decided, act the part of good patriot and prudent politician. Urged by Norfolk and Cecil he came out for the Archduke. His colleagues welcomed his conversion with tempered enthusiasm ; they could not yet feel unqualified confidence in the convert. But despite an occasional backsliding when Elizabeth's frown relaxed for a little, and perhaps a little wavering when the stiffly Protestant and nationalistic faction in the Council petitioned her " to follow her own inclination," he clung to the position he had taken. The meeting of the Parliament that autumn found him firmly on the side of conservative respectability through as difficult and bitter a session as Elizabeth's personal government ever survived. In the course of a furious debate it was even proposed that a husband should be forced on her, or a successor named by Act of Parliament, before a penny was voted her to carry on with. When the two Houses, in the hope of avoiding so extreme a course, with virtual unanimity petitioned her to declare her successor, she turned on Norfolk, leader of the Committee bearing the petition, with the deadly insult of " traitor " ; and when an overwrought member of the Commons, ignoring her injunction to air the matter no further, insisted on delivering a harangue as emotional as if less critical than the sort Charles I was one day to be subjected to, she went Charles one better by promptly flinging the offender into prison.

The situation began to threaten not only the breakdown of government but open violence. To prevent it from degenerating further a delegation of Lords including the Marquis of Northampton, husband of her closest woman friend, the Earl of Pembroke, of the faction opposed to Norfolk, and the Earl of Leicester waited upon her with proposals of moderation. She would have none of them. Pembroke's protest that she had been unjust to Norfolk she silenced with the observation that he talked like a swaggering soldier. To Northampton she remarked that he had better save his breath to explain how he had managed to marry a second wife with the first still living. When Robert tried to intervene, she cut him short by saying she had always thought that if the whole world abandoned her, he would not have done so ; and when he professed his readiness to die at her feet, irritably informed him that that had nothing to do with the matter. The interview ended with her walking out on the threat to arrest the lot of them if they meddled further. Railing against them shortly afterwards to de Silva, she remarked with particular resentment of Robert " that even her honour had suffered in honouring him," but that she was now through with him and the Archduke might come free of suspicion.

In the end she had her way. Before the session was over she was actually threatening Parliament that she would marry out of sheer need of masculine protection against it, but that it would little like the husband she would choose or he it for treating her so. Handsomely admitting herself in the wrong over the offending member's imprisonment, she released him with the disarming confession that nothing had been further from her mind than to violate the constitutional rights of her loyal Commons—an act of grace which an awed House rewarded by voting the money she required ; and which she acknowledged by returning to them a fourth of the sum in an address compounded of motherly severity and royal benignity. After which the Archduke was put off by a conscientious—and generally popular—scruple about allowing him a private chapel for his Papist devotions.

Only Robert remained to be forgiven. To the others whom she had offended by harsh words she made amends by giving them credit for good intentions. Even of him she privately admitted " he acted for the best, but was misled " ; and that she was " quite certain that he would sacrifice his life for her, and that if one of them had to die he would willingly be the one." But openly she still complained of him ; nor would she humble herself to make the first overtures. At least directly, though on thinking it over she seems to have come to the conclusion that there was no harm in letting him know how badly he had behaved. And so during the following Spring she sent him a note, unfortunately lost like nearly all letters to him,[1] through his friend Throckmorton. His

---

[1] Many are supposed to have been destroyed in the sack of Kenilworth during the Civil War.

answer, too, is lost, the gist of it survives in his acknowledgment to Throckmorton, and her response in Throckmorton's subsequent covering letter to him.

His to Throckmorton is dated May 4th (1567), from Norwich, presumably the one near Ashby in Leicestershire. The difference over Lettice still rankles, through all the awkward complication of language involved in trying to establish intimate communication with one person through another :

"I have received yours (he tells Throckmorton) and another enclosed from one from whom it had always been my greatest comfort to hear from, but in such sort that I know not what to impute the difference to . . . I may have many ways offended, but as we all justified by grace and not by desert, so I protest my faith was before my works, and my full trust was that my imperfections—not proceeding of malicious arrogancy —should have been cleansed through the righteousness and clemency of others. Foul faults have been pardoned in some ; my hope was that only one might be forgiven—yea, forgotten to me. If many days' service and not a few years' proof have made trial of unremovable fidelity enough without notable offences, what shall I think of all that past favour which in some unspeakable sort remained towards me, thus to take my first oversight as it were an utter casting off of all that was before. . . .
"It would have been great comfort to me, as in times past, to answer what is enclosed ; so is the case so changed as I dare scarce now think what I have been told before to say and write. I entreat you to give humble thanks for the pain taken with their own hands, although I could wish it had been of any other's report or writings ; then I might yet have remained in some hope of mistaking. It makes me another man, but towards them ever faithful and best wishing, whilst my life shall last.
"P.S.—I see I need not to make so great haste home, when no good opinion is conceived of me ; either a cave in a corner of oblivion, or a sepulchre for perpetual rest, were the best homes I could wish to return to."

The postscript is characteristic. It is good Elizabethan—and perfect Leicester. Throckmorton's answer, dated May 9th, 1567 (no place given), needs no comment :

" Mr. Colshill arrived from your Lordship the 8th of this month, in the morning. He delivered your letter, and presented your writing, what time no person was present (by the Queen's order), but my lady Knolles. Her Majesty read your letter over thrice together, and said you did mistake the cameleon's pro-perty, who doth change into all colours according to the object, save *white*, which is innocency. At your cypher, the black heart, she shewed sundry affections, some merry, some sorrowful, some betwixt both. She did much commend the manner of your writing. Then she willed me to show her what your lordship had written to me. She read my letter twice and put it in her pocket. Then I demanded of her whether she would write to your Lordship. She plucked forth my letter and said, ' I am glad at the length he hath confessed a fault in himself, for he asketh pardon.' I said, ' Madam, do you mean in your letter or in mine ? ' ' In yours,' she answered. I said, ' That which you mean is but a conditional supposed proposition.' Then she read again my letter and said, ' This is enough to suffice me.' ' Yes,' said I, ' and to accuse your Majesty also.' ' Whereof ? ' said she. ' Of extreme rigour,' said I. Then she smiled and put up my letter. I asked again whether her Majesty would write to your Lordship. She said, ' I will bethink myself all this day.' I do judge by Sir H. Lee she meaneth to send your Lordship a token and some message . . . since she hath said you have confessed at length a fault in yourself."

The incident was closed. Like two cruel and brilliant children they had made their peace after a quarrel in which the peace of England and of Europe had played something of the part of a disputed toy ; and Elizabeth was left rejoicing in her " triumph over arrogancy."

Chapter Eight

DOMINUS FACTOTUM

FIVE of the most eventful years of Elizabeth's reign followed. At about the time Robert was taken back into favour, Mary Stuart was driven from her throne and imprisoned for marrying the lover who had recently murdered her husband. Twelve months later she escaped and fled into England. While Elizabeth and her ministers deliberated what to do with her, Catholic discontent in the North took fire from her presence and blazed out into a fearful insurrection fearfully suppressed. Almost simultaneously the Netherlands broke into their epic revolt against Spain, while England and Spain began those acts of violence and treachery upon one another by which they tried for a generation to achieve the results without incurring the risks of war. It was one of those acts, nevertheless, that brought this period to its close. It took the form of a plot, hatched out by a Florentine in Spanish pay, to assassinate Elizabeth, and its unravelling led to the arrest of the Duke of Norfolk, chief of her nobility and of her malcontents, on a charge of treason. His trail and execution in 1572 cleared the air and a comparative quiet descended once more.

In those five stormy years the courtship naturally receded into the background. There were other more urgent matters to occupy the attention of the two principals and of the public. Once indeed it came into brief prominence when Robert supported a project for the marriage of the Duke of Norfolk to the Queen of Scots in the hope that the example would stimulate Elizabeth to marry him, but since Elizabeth harshly declined to hear of a closer alliance between her first nobleman and her chief enemy, his meddling did him more harm than good. Then, with the return of quieter times, the courtship with its fevers and frivolities was found to have at last dissolved into the soberer and more tenderly humorous companicnship of middle age. Occasionally it would be brought out again and inspected like some ancient curiosity, to see if there was further use in it, but never again would it be capable of evoking the same emotion in the beholders.

Nor was Robert any longer the same ; no longer merely Elizabeth's favourite and supple foil but her minister and man of affairs standing on equality with the other administrators of her kingdom. Something of his new status was already reflected in another passage in Throckmorton's letter describing his interview of reconciliation in May, 1567. Certain rumours had been circulating in London that spring to the effect that Amy had in fact been murdered and the truth suppressed by Robert's agency. These rumours Robert, acting again through Blount, had succeeded in tracing to John Appleyard, Amy's half-brother, whom he had summoned at the time of the inquest to be present as her next of kin ; with the result, as Throckmorton informed him with satisfaction, that Appleyard had been arrested and held for examination by the Privy Council. Interrogated first by Cecil, then by other members of the Council, including the two known to be most hostile to Robert, Norfolk and Sussex, the prisoner admitted that he had received many favours both in money and employments from his brother-in-law, until the latter, irritated by importunities which began to resemble threats, had cast him off ; that he had brooded revenge and when a couple of ambiguous characters previously unknown to him had approached him with an offer of money to reopen the old scandal, he had agreed. In his defence he urged that he had never said that Robert was guilty of murder, merely that the jury had neglected to sift to the bottom of the affair. A copy of the Minutes of the inquest being given him he confessed his inability to read it, but after it had been read to him and time allowed him for reflection, he acknowledged that he had been wrong and was presently discharged with a warning. From this stout rallying round the maligned favourite it would seem that the governing body of the realm had fully accepted him as one of themselves.

For nearly twenty years he and Cecil, with the addition in 1573 of Sir Francis Walsingham—brought home from France to be

Principal Secretary after Cecil's elevation to the office of Lord Treasurer and the Barony of Burghley—virtually governed the kingdom between them for and on behalf of the Queen. The acknowledged leaders of the Privy Council, they three—to whom was added towards the end for the sake of balance the Queen's cousin, Lord Hunsdon—constituted a kind of sub-committee often meeting without the other councillors to advise Elizabeth and to reach decisions with the purely nominal consent and not infrequently without the knowledge of their colleagues. The labours of the trio ranged over all the countless and complicated affairs of an active, truculent and imperilled state. Finance and fiscal policy, the maintenance of the army and navy, the building of fortifications, the instruction of diplomats abroad and negotiations with foreign diplomats at home, the tragic confusion of Ireland, questions of alliances and war and peace, education, internal order and the system of justice, the multifarious and insoluble problems of religion, the management of Parliament, appointment to and removal from office, the fostering and protection of commerce, agriculture, forests, fisheries, etc., all these and a host of others formed part of their daily routine.

Nor were their activities confined to matters of high and general importance. Petitions, complaints, appeals, requests poured in on them from all corners of the realm—individuals who clamoured to have a wrong redressed, a property granted or restored, a friend or relative rewarded, a neighbour punished or released from punishment, a local scandal ventilated, a missing person traced. A typical instance taken at random shows Robert, Cecil and Sir Edward Rogers, as Lords of the Council transmitting to Sir John White, Lord Mayor of London, the complaint of a Frenchman named Bryart against a Portuguese, "who under colour of being the Queen's grocer would put him out of his house" :

"We pray you," runs the accompanying letter, "to call the parties before you, and finding it as pretended, to take order that no colour of Her Majesty's service wrongs the Frenchman, and send order that the party complain no further hither ; or

if there be not right on the Frenchman's side, certify the same
to us, to be answered him upon further complaint."

All these had to be considered, answered, investigated, answered
again—often many times again ; parties sometimes interviewed ;
the urgencies of the important patron they had invoked in their
support appeased or evaded with the tact appropriate to his
importance.

So passed many hours of many days on end of those twenty-
odd years. In the course of them the gilded courtier underwent
the not uncommon evolution into the knowledgeable and versatile
public servant : a process heightened in Robert's case by activities
so far-reaching as to comprise a fairly comprehensive history of
the whole range of Elizabethan government during that period.
Yet the duties of the Queen's minister occupied only a comparatively minor portion of his time. He was Constable of her Majesty's
Castle and Forest of Windsor and Ranger of Snowdon ; he
remained Master of the Horse, an office which in addition to its
regular duties devolved upon him the responsibility of improving
the English stock by breeding and import, and of preparing a
cavalry for wars. Thus the early months of 1581 find him taking
the musters of horses and horsemen in the shires, and judging endless
disputes between individuals and the local commissioners over the
latter's estimates of the former's ability to supply the Crown's
requirements. A little later he took on as well the responsibilities
of Lord Steward to Elizabeth's populous, costly and roving
household.

And with all this there remained the high ceremonial function
which gained him the familiar title throughout Europe of " The
Great Lord," together with the equally appropriate nickname of
Dominus Factotum. He met princes and ambassadors on the
Queen's behalf and conducted them into her presence, often standing for hours to give and receive addresses of welcome ; he accompanied hunting-mad visitors of rank through slaughterous days in
field and forest and sat with them through the night watching them
eat and drink themselves into a stupor. He draped the insignia of
the Garter round their necks and knees and showered them with

gifts of gold cups and geldings and palfreys, hawks and hounds and crossbows for the chase and broadcloth for winter and summer sporting garments.

In addition he had what one might call his low as opposed to his high ceremonial routine, the many occasions, that is, on which the Great Lord represented himself rather than his sovereign. On these occasions there were also the exchanges of gifts and speeches, the pageantry and the dressing-up ; but, on the part of the boroughs so honoured, worried computations of resources and painful misgivings as to precisely what welcome might be given him and expense lavished without overstepping the limits of what was due to Majesty alone. Then there would be offence on the part of the haughty earl, consternation on the part of the townsmen . . . hasty consultation and a raising of the quality both of the ceremonial and material aspects of the welcome by the latter and a gracious relenting by the former.

It was a dramatic as well as decorative existence—no drawback to an Elizabethan and least of all to this particular Elizabethan. Like his young admirer and, in some respects, successor, Sir Walter Raleigh, he loved making these sudden appearances in " white satten embrowdered with gold a foot brood very curiously, his cap black velvet with a white fether his colour (collar) of gold besett with precious stones and his garter about his legg of Saint George's Order " and to know that he was " a sight worth beholding . . . all this costly and curious apparell . . . not more to be praised than the comely gesture of the same Earle whose stature . . . with all proporcion and lynaments of his body and parts answerable in all things so as in the eis (eyes) of this writer he seemed the only goodliest personage made in England . . ."

Nor did his feeling for drama and display end with himself in the role of principal actor. In recognition of his unique skill in organising theatrical entertainment the Society of the Inner Temple —scene of at least one unforgettable First Night—made him Constable and Marshal of the Court of Merriment, with the title of Palaphilos, and enacted that no person of their Society should ever be retained as counsel against him or his heirs.

Of considerably greater importance was his taking into his

service the first of those private companies of players so largely responsible for the spreading of the gospel of the new-born Elizabethan drama. Actors were then—and intermittently for long afterwards—regarded with the same official and popular distrust as rogues, vagrants and suchlike "masterless men"; and it was a long step forward for them—and for the ten-year-old Shakespeare and Marlowe—when on May 7th, 1574, the Earl of Leicester procured a royal patent according certain of his servants the privilege of performing plays. Back of this patent lies a petition from "his humble servants and daily orators your players" praying him in view of a recent Proclamation "for a reviving of a Statute touching retainers" that he would incorporate them into his household—"not that we mean to crave any further benefit or stipend at your Lordship's hands, but our liveries as we have had . . . and also your honour's licence to certify that we are your household servants when we shall have occasion to travel among our friends as we do usually once a year . . ." At the head of the five signatures to the petition stood that of James Burbage,[1] originally joiner by trade and builder of the first theatre in England of " wood and timber " near Finsbury Fields, and father of the Richard who was first to create the parts of Hamlet, Macbeth and Coriolanus.

The distinguished patron of drama apparently made a less successful patron of education. For nearly twenty-four years, from the last day of 1564 until his death, the Dominus Factotum held the office of Chancellor of Oxford and the University was in general not thought to have flourished under his patronage.

" All good order and discipline are despoiled in that place," laments a contemporary critic, " and the fervour of study extinguished; the public lectures abandoned (I mean of the more part), the Taverns and Ordinary Tables are frequented, the apparel of the students grown monstrous; and the Statutes and good Ordinances, both of the University and every college and hall in private, broken and infringed at our Lord's good

---

[1] His company actually existed as early as 1559 and performed before the Queen at Saffron Walden in 1571 and on tour in Ipswich in 1572.

pleasure. . . . The head officers are put in and out at his Lordship's discretion and the scholars places either sold or disposed of by his letters and those of his followers. . . . It is as common buying and selling of places in that university as of horses in Smithfield."

There seems to have been some substance in these charges ; certainly various of Robert's appointments and his motives for them fell short of the highest academic standards. But it must be remembered that well before his time Oxford had been torpidly sinking and Cambridge exuberantly rising : and Cecil's much-praised chancellorship of the younger university probably had as little to do with the contrast as Robert's shortcomings in the equivalent post at the elder. So far as disorder and indiscipline went, the riots, wreckings of public houses, gaol deliveries, and the assaults on peaceful citizens, " so that no one can carry a winepot in the street but it is taken away, or a lantern but it is smitten out of his hand " complained of at Oxford could be matched at Cambridge, where Cecil had now and then to deal with uproar among the Fellows themselves.

Whatever Robert's failings they did not include indifference. If his patronage was sometimes corrupt, it was also zealous ; and later critics, less partisan, have spoken well of various of his teaching appointments and curricular reforms, especially in theology and the classics. At his first installation he tried to enforce better habits of study, both by statute and visitation, and when things appeared to grow slack again wrote six months later from court how he was in a

" marveil, at the mindes of learned men so soon altered from their own device and purpose ; and sorrie, for the evident hurt of that Universitie, which hath heretofore been compted the right eie of England and a light to the whole realme . . . and therefore these (presents) are to pray you and to require you to looke more straightly to your owne orders, and to put them in better execution than hath hitherto been done. Naimlie to the principal orders which directly touch Learning and Religion, as Sermons, publick Exercise and Disputations, whereby all Universities stand and kepe their name . . ."

Unless this were done, he threatened the venerable scholars that they would have to find another Chancellor—a threat which they meekly answered with a promise to do better.

It was not an easy life. The calls upon him both as politician and prince multiplied from year to year, while his social obligations at court and at home grew no less and his travels, necessitated by business and the deterioration of his health, ramified more and more. One wonders how he managed on twenty-four hours a day. Nor was it a cheap life. Duties and dignities brought in something but nothing like what they cost, and money was a constant and pressing anxiety. So a great deal of his time had to be devoted to making ends meet. The lands which were his principal source of income required the most anxious and careful attention : long reports from his many stewards—loyal and able men often chosen from amongst his kin—to be studied and intelligently answered ; journeys of inspection involving at times heated disputes with his tenants and local officials ; improvements to be ordered, markets for produce found, manors to be exchanged, titles to be fought out in the courts—one of these litigations, a dispute over the Berkeley estates in the West Country into which he was plunged soon after receiving his peerage, had been going on since 1410 and would not end until 1604, sixteen years after his death.

" A brief abstract of the Rents and Revenues of Robert, Earl of Leicester." compiled in the 1580's shows him as having lands scattered through over a third of the counties of England and Wales from which he derived an annual income of over £5500. The list is incomplete, several pages being missing under the heading of " Warwickshire," where some of his best properties were located; and his lands by no means accounted for all of his income. There were in addition special gifts from Elizabeth, not only of plate, costumes and the like, but sums in cash when he was hard pressed ; there were his percentages on the import and export of certain articles granted in monopoly to different trading companies ; his profits in various business ventures by land and sea, including a substantial interest in Drake's fabulous voyage of circumnavigation ; his allowances from a wide range of offices—wardenships, rangerships and the like, tributes from seekers of his, or through him, of Elizabeth's favour, and a host of miscellaneous perquisites.

But of this golden flood had to be found the wherewithal to sustain a princely dignity, and the greater the volume of the flood, the larger and more insatiable grew the demands upon it—the largesse to be distributed, the entertainments involving thousands of pounds for their scenic preparation alone, gold cups at £300 each, blooded stallions and jewelled Orders to foreign royalties, diamond and ruby studded knick-knacks for Elizabeth's New Year gifts, hospitals and other institutions to be endowed, as well as several costly households to be maintained whether he was using them or not. On Kenilworth alone, a small and inferior estate when it passed into his hands, he is estimated to have spent £60,000 in a few years on enlarging and improving it until the circuit of castle, manors, parks and chase extended to nearly twenty miles, according to a survey made after his death, " the like, both for strength, state and pleasure, not being within the realm of England." There were also Denbigh, his seat in Wales, Leicester House in London, and later his favourite residence of all, Wanstead in Essex, to be enlarged and beautified.

The appointments of these several mansions are what one would expect. The inventory made of them by his servant Thomas Underhill in 1583 conjures up vistas of endless rooms bulging with the results of their owner's effort to spare nothing in the way of variety, fantasy, colour and cost. One strides across acres of carpet of which the masterpiece in " crimson velvet, richly embroidered with my Lord's posies, bears, ragged staves, etc., of cloth of gold and silver " is only one of the more opulent specimens. One stares at miles of tapestry : " 8 pieces of Judith and Holofernes . . . 7 pieces of Jezebel . . . 5 of the story of Samson, old stuff," and so on through the Bible and all classical antiquity, with flowers and beasts, hawking and hunting pieces to fill in. One studies respectfully the countenances of the illustrious living like Elizabeth, Philip II, Mary Stuart and the Prince of Orange, and with interest at the family likeness of the owner " in whole proportion, the one in armour, the other in a sute of russet satten and velvet welted " and another " with boye his dogge by him," of his third wife " with Blackamorrs by her " and of his young son " the Lord of Denbigh, naked " ; many oft repeated and the whole of an astronomical total.

A roving inspection of the furniture gives a strong impression of the owner's fondness for his colours, crimson and silver, and of his diverse heraldic labels. They are to be seen on the

> " caborett of crimson satin richly embroidered with a device of huntinge the stagge in gold silver and silke with IIII glasses in the tope thereof and XVI cups of flowers . . ."

in the chair of

> " crimson velvett in clothe of golde, and the beare and ragged staffe in cloth of silver, garnished with lace and fringe of gold silver and crimson silk, the frame covered with velvett bounde about the edges with golde lace and studded with gilte nailes "

or in the

> " instruments of Organs, regalles and virginalles covered with crimson velvet."

The same is true of his napery and table services of which specimens were given in Chapter I, and of the binding of his books—of which there is a startling dearth—a Bible and 3 psalters bound in " redde leather gilte " at Kenilworth and a few of the same at Wanstead, " old, torn."

In the sleeping apartments above, the showpiece was undoubtedly a

> " faire, rich, newe, standing square bedstedd of walnuttre, all painted over with crimson and silvered with roses, fowre beares and ragged staves all sylvered standing upon the corners."

Of the tester and " ceeler," the 3 bases and double " vallaunce " and the 5 curtains " of crymson satten of XIIII breadthes " all one can say is that they harmonized ; so did the " faire quilte of crimson satten . . . all lozenged over with sylver . . . within a garland of ragged staves." Twenty other bedsteads of similar exuberance served the adjoining chambers. The quantity of bedding—sheets, quilts, blankets, counter-quilts, mattresses, " pillowbeeres wrought in braunches of roses, ragged staves, scutcheons of arms "—all " the sweete bagges of green satin richly embrothered "—of " close stooles," some of them black velvet, quilted, with pewter pans, dozens of others less elaborate—of nightcaps " of holland clothe wrought with flowers of gold and silver . . ." could have furnished simultaneous hospitality to at least half the peerage of England.

As it sometimes had to, or very nearly. No wonder that at his death he left liquid assets of less than £30,000 with which to confront almost unassessable debts.

The Queen of England herself, unable to maintain her state upon her official revenues and private rent-rolls, was forced to eke out her income by commercial enterprise. So were her principal servants, domestic and diplomatic, driven to their wits' end to support the heavy charges laid on them from the inadequate and erratic allowances granted them out of her exchequer. This participation in the nation's expanding business was of two kinds, one old, one new : one resting upon traditional privilege, the other upon competitive enterprise. Among the Crown's financial resources were the Customs duties upon exports and imports, and the right to grant monopolies at a price to merchant companies in the exploitation of specific articles like wool, finished cloths and various categories of wine. Of this right Elizabeth made use to reward useful, favoured and needy servants to their material profit and proportionate unpopularity, since their gleanings added to the consumers' costs and the traders' difficulties ; and of both the profit and the unpopularity Robert received his undue share.

Through the records of the period runs a kind of antiphony of payment and complaint : an association of Merchant Adventurers grumbling at the impossibility of disposing at a suitable price of an annual shipment of " 50,000–60,000 white cloths above the value of £4 apiece" when, in addition to other vexatious restrictions, 3s. 4d. to 4s. had to be paid for Robert's licence . . . manifestos against his licensed impositions on barrel staves and such like wares, sweet wines, oils, currants and the like, silks and velvets, etc., etc. Some idea of what these perquisites were worth to him may be gained from his sale of his licence for transporting cloths to a group within the Merchant Adventurers for £6260 13s. 4d., and an inkling of the scale of his transactions by a remittance from Sir Thomas Gresham in Antwerp in March, 1570, for the Earl of Leicester and others of £105,832.

Apart from this authorised rake-off on the country's trade, he gained from his contact with it an insight into its possibilities which naturally led him to try what he could make out of it on his own account. He dealt in shipments of wool by royal licence to the rage of competitors who were already paying him a tax on their own business ; he bought up French vintages for import into England, chartered vessels, studied markets, haggled with Customs officials ; his correspondence with his agents over these transactions constitutes a substantial proportion of his surviving papers. And like many a modern capitalist he kept a shrewd eye upon the industrial possibilities of science—one of several such memoranda amongst his papers shows him, Burghley and others financing a syndicate to encourage experiments extending over several years " for turning iron into copper by alchemy."

But there was another more adventurous sort of commercial enterprise that elevated business to the sphere of high policy and ultimately to the sphere of world-wide imperialism. During the earlier part of Robert's active life it remained unclear to the mind of Protestant England whether Catholic Spain, the jealous mono-polist of the riches of the West by right of prior discovery and a papal grant, was to be regarded as a friend or an enemy, with the result that in practice she was treated to official peace and private war. English merchantmen sailed the Atlantic to force her mono-poly and in the process often scooped up Spanish merchantmen returning to Europe bearing its rich assorted fruits : and English-men of money provided them with the funds to do so on a profit sharing basis.

Of these new style capitalists the Earl of Leicester was a distinguished pioneer. Ship after ship set forth financed either by him alone, if the venture were a small one, or by him at the head of a syndicate if it were a large one. It was not only his own money but that of his friends, borrowed or begged, that he flung into the good cause. What he owed to Elizabeth amounted to so impressive a total that her determination to have it back reduced him before setting out for the Netherlands, and his widow after his death, to hunted despair.

For his voyages did not always prosper, though his sanguine temperament invariably expected them to. Barely had Drake returned from the voyage of circumnavigation with its dividend of 4,700 % than Robert began preparing the voyage to Calcutta which Sir Julian Corbett thought should "entitle him to be remembered amongst the fathers of the Indian Empire." To his friend the Earl of Shrewsbury he wrote :

"For our voyage, my lord, we are now at a point for two other ships which shall be sent forth by the Company for Muscovia, and I am sorry your lordship is no deeper adventurer: for surely, my lord, I am fully persuaded it will fall out the best voyage that ever was made out of this realm, Drake or any other ; but thank your Lordship that you do venture that you do for company of me ; I assure you if I had X^m (10,000) pounds in my purse, I would have ventured it every penny myself."

The design was a grand one. Spain had annexed Portugal—it was Robert's purpose, in the name of the Portuguese Pretender, to annex the Portuguese Indies for England. But the Merchants of the Muscovy Company overruled him and Drake, his intimate colleague in the affair, in their choice of captains, the voyage ended in disaster and he lost every penny he put in, more than he had gained in several lucky adventures. Yet never for a moment did his enthusiasm flag. He went on with his brother Ambrose as partner if he could find nobody else, and before his death the adroit agents of the two brothers were sailing their ships in and out of

he North African ports in most amiable co-operation with the
ocal deys and beys—foundation of the invaluable Barbary trade
of the centuries to come.

The object of all this activity was, of course, to make money.
But it was not the only object. The Elizabethan crass enough for
that was rare, however feverish his greed. In Robert the specu-
lator's mind, as in Drake the buccaneer's, or Raleigh's who stood
somewhere in between, were other considerations larger than his
own pocket—his Queen's fame in the world, his country's prosperity through power at sea. His interest in the ships that bore his
fortunes did not end when he had paid in his subscription. During
the Portuguese expedition his "chaplayne" from aboard the
Edward Bonaventure wrote him, together with commendation of
Captain Ward, a report on the health and discipline of the men and
the state of the ships, assuring him that

> "we have daily morning and evening prayer, besides other
> special prayers at other times of the day. Every Sunday I
> preach, and after dinner we have conference in the scriptures,
> wherein the mariners, who never heard sermons in their lives,
> are marvellously delighted."

Robert may not have been personally addicted to prayer, but
his correspondence shows him strongly attached to the moral as
well as to the material welfare of the seamen whose efficiency owed
no less to their pride in the flag under which they sailed and the
cause of militant protestantism which they represented than to the
treasure they meant to bring home.

In fact, reflecting upon the activities of Robert in general, one
finds it next to impossible to draw the line between his public and
his private self. On the occasion of his going to Warwick in his
capacity of regional magnate, to receive the title-deed of the house
he was to establish as a hospital, he put the Bailiff through a long
and searching examination on the state of the town's textile industry,
ranging with intimate knowledge over the problems of raw
materials, skilled labour and competition, and ending with a
promise to look into the possibility of obtaining governmental

assistance. Merely on his way to a holiday and cure he would look shrewdly round him and write Burghley informative letters, describing economic conditions and popular religious and political feelings in the country through which he had passed. Much has been made of Elizabethan versatility, not enough of the underlying Elizabethan unity. This was the form it took. The energy and enthusiasm with which the Queen's servants pursued their diverse and individual interests somehow radiated over the whole field of national activity . . . in time of national need so intensely as to transform their very dissensions into an added potential of force. It is this quality in even rampant egotists like Robert Dudley which perhaps explains why the public business of the reign was, despite many glaring failures, characterised by so much and such conspicuous success.

Chapter Nine

MIDDLE AGE

ELIZABETH—the woman as distinct from the Queen—took up less of his time in these middle years than formerly, though she still occupied a good deal. His health took some, and other women more.

Their correspondence, more frequent than before because of these intervals of separation, enables us to see better into their feelings during these years than perhaps at any other time. So much of their earlier intercourse had been conducted by secret or murmured conversation, so much of it later was to consist of letters full of fume and fury over great political and military differences—though the last letter of all, his, with her comment on it, is perhaps the most revealing of all. But from the time of their reasonable certainty that they would never marry until his departure for the Netherlands, and in particular during the golden peace of the 1570's, their letters reflect the frank and unconstrained intimacy of two lovers who had successfully weathered the trial of each other through many and stormy circumstances.

But his letters show more. They show an independence of his background which make them singularly readable compared with the ordinary letter-writing of his time. The age was not only one of fantasy but of what would appear to us fulsome hyperbole, its taste more nearly expressed in Lyly and the Euphuists than in Shakespeare, especially so where royalty and supremely so where Elizabeth was concerned. To speak of her as " hunting like Diana, walking like Venus, the gentle wind blowing her hair about her cheeks like a nymph, sometimes singing like an angel, sometimes playing like Orpheus," as Sir Walter Raleigh did, was an exercise in restraint ; Sidney and Spenser, and Raleigh himself, when he really let himself go, could and did far outdo it. Leicester's stepson and successor, Essex, would write—when he was twenty-five and she sixty—" since I was first so happy as to know what love meant, I was never one day, one hour, free from jealousy," and swear that in her absence " I spiritually kissed her royal fair hands and thought of them as a man should think of so fair flesh." It was the sort of thing she asked for and increasingly got. An even better example would be a letter addressed to her by Sir Christopher Hatton, the able dancer who was to become a quite acceptable Lord Chancellor, while on the same sort of journey for health from which Robert so often wrote her :

" The time of two days hath drawn me further from you than ten when I return can lead me towards you. . . . No death, no, nor hell, no fear of death shall ever win of me my consent so far to wrong myself again as to be absent from you one day. . . . My spirit and soul (I feel) agreeth with my body and life, that to serve you is a heaven but to lack you is more than hell's torment to me. My heart is full of woe. Pardon, for God's sake, my tedious writing. It doth much diminish (for the time) my grief. I will wash away the faults of these letters with the drops from your poor Lydds (for he was Elizabeth's ' lids '—when he was not her ' sheep ' or ' mutton '—as Robert was her ' eyes '), and so enclose (close) them . . .

" Bear with me, my most dear sweet Lady, Passion over-cometh me. I can write no more. Love me, for I love you . . .

" Your bondman everlastingly tied,

" CH. HATTON."

and ending with the cipher of three lids △ △ △.

The signature of R. Leycester was never attached to effusions like these. They were almost invariably straightforward, brisk and businesslike. Writing to Randolph, who was on a mission to Russia in 1569, to keep him abreast of current European news, he starts off with a paragraph on France, then goes on : " Hitherto of France, now of Flanders. . . . Now a little of Scotland. . . . For lack of other matters I end." And even his love-letters to Elizabeth quite lack the flourishes, the over-blown rhetorical blooms, so favoured by his rivals and contemporaries. Perhaps his pen did not

run that way because his mind had not been formed that way :
it had been shaped, one remembers, to historical facts and mathe-
matical figures rather than to the modish classical festoons. His
literary images and allusions are comparatively rare ; his meta-
phors when they occur are nearly always spontaneous and original,
like the " cave in a corner of oblivion " at the end of his letter to
Throckmorton already quoted, or his statement that the Queen
of Scots, now a helpless prisoner in England, " hath broken all the
strings to her bow." Virtually the only foreign influence regularly
apparent in his style is his use of English words in their original
French sense, like " defends "—from *defendre* signifying " to
forbid "—in the letter below.

The best way to convey both the tone of his correspondence
with his royal mistress and the style that reveals the man is to give
a couple of examples, of average length, in full. The first is dated
January 16th, 1570, " from your house at Kenilworth " :

" If it lay in the power of so feeble a creature to yield you what
our will would, you should feel the fruits of your wishes as well
as the continual offering of our hearty prayers. We two here,
(his brother Warwick and himself), your poor thralls, your
ursus major and minor, tied to your stake (a reference to the
family emblem of the bear chained to the ragged staff), shall
ever remain in the bond-chain of dutiful servitude, fastened
above all others by benefits past and daily goodness continu-
ously showed, the last not the least, whereto our stake there
stands so sure a staff as defends curs from biting behind : and
then so long as you muzzle not your beast, nor suffer the match
over-hard,[1] spare them not ; I trust you shall find they fear not
who shall come before. And herein is the best and most indifferent trial, and to this end did I receive your gracious remem-
brance (of) the humble suit I made at my coming away.

" Now if it please your sweet Majesty that I return to my
wonted manner, your old eyes (here a pair of eyes are sketched
in place of the word) are in your old ill-lodging here, very well
and much the better for the great comfort I have lately received,

[1] A reference to the current sport of bear-baiting.

first by your Treasurer, and next by Mr. Topcliffe, of your
healthful estate, which is what I most pray for, not doubting
but that God will add to it such continuance as we poor
creatures have need, chiefly we that are left to your protection,
as ursus major and minor, Sister Mary and Sister Kate[1] who is
here with me, and well amended, whose life stands only on
your good comfort.

"You may see how boldly I enter into my wonted manner,
but not believe how gladly I would be in my wonted place.
Well, God, who has hitherto done for you the best, makes me
yield gladly to what I think shall be for your best, and only
yourself I prefer at his hands before myself which I have ever
done and continue to do."

The conscious transition from the stylised metaphor of the first
paragraph to "my wonted manner" in the second reads like a
quiet bit of fun at the expense of the epistolary idiosyncrasies of
the time. It points up the better his genuine reverence for the
Majesty in his reader of which he is so conscious. The second letter,
dated four weeks later in apparently the same year, from
Teddington, runs :

"Thanks for sending so graciously to know how your poor
eyes (ʘ ʘ) doth ; I have hitherto so well found myself after
my travel, as I trust I am clearly delivered of the shrewd cold
that so hardly held me at my departure from you. I have
always found exercise with open air my best remedy against
those delicate diseases gotten about your dainty city of London,
which place, but for necessity, I am sorry to see you remain
about, being persuaded it is a piece of the sacrifice you do for
your people's sake, seeing it is not profitable for your own
health or to prolong your life, which ought to be most dearest
to us, your poor servants, how little soever esteemed of yourself.
My daily prayer shall be that God will make us that way blessed,
and I trust you will use those means by which it may be hoped
for. I would gladly wish you were ever where your ʘ ʘ are.

[1] Lady Sidney and Lady Huntingdon.

but the ways are too foul for your travel ; a few fair days will amend this want ; if when the seasons serves, your determination holds to spend some time abroad further from London, it shall be well begun now, but I wish it had long before been put in proof. God grant you may find as much good thereof as hereafter to reap the benefit of the good continuance of your desired health.

" You see, sweet lady, with how weighty matters I trouble you ; if there were other matters in me than well-wishing, I would be as ready to pour it out to do you the least good as I will ever have a most dutiful heart to wish you the most and greatest blessings that God can give his anointed ; so with humble pardon craved for your poor old ⊙ ⊙, they reverently offer themselves as your vassals and creatures, praying the almighty to prolong your days with the longest that ever lived, and bless your reign with the happiest that ever he made most happy.

" I have your command to the lady of this house, who thinks herself most happy to stand so far in your thoughts for so small deserts, and is greatly comforted that you esteem her poor present."

Many of the letters were written from Buxton in Derbyshire, where courtiers and statesmen took the waters to ward off the pains of gout and corpulence. There was great faith in those waters : statesmen detained at court on business gratefully acknowledged the gift from their luckier colleagues of barrels of it to be drunk daily according to doctors' prescriptions. There was also great hospitality in the palace of the Earl of Shrewsbury, within whose territory Buxton lay, for the more exalted of these visitors, who upon the windows of the great hall of the palace scratched sententious tags and simple drawings of roses and arrow-pierced hearts as memorials of their stay. Most of these inscriptions were straightforward and (so far as we can judge) irrelevant borrowings from the classics, like E. (lizabeth) R. (egina)'s.

Fides ut anima ubi semel abiit munquam reddit

and " R. Leycester's "

> *Qui fidus idem Phoenix*
> *Qui se invidia aponit, Aethiopem lavat*

but there are also cryptic snatches of autobiography like " L. Essex's " (the former Lettice Knollys and future Countess of Leicester)

> Faythful, faultelesse, yet sumway unfortunatt.
> Yet must suffer

or Mary Stuart's lines written in 1573 during her captivity under Shrewsbury's care :

> *Bien que l'on aye tant dict de mal de moy*
> *Bien que l'on aye mal jugé de ma foy*
> *Dieu seul qui a de mes coeurs cognoissance*
> *Rendra un jour clere mon innocence.*

Of Elizabeth's answers to her absent favourite there are various commonplace messages of goodwill for his relief from pain and his speedy recovery. But the most interesting, and far the most amusing, of her communications, illuminating both herself and one aspect of her relationship with him, is a letter addressed to Shrewsbury in her own hand after Robert's departure from a visit in 1577 :

> " Right trusty, Being given to understand from our cousin[1] the Earl of Leicester how honourably he was lately received and used by you and our cousin the Countess at Chatsworth, and how (not only) his diet is by you both discharged at Buxton, but (he) also presented with a very rare present, we should do great wrong holding him in that place in our favour which we do, if we did not let you know in how thankful sort we accept the same at your hands, not as done unto him but our own self ;

[1] So-called because of the feudal fiction that the higher peerage were cousins —*consanguinis*—to the sovereign.

and therefore do mean to take upon us the debt. . . . Wherein
is the danger unless you cut off some part of the large allowance
of diet you give him, lest otherwise the debt Thereby may grow
to be so great as we shall not be able to discharge the same and
so become bankrupt. And therefore we think it for the saving
of our credit meet to prescribe unto you the portion of diet
which we mean in no case you shall exceed, and that is to allow
him by the day, for his meat, two ounces of flesh, referring the
quality to yourselves, so as you exceed not the quantity, and for
his drink the twentieth part of a pint of wine to comfort his
stomach, and as much of St. Anne's sacred water as he listeth to
drink. On festival days, as is meet for a man of his quality, we
can be content you shall enlarge his diet by allowing unto him
for his dinner the shoulder of a wren, and for his supper a leg
of the same, besides his ordinary ounces. The like proportion
we mean you shall allow to our brother of Warwick, saying that
we think it meet, that in respect that his body is more replete
than his brother's, the wren's leg allowed at supper on festival
days be abated, for that light supper agreeth best with rules of
physic. . . ." [1]

As a pendant to the complacent gibe of the safely thin person at
the threateningly fat, one might add Robert's own boast—equally
familiar in its smugness—to his fellow-sufferer Burghley that his
treatment was beginning to show results :

"We (he and his brother) observe our physicians orders
diligently and find great pleasure both in drinking and in bathing
in the water. I think it would be good for your Lordship, but
not if you do as we hear your Lordship did last time, taking
great journeys abroad ten or twelve miles a day, and using
liberal diet, with company dinners and suppers. We take another
way, dining two or three together . . . having but one dish or
two at most, and taking the air on foot or on horseback
moderately."

[1] The letter as here given is taken from a "Minute"—presumably a draft in
the Calendar of State Papers Scottish. There is another and shorter version of it
as actually sent in Lodge's Illustrations, which gives the date correctly as June
25th.

Nevertheless his forty-fifth birthday was to find him already red in the face and round in the girth, his thinning hair and swelling beard rapidly silvering.

He was no longer simply an official of Elizabeth's household, but now and then her host either in a public or private capacity ; easily the most princely both in the quality and quantity of his hospitality of all the hosts who courted bankruptcy for the privilege of entertaining her during her many summer tours, or "progresses," through the southern and central parts of her realm. It was he who as Chancellor arranged for her reception at Oxford in 1566, during one of the lulls in their stormy passage from courtship to friendship ; and who nine years later at Kenilworth treated her to nineteen days of apparently inexhaustible invention and expenditure which his contemporaries (including an eleven-year-old boy from the neighbourhood called William Shakespeare) and future generations would recall as the climax, socially speaking, of her reign.

The Oxford visit, awaited with intense expectancy since Elizabeth's descent upon Cambridge two years before, began unfortunately. On August 29th Leicester, attended by a brilliant company, rode in to see what provision had been made for the Queen's entertainment. The Vice-Chancellor, Dr. Kennal, and the heads of the Colleges rode out to meet them and bring them to Christ Church quadrangle, where the students stood drawn up to give them an appropriate welcome. But as they prepared to enter a sudden downpour of rain drove them pell-mell to the shelter of Dr. Kennal's lodgings, where in crowded dampness Dr. Pottes of Merton delivered his set oration to Leicester and Mr. Robert Benson his to Cecil ; and the latter became involved in a heated cross-argument with Dr. Pottes as to why Aristotle, in his Poetics, wrote *de monarchia*, there being at that time no monarch in the world ; the argument ending only by all going in to dinner.

More disputations followed before the visitors rode off to Woodstock, and more again the following day on their return ; and in the evening all rode out again, the doctors in their scarlet robes and goods, the Masters of Arts in black, to meet Elizabeth " with a whole retinue " at Woodstock, the boundary of the University's jurisdiction. Leicester as Lord Chancellor received the staves of the three Esquire Beadles in sign of submission and handed them to Elizabeth who handed them back in token of confidence ; and from then on she was drenched in learned outpourings in both the classic tongues, her responses to which give an inkling of the reason for her hold on the hearts and imagination of the subjects who came in contact with her. To one wordy Canon of Christ Church she responded with a graceful "We have heard of you before, but now we know you," to Dr. Humphreys, the severely puritanical President of Magdalen, with a smile as he bent to kiss her hand, " Master Doctor, that loose gown becomes you well ; I wonder your notions should seem so narrow."[1] To another Calvinist who in his speech thanked her for kindness she had shown to his brethren she remarked, " You would have done well, had you had good matter," and to the Regius Professor of Greek, after acknowledging his address of greeting at Carfax in the same language, " that it was the best oration she ever heard in Greek ; and that we should answer you presently, but with this great company we are somewhat abashed ; we will talk more with you in our Chamber."

It would have been easier to enter in the " rich chariot " sitting upright with a fixed smile ; to have received with mechanical graciousness the Corporation's gift of " a cup of silver double-gilt, worth £10, and in it about £40 in old gold " ; to have replied to the kneeling students' shouts of " *Vivat Regina* " with an intermittent and perfunctory " *gratias ago* " ; to have made a set speech instead of her charming little valedictory in Latin at the end of the week's visit—to have gone through the motions, in short, of a puppet Majesty in the face of this delirious crescendo of enthusiasm rather than to remain herself—alert, shrewd, caustic, appreciative. . . . The students of Christ Church, where she was lodged, gave a performance for her of the comedy *Palamon and Arcite*, in the course of which " a cry of hounds in the Quadrant, upon the train of a fox in the hunting of Theseus, with which the younger scholars who stood in the window were so much taken supposing it was real, that they cried out, ' Now, now ! There, there ! He's caught ! He's caught !' All of which the Queen merrily beholding said, ' Oh,

[1] Jebb. Nichols' *Progresses* makes the same point in slightly different words.

excellent ! Those boys are, in very truth, ready to leap out of the windows to follow the hounds ' "—a feeling with which she herself could acutely sympathise.   Unluckily the comedy " had such a tragical success as was lamentable," for owing to the " great press of the multitude " a wall and a flight of stairs collapsed, killing three persons and injuring many others.

The nineteen days of Elizabeth's second visit to Kenilworth, from July 9th to July 27th, 1575 (she had been there briefly ten years earlier), are probably more familiar than any other royal visit in English history from the very full description of them in Sir Walter Scott's enduringly popular novel.   The success of the novel caused his principal source of information to be immediately reprinted under the title of " Kenilworth Festivities, comprising Laneham's Description of the Pageantry and Gascoigne's Masques, represented before Queen Elizabeth at Kenilworth Castle, anno 1575 "—Robert Laneham, a court servant, being an eye-witness and George Gascoigne the poet charged with preparing the literary portion of the entertainment.   To the modern reader the chief wonder would probably be how the participants in those nineteen days survived them without perishing or at least going out of their senses from surfeit.   The mountains of rich food and oceans of sweet heady drink—320 hogsheads of ordinary beer alone were consumed at the time ; the trumpets and the fireworks, the pageants and the masques alternating with recitations in English and Latin in between the rapid changes of clothes and the constant thrumming of music ; the furious chases across the uneventful countryside under the hot July sun, the intermittent roar of the artillery Robert had liberally stocked for the occasion to greet his sovereign's coming in and going out, the pushing and jostling and cursing of 10,000 sweaty men at arms and horses which, with the artillery, he kept by for his royal guest's security—in this fashion were the Elizabethans apparently able to take their summer relaxations.   The cost to the host was estimated at the fantastic rate of £1000 a day in contemporary spending power.

Chapter Ten

" THE LITTLE WESTERN FLOWER "

THE eleven-year-old boy from Stratford, remembering, it is
supposed, the Kenilworth festivities in his young manhood,
distilled his recollections into his early play *A Midsummer Night's
Dream.* In it (Oberon's vision, Act II, Scene 2) he writes of

> Cupid all armed : a certain aim he took
> At a fair vestal, throned by the West ;
> But the bolt missed her, and passing on
> It fell upon a little Western flower,—
> Before milk-white, now purple with love's wound,—

The fair vestal throned by the west was, it is surmised, Elizabeth,
the little western flower another lady with whom Robert had
become involved to her sorrow. Whether the allusion is deliberate
or not, Shakespeare was much nearer the truth of the situation at
Kenilworth than Sir Walter Scott two hundred and fifty years later.
For Scott has the long-dead Amy secretly present as Countess of
Leicester, which she never was ; while there is no doubt at all that
there was present an unhappy young woman not only in love with
Robert and the mother of his son, but holding herself to be his wife.
Her name was Douglass Sheffield, a Howard by birth of the
Effingham branch of the family—her brother Charles was to command the fleet that defeated the Spanish Armada—and widow of
John second Baron Sheffield. Exactly how and when Leicester
became involved with her is not very clear, like so much else in
his private life, though there are suggestions in plenty. The first
open notice of the affair seems to be a reference in a letter from the
indefatigable gossip Gilbert Talbot to his father the Earl of Shrewsbury, dated May 11th, 1573 :

" My Lord of Leicester is very much with her Majesty, and

she shows the same great affection to him that she was wont ;
of late he hath endeavoured to please her more than heretofore.
There are two sisters now in the Court that are very far in love
with him, as they have been long ; my Lady Sheffield and
Frances Howard ; they of like striving who shall love him are
at great war together, and the Queen thinketh not well of the
and not the better of him ; by this means there are spies over
him."

But by May, 1573, the affair was already an old story, as the
pharse "as they have been long " shows ; it was in this same month,
according to Douglass's claim, that he married her, and six months
later that she conceived the child whom he at once acknowledged
and caused to be christened Robert on his birth in August, 1574.
It was only afterwards that the details began to be filled in, largely
by a connection of the Sheffields called Gervase Holles, who was
the ward of one of Sheffield's nephews ; and though some of the
story is pretty obviously false, even its falsehoods are part of the
truth of the age and Leicester's reputation in it.

According to Holles (repeating family tradition) Lord Sheffield
and his bride had lived together some years in content when
Elizabeth in a progress northward spent some days with the Earl of
Rutland at Belvoir Castle, accompanied by Robert. " Thither the
principal persons of Lincolnshire repaired to see their Queen and
do their duty. And among others the Lord Sheffield and the fair
young lady of his who shone like a star in the court, both in respect
of her beauty and the richness of her apparel. Leicester (who was
Cauda Salax) seeing her, and being much taken with her perfection,
paid court to her and used all the art (in which he was master
enough) to debauch her." But Sheffield, it appears, " was a gentleman of spirit," not at all the sort to condone the dishonour if he
found out about it ; and to reassure his frightened wife that he
never would find out, Leicester wrote her " that he has not been
unmindful in removing that obstacle which hindered the full fruit
of their contentments ; that he had endeavoured by one expedient
already, which had failed, but he would lay another which he
doubted not would hit more sure."

LETTICE, COUNTESS OF LEICESTER

From the Collection at Alnwick Castle; by the kind permission of Her Grace the Duchess of Northumberland.   Painter unknown.

This letter Douglass accidentally dropped from her pocket : missing it, she frantically examined all her women (including the gentlewoman from whom Gervase Holles later claimed to have had the story) " at first with entreaties, then with severities and cruelties," but as they knew nothing, she turned in dread to Eleanor Holles, her husband's sister, and " besought her on her knees to restore it, if she had it," assuring her that the contents did not seem to mean what they appeared to. Mrs. Holles, denying all knowledge of it, passed it on to her brother who " that night parted beds, and the next day houses, meditating in what way he might have just and honourable revenge." For that purpose he posted to London : but Leicester, moving faster, " bribed an Italian physician in whom Lord Knolles had confidence to poison him, which was effected immediately after his arrival. . . ."

It is pure Renaissance melodrama, Italian physician and all. Lord Sheffield was no man to be feloniously poisoned without serious official inquiry, which was apparently never even suggested : and the charge of murder may be dismissed as a product of family hatred natural enough in the circumstances, partisan malice (of which more will be said later) and popular credulity. Even some of the other details are not above suspicion. Elizabeth's progress into Lincolnshire took place in 1565, whereas Sheffield did not die until 1568, so that the element of speed would seem to have been introduced into the tale for the sake of art rather than of accuracy. And the gentlewomen from whom Gervase Holles had the tale must have been somewhat over a hundred when she transmitted it to him, with perhaps a touch of that selective power in her memory sometimes associated with very great age.

But even without the letter and the poisoning there remains enough in the way of intrigue, fear, love betrayed and grudges unforgiven to have engaged the theatrical attention of John Webster. In 1604, sixteen years after Robert's death, his son by Douglass brought a suit in the Court of Star Chamber to have himself declared Earl of Leicester and heir to his uncle Ambrose's estate of Warwick Castle ; and Douglass, to help her son, submitted to examination and under oath gave her version of the story. Without confessing adultery in Sheffield's lifetime—or alluding to the tale of his murder—she swore that Leicester had solemnly contracted to marry her in Cannon Row, Westminster, in 1571 ; that her marriage to him had taken place at Esher, in Surrey, in May, 1573, in the presence of Sir Edward Horsey, who gave her away, of Dr. Julio, Robert's friend and medical attendant (the prototype, doubtless, of the " Italian physician " of the poisoning) and several other persons more or less well known ; and that he had at the same time presented her with a ring " set with five pointed diamonds and a table diamond," which had been given him by the grandfather of the present Earl of Pembroke (his nephew by marriage) on the express condition that he should bestow it on no other than his wife. The reason for the close secrecy in which the whole affair had been wrapped, she explained, was Robert's declaration that " if the Queen should know of it, I were undone and disgraced and cast out of favour forever "—a plausible enough explanation considering Elizabeth's almost pathological reaction to the marriage of her favourites, and to be impressively confirmed by her fury when Robert later came to marry Lettice Knollys. In support of her contention that Robert regarded their marriage as valid, Douglass cited witnesses and letters, including one in which he " did thank God for the birth of their son, who might be the comfort and staff of their old age " and subscribed it " Your loving husband." By way of further confirmation she told how she had had herself served in her bedchamber as a Countess until he interfered for fear of disclosure. Finally, having decided to repudiate the marriage altogether, he had arranged an interview in the Close Arbour at Greenwich, where he offered her £700 a year in the presence of witnesses to disclaim it, and when she refused tried to terrify her into consent with threats never to see her again or give her another penny.

Nevertheless the Court of Star Chamber found against her son's claim. It did not directly pronounce upon the validity of the marriage, but very definitely rejected the evidence by which she attempted to prove it ; the chief witnesses whom she cited were either dead or not summoned, and of the rest several were arrested and fined for perjury or subornation, and the papers in the case impounded in the interest of public policy to prevent the issue being raised again. Reading the testimony it is, in fact, impossible to avoid the impression that the plaintiff's witnesses were a pack of rogues who had instigated the suit for what they might get out of it; and Douglass's own evidence is hardly more satisfactory. The ring and the letters she referred to were never produced. More significant still, not only did she make no protest when Robert publicly married Lettice Knollys in 1578, but not long afterwards herself married Sir Edward Stafford, who presently removed her to Paris on his appointment as Ambassador to the Court of Henry III. It may be, as she explained in her deposition to the Star Chamber, that she was driven " to secure her life " from Leicester's professional poisoners, " having had some ill potions given her which occasioned the loss of her hair and nails." But whether she really believed this, or was merely overwhelmed in her not too strong intellect by her ex-lover's sinister reputation, it is next to impossible to believe that a Howard—and as a Howard a kins-woman of Elizabeth—would have lacked the means to protect herself and vindicate her rights, particularly against a Robert deep in Elizabeth's black books after his marriage to Lettice. In fact her next husband himself, whose hatred of Robert at times resembled insanity, testified that Elizabeth had promised Douglass to force Leicester to keep his contract to marry her if she could prove it and that she had been compelled to admit in tears that the proof was beyond her though her alleged witnesses were at the time still alive. Nor can it be overlooked that in the very month she claimed the nuptials had taken place, her own sister was reported as flirting with Robert on terms of equal rivalry.

But there is still another witness to be heard : Robert himself. His testimony consists of what appears to be a copy of a letter to a lady, without address, date, or endorsement, and signed merely with his initials R.L. That the original was written to Douglass Sheffield seems unarguable. The copy, in Robert's own hand—the contents were much too delicate to entrust the copying to a secretary —form part of the collection of papers left by Sir Thomas Egerton, first Baron Ellesmere, who as Lord Chancellor tried the case in Star Chamber. How it came there is unknown, but not unlikely as the result of a search amongst his late uncle's papers by Robert's nephew and heir, Sir Robert Sidney, whom Douglass and her son were trying to dispossess.[1]

The document does not settle the question of whether Robert ever really married Douglass, but it does much more—in revealing the nature of their relationship and of his feelings towards her it reveals him better than any other single piece of his surviving correspondence. The internal evidence shows that it was written after Sheffield's death in 1568 and before the alleged marriage in 1573, perhaps even before the marriage contract of 1571, since neither is referred to.

" My good friend " (it begins) " hardly was I brought to write in this sort to you lest you conceive otherwise thereof than I mean it, but more loath am I to conceal anything from you that both honesty and true good will doth bind me to impart to you.

" I have, as you well know, long both loved and liked you, and found always that earnest and faithful affection at your hand again that bound me greatly to you. This good will of mine, whatsoever you have thought, hath not changed from what it was at the beginning towards you. And I trust, after your widowhood began upon the first occasion of my coming to you, I did plainly and truly open to you in what sort my good will should and might always remain to you, and showing you such reasons as then I had for the performance of mine intent, as well as ever since. It seemed that you had fully resolved with yourself to dispose yourself accordingly, without any further expectation or hope of other dealing. From which time you have framed yourself in such sort toward me as was very much to my contentation."

A state of affairs, which, however agreeable to him, was naturally less agreeable to her. A year before the letter was written she had

[1] The Egerton papers are now in the Huntington Library in California; and the letter in question was printed, edited, and critically examined in its Bulletin for April, 1936, by Mr. Conyers Read, one of the greatest living authorities on the period. The conclusion that the original letter was addressed to Douglass Sheffield is there fully argued and appears irresistible.

begun to press him "in a further degree than was our condition" and though "I did plainly and truly deal with you" a period of "unkindness began and after, a great strangeness fell out." Nevertheless they continued to meet "in a friendly sort and you resolved not to press me more with the matter." Apparently she did not keep her promise. A new estrangement arose, lasting five or six months, and though he tried to explain to her that he still felt the same towards her, she suspected that "the good will I bare you had been clean changed and withdrawn, in such sort as you often move me by letters and otherwise to show you some cause or to deal plainly with you that I intended toward you." Feeling himself unable to do so because of the situation he was in (on this he does not dilate, though it is clear it had to do with Elizabeth), he offered no explanation at the time and she, as he gratefully acknowledged, waited patiently for "one answer or other till time conveniently for me might issue." In the end he had to tell her the cause of his hesitation and to confess that he could see no possibility of any change in their relationship such as she was insisting upon—in other words marriage. A reconciliation took place; he understood her to have agreed to go on as before; but reflecting later on what she had said at this meeting of reconciliation a few days before, he fears she is still in the same exacting and reproachful mind and for that reason is writing her to make the position plain once and for all.

"My affection," he asserts, "was never greater toward you otherwise since my first acquaintance with you than it now is. . . . For albeit I have been and yet am a man frayll, yet am I not void of conscience toward God, nor honest meaning toward my friend; and having made special choice of you to be one of the dearest to me, so much the more care must I have to discharge the office due unto you. And in this consideration of the case betwixt you and me, I am to weigh of your mind and my mind, to see as near as may be that neither of us be deceived." He feels bound, therefore, to repeat, and to make her understand, that "to proceed to some further degree than is possible for me without mine utter overthrow" is as far from his own mind as ever : ". . . no other or further end can (yt) be looked for." The decision is no less painful to him than to her "that forceth me thus to be the cause almost of the ruin of mine own House ; for there is no likelihood that any of our bodies are (like) to have heirs ; my brother you see long married and not like to have children, it resteth so now in myself ; and yet such occasions is there, as partly I have told you ere now, as if I should marry I am sure never to have favour of them that I had rather yet never have wife than lose them, yet is there nothing in the world next that favour that I would not give to be in hope of leaving some children behind me, being now the last of our house."

Now for her side of the matter. Leaving out " your casual depending on me, for all men be mortal " he advises her to " look to your person, your youthful time to be consumed and spent without certainty . . . the daily accidents that happ(en) by grieving and vexing you, both to the hindrance of your body and mind ; the care and cumber of your own causes ungoverned ; the subjec- tion you are in to all reports to the touch of your good name and fame." On the remedy for this unhappy state of affairs he is hesitant to speak, it being a matter for her " disposition " of which he con- fesses himself " no competent judge." Nevertheless he cannot refrain from reminding her " that for my sake you have and do refuse as good remedies as are presently in our time to be had. The choice falls not oft, and yet I know you may have now of the best ; and as it is not my part to bid you to take them, so were it not mine honestly, considering mine own resolution, to bid you refuse them . . . to carry you away for my pleasure to your more great and further grief were too great a shame for me. . . ." And so, after urging her " to consider thoroughly and deeply of this matter," and committing her " to the Almighty who always preserve and keep you as I would myself," he signs himself " Yours as much as he was, R.L." A short postscript repeats the cause of his writing and the assurance of his eternal good will.

A man asserting his rights in a detestable situation arising out of his own act is not apt to cut a sympathetic figure. Nevertheless the underlying facts of the situation seem plain, since there could have been no motive for falsifying them in a letter designed to create an agreed basis of understanding between two persons equally privy to them. As Robert indicates he was " a man frayll " where women were concerned, and not less so for years of subservience to Elizabeth's exasperated jealousy. The lady seems to have been both soft and clinging—another Amy, in fact : qualities all the more flattering in an exceptionally pretty woman of exceedingly high birth—until they ended by becoming merely irritating from overmuch familiarity with them. The affair probably started in Sheffield's lifetime and became formally established " after your widowhood begun upon the first occasion of my coming to you " by mutual agreement on the condition that she would be satisfied with his affection and support and not press for a marriage which would be the end of him so far as Elizabeth was concerned. There is no reason to suppose that he still seriously hoped to marry Elizabeth himself ; her displeasure, amounting sometimes almost to frenzy at the marriage of her favoured unwedded courtiers, was enough to give pause to all but the bravest or most love-besotted.

That Douglass, ever more infatuated as he grew less so, ever aware of the ambiguity of her position, should have rigidly abided by the letter of their agreement, was, one would have thought, too much for him to expect. Nevertheless he did expect it ; and the alternations of estrangement and reconciliation referred to in his letter reflect the growing impossibility of both of them being happy in the arrangement. The letter clearly comes at a time when an uncomfortable conscience was in conflict with a diminishing affection to keep the affair going : it is the very climax of disingenuousness for him to plead how painful it is for him not to fall in with her wishes if only for the sake of the sons he longed for and how hard it will be on him if she follows his unselfish advice to marry somebody else. What followed is less plain though not too difficult to guess. They made it up on his own terms as before until, worn down by her persistence, he gave in to some form of ceremony which would quiet her, and yet be open to repudiation later if he so chose. By the time their son was born he had already so chosen : whether out of sheer weariness of her or continued dread of Elizabeth, or because Lettice Knollys had come back into the picture, one cannot be sure, though from what followed it seems not unlikely that all three elements had their weight. And Douglass, recognising with female shrewdness when she was beaten, kept her son and married Stafford—whose death opened the way for the pack of rogues to intervene in the reopening of the matter for the son's sake.

She did not keep him long, this son whom Robert had so deeply yearned for and yet irrevocably repudiated. After his mother's marriage to Stafford, and the death in infancy of Lettice's only child, Robert reclaimed him with the paternal intention of giving him a proper start in life. His correspondence with the boy's masters shows that he gave close thought to the young Robert's early instruction before entering him at Christ Church, Oxford, with the status of an earl's son. But then he died when the boy was only fourteen, leaving him a not inconsiderably property by will.

At nineteen the young Robert married a sister of Sir Thomas Cavendish, the famous sailor who circumnavigated the earth a few years after Drake, and from him inherited a couple of ships with which he proposed to join in the popular sport of harassing Spaniards in the Southern Seas. The government disapproved—ships were valuable and he was only twenty—but he managed to slip away to the West Indies for a raid on Spanish shipping at Trinidad and a cruise to the mouth of the Orinoco River—not yet explored by Sir Walter Raleigh—where he discovered an island which he named Dudleiana. From there he returned to join in Essex's immortal expedition to Cadiz where he gained a knighthood. His first wife having meantime died, he married Alicia Leigh of Warwickshire by whom he had a rapid succession of daughters.

So far he had followed the conventional Tudor pattern, if in its more exciting aspects. But thereafter he completely abandoned the path of riches and power thrice traced for him by his forebears across the Tudor landscape. The failure of his suit in Star Chamber marks the transition. Tiring of Alicia and her many daughters, he abruptly quitted England forever, taking with him, disguised as a page, his lovely cousin Elizabeth Southwell. Long afterward the government of Charles I compensated Alicia for her husband's disappointment at not being recognised as an earl by making her a duchess in her own right. By then, however, the husband had long since turned Roman Catholic, married Elizabeth Southwell by a papal dispensation and settled in Florence. From there he addressed voluminous letters of advice to James I on the art of controlling refractory Parliaments and to Henry, Prince of Wales, on navigation and shipbuilding. In this last respect he practised what he preached. His fame as a shipbuilder, as well as mathematician and engineer—he drained the marshes between Pisa and the sea, a really remarkable feat which laid the foundation for Leghorn's future prosperity—at length won him the recognition abroad he had been refused at home : he was made Duke of Northumberland and Earl of Warwick in the Holy Roman Empire, as well as a papal Count. He died in 1649 at the age of seventy-five, leaving thirteen children by his last and surviving wife, a fine Florentine mansion of his own design and an example of successful transplantation to Italian soil which generations of restless Englishmen were to follow.

Chapter Eleven

"THAT SHE-WOLF"

Aliquando mulierosus, demum supra modum uxorius, writes William Camden in his obituary notice of the Earl of Leicester, a verdict which the historian himself renders less pithily in his English edition "given awhile to women and in his latter days doting above measure on wiving." A partial cause of the gallant's reformation—though the number of his gallantries seem on the evidence to have been somewhat exaggerated—may perhaps be put down to increasing age and responsibility, but a share of it must be credited to his third (or, according to him, second) wife Lettice Knollys . . . the two being associated in the public mind as his Old and New Testaments.

He had, it may be remembered, been attracted to her at the time of Elizabeth's flirtation with Heneage and Throckmorton's advice to make her jealous by looking elsewhere. This advice he had taken only too well : not only had he annoyed Elizabeth with his practical illustration that what was sauce for the goose was also sauce for the gander, but he had apparently got himself deeply and permanently involved with the then Lady Hertford. How close the intimacy remained it is difficult to guess. They seem to have seen little of each other between Robert's restoration to favour after 1566 and the departure of her husband, by then Earl of Essex, into Ireland on Elizabeth's service a few years later—an interval during which Lettice's son Robert, Elizabeth's last, unluckiest and most over-written favourite, was born. It was widely believed that her husband's somewhat grudging return to Ireland after a leave of absence at home was forced upon him by Leicester's influence in the Queen's councils—and here the evidence of the debates in Council seem to support the belief, though the cause of Essex's reluctance to go was at least as likely to have been the universal dislike of the Irish service as his domestic suspicions.

The gossips held that the affair was resumed at this time. There is reason to believe that Lettice was present at the Kenilworth festivities in 1575, which would have provided Douglass with another cause of uneasiness ; and it is almost certain that she was amongst the guests of the Shrewsburys the following year when he went to take the waters at Buxton. That he was by then in hot pursuit of her can hardly be doubted, so that it came as a surprise to few when Essex suddenly died in Dublin only a month or two later. The world naturally murmured poison, and a few individuals close to the scene blurted it outright ; though an inquest conducted with apparently the most scrupulous care and impartiality by the Deputy for Ireland declared that the Earl had died of a flux—a disease common enough in those parts, and in Essex's case aggravated by medical treatment gross even for those times. Nevertheless it did not help Robert that the Deputy was his brother-in-law Sir Henry Sidney—nor that the loudest of his accusers expired of a similar malady shortly thereafter.

Lettice and Robert were married at Wanstead on September 21st, 1578. There was apparently an earlier, clandestine wedding at Kenilworth, but the bride's relatives, in view of the groom's reputation, were taking no chances : they insisted on the ceremony being formally repeated, and Robert later volunteered, or was induced, to have the witnesses swear before a notary to its having been performed in their presence. The precaution seems redundant. Not only was Lettice well able to look after herself, as after events (or a glance at her portrait) prove, but his affection for her was and remained so strong that no shadow of another woman crosses the brightly-lit stage of his life again. It would be hard, in fact, without considerable character on her part and affection on his, to believe in the transformation from *mulierosus* to *uxorius* ; a change hardly less remarkable than his daring at last to brave the possible consequences of his ageing mistress's royal fury.

Elizabeth took it badly. The marriage seems to have been kept from her for eleven months, until the late summer of 1579 ; possibly the Knollys family agreed to the private ceremony at Wanstead out of consideration for Leicester while insisting on the elaborate legal paraphernalia for the protection of their daughter. But in that summer the long drawn negotiations for the marriage between the Queen of England and the Duke of Alençon, brother and heir ro the King of France, reached their climax.[1] The Duke, resolved to press his suit in person—a procedure which Elizabeth had always, though often vainly, favoured with her suitors—sent over one of his gentlemen named Simier to prepare the way and apply for the necessary passport. The conservative majority led by Cecil wanted to grant it both because they still desired to see the Queen married and because they wanted to embroil France in a conflict with Spain over the Dutch struggle for independence rather than have England take the lead in that dangerous enterprise herself; the aggressive minority headed by Leicester and Sir Francis Walsingham, eager for England to challenge Spain upon the continent as she was already doing upon the oceans, fiercely opposed Alençon's coming. Elizabeth herself remained poised in characteristic irresolution between an almost hysterical loathing to enter upon a war and an exhilarating excitement at the prospect of putting a genuine flesh-and-blood royal wooer through his paces. Meanwhile she practised upon Simier, whom she took (literally) to her breast, fondly nick-named him her Monkey, and in general—perhaps the shock of the Douglass Sheffield affair had something to do with it—made a spectacle of herself over him.

The temperature of the country grew dangerously sultry. A gentleman named Stubbs began a pamphleteering campaign against Alençon which led to the public removal of his right hand; prominent courtiers, including Sir Philip Sidney, got into trouble and were banished the Court for speaking their opinion too frankly; a sudden illness of Simier and a stray shot at him while he was with Elizabeth in her barge were widely and spontaneously attributed to Leicester's inspiration. The matter came to a head when Simier learned of his enemy's marriage. During a stormy and critical dispute before Elizabeth as to whether or not his master should be given a passport for England he produced his information : where-upon she drew the passport to her, scrawled her signature upon it

[1] Francis, Duke of Alençon, had by now succeeded to the title of Duke of Anjou; but since his older brother, Henry III, had formerly courted Elizabeth when Duke of Anjou, the title of Alençon has here been retained for the younger brother to avoid confusion.

and was reported to have placed Robert under close arrest at Greenwich with the wild threat to send him to the Tower.

For a moment Lettice Knollys seemed to have changed the course of history. Alençon came—in fact he came twice : an ugly little man with a huge nose and deep pock-marks. But he was young, a practised hand with women, and a prince whose ancestors had been reigning in France when Elizabeth's were still waiting to be admitted to the service of the gentry in Wales. Elizabeth mooned over him in corners, publicly kissed him, and succeeded in convincing everybody, including more than probably herself, that the long looked-for love which might be consummated in marriage had at last overtaken her. But she still remained Elizabeth. Only her heart fluttered, not her head : the emotion which Alençon provoked in her stopped short of plunging England into war for him. So in the end she lent him a large sum of money, by way of compensation for wasting his time and toying with his affections, to enable him to go off to the Netherlands and try to wrest its crown from Spain as the King of France's brother rather than as the Queen of England's husband. In addition she gave him an escort consonant with his dignity to see him over the North Sea ; its chief was the Earl of Leicester, who returned to report gravely—and as events turned out, truthfully—that he had left the Duke stranded like an old hulk on a sandbank.

In this wise was Robert forgiven, to take up presently the task of freeing the Netherlands at which his rival failed. But his wife was never forgiven ; in Elizabeth's menagerie of endearing nick-names she occupied a sort of isolated cage labelled " that she-wolf " while her royal cousin lived. Once again she nearly changed the course of history when Elizabeth thwarted Leicester's designs in the Low Countries partly out of hatred for her. And after he died, and Elizabeth fell to doting upon her young son by Essex, she saw to it that Lettice should derive the least possible benefit from what was left of his estate.

Perhaps had the marriage turned out badly, Elizabeth might in time have relented. But from Robert's point of view it was only too distinctly a success. Of its domestic side not much can be known, because the conjugal letters exchanged during Robert's long absences at court and abroad seem not to have survived. Yet there is enough—in his many tender allusions to her, in the language of his will and his delight in surrounding himself with her portraits— to confirm the impression, gleaned from others besides Camden, of how complete his emotional dependence upon her became in the course of their ten years together. Her response, one gathers, was less than perfect. After his death she exhibited a devotion unmistakable greater and more tenacious to his property than his memory. Even while he lived gossip coupled her name with that of a much younger man, one of her husband's followers and her son's friends, whom she subsequently married. It would be ironic, but by no means unnatural, to surmise that one cause of Elizabeth's unforgiving hostility was this suspicion that Lettice had betrayed the man Elizabeth had loved and lost to her. She lived to plead in vain with Elizabeth for her son's life, and then on to such old age as to see her grandson General in command of the Parliamentary Army in the Civil War.

What was perhaps the main purpose of the marriage was defeated. There was only one child, a boy, Robert, who died in 1584 at the age of four, " the noble impe " as he was described in the inscription on his tomb in the Beauchamp Chapel at Warwick. What he died of is not known—of poison administered by a nurse at his father's instigation because he was hunch-backed, Robert's enemies appear to have discovered later. The volume of letters of real and deep sympathy which Robert received on his loss from the greatest in the land of all parties gives one indication of how his stature had grown since the death of Amy ; and his own letter of acknowledgment to Hatton (by then one of his rivals for the Queen's favour), though full of a genuine unaffected sorrow, compresses into a few words perhaps better than anything else he ever said or wrote the feelings of a world of which he was so thoroughly, often shockingly, representative :

> " . . . I must confess that I have received many afflictions within these few years, but not a greater, next to her Majesty's displeasure ; and, if it pleased God, I would the sacrifice of this innocent might satisfy ; I mean not towards God (for all are

sinful and most wretched in His sight, and therefore He sent a most innocent lamb to help us all that are faithful). The afflictions I have suffered may satisfy such as are offended, or at least appease their long, hard conceits : if not, yet I know there is a blessing for such as suffer : and so there is for those that be merciful. Princes (who feel not the heavy estate of the poor afflicted that only are to receive relief from themselves) seldom do pity according to the true rules of charity, and therefore men fly to mighty God in time of distress for comfort. . . . I beseech the same God to grant me patience in all these worldly things, and to forgive the negligence of my former time, that have not been more careful to please him, but have run the race of the world. In the same sort I commend you, and pray for His grace for you as for myself ; and, before all this world, to preserve her Majesty forever, whom on my knees I most humbly thank for her most gracious visitation by Killigrew. She shall never comfort a more true and faithful man to her, for I have lived and so will die only hers . . ."

One begins to understand what the age meant by " our God on earth " when a sorrowing father can conceive of his only son as a " sacrifice " which may cause the Almighty to appease a Queen's passing displeasure . . . and of a repentance for having too much " run the race of the world " as a possible means of gaining divine intervention towards regaining royal favour.

Chapter Twelve

" LEYCESTER'S COMMONWEALTH "

IT WAS NOT only for marrying Lettice that Robert offered to the God of Abraham the sacrifice of his son in appeasement of Elizabeth's displeasure. That act she had condoned because, however much it hurt, she could no more bear to put an end to their friendship than he to lose her favour. But in marrying Lettice he had gone beyond a declaration of personal independence : he had espoused for better or worse a cause in utter opposition to her will.

It was the cause of independent, militant Protestantism, coming to be generally known in England as Puritanism. Like its equivalent in France, Huguenot Calvinism, it numbered amongst its adherents a large part of the rising middle class and an important group within the aristocracy. Of this group Sir Francis Knollys was one of the earlist and most prominent members : and in taking his daughter to wife Robert had in the eyes of the world all but made an irrevocable profession of faith. For in that time, and especially in that small social circle, religion, politics and sex often composed a trinity not readily separable from one another, and the choice of a mate, whether inside or outside wedlock, could as easily be traced to the partisan as to the more domestic emotions. It was in accordance with this principle that Robert's gifted nephew Sir Philip Sidney should marry the daughter of Sir Francis Walsingham, Puritanism's political genius, and that his sister,—immortal companion of his *Arcadia*—should marry their uncle's high-born follower the Earl of Pembroke. Thus was the Puritan circle drawn tight. Its tightness was its strength and at its centre, the brilliant focus of its radiating lines of force, stood the Earl of Leicester.

It was there he began and there he ended. There was no other possible place for him. No one could imagine him as anything else than the central figure, the uncrowned monarch, of the enterprising sect with whom he had chosen to join his fortunes. He would not have had them, nor they have found much use for him, on any other basis. Brains, experience, fiery conviction and drive they could command in plenty ; what they lacked was the standing at court and in the eyes of the world, the direct and unfailing access to the ultimate source of power, which no ambitious and unpopular new political grouping could in the circumstances of the age do without and which the Favourite was in a unique position to supply. If his role could not be precisely defined as that of leader, it was considerably more than that of a mere decorative figurehead. His contemporaries perhaps defined it best when they alluded to Walsingham, the swarthy director of the party's operations, as Leicester's " spirit."

Throughout its brief history Puritanism had on the worldly level represented the successful combination of plain living with high finance. Throughout his life Robert had pre-eminently stood for personal magnificence and pride of caste. Yet their fusion seems to have struck no one as incongruous, so slow and apparently inevitable had the process been. His early flirtation with the Catholics had proved unfruitful because from the outset they had not trusted him and because their later programme of counter-revolution by force with help from abroad smacked too much of the treasonable. Even at that time certain ties of interest and sentiment had linked him to the Puritans, for whom he had done favours as he now continued to do them for individual Catholics. The Puritans remembered his father, their " Moses and Joshua," who had overthrown the too moderate Somerset for them and before his own fall set in motion the first of English business explorations by sea with Willoughby and Chancellor's voyage to Arctic Russia. Robert's own maritime enthusiasms had drawn the bond closer, for in this department of Elizabethan life the Puritans, whether as sea-captains or merchant capitalists, were pre-eminent. Marriage, his own and his relatives', helped to ratify the compact, though which was cause and which effect was, as in most such affairs, not altogether clear : whether the community of interest furthered the social and religious connection or the connection was made to further the interest.

But so far as Robert was concerned his Puritan connection was a political arrangement pure and simple. God was by tacit agreement left out of it. Some sort of God he undoubtedly believed in, not being like the Scottish Lord of Lethington, who considered Him " ane bogle of the nursery " ; a God, so far as one can judge, very like the Puritan Jehovah whose approval was success and of whose frown one's failures and discouragements were a frightening reminder. But to their theological doctrines he was seemingly indifferent and from their theocratic notions of society, which were to cause so much trouble in the next century, he held prudently aloof.

Nevertheless God came into it if only because nothing less than divine assistance—his letter to Hatton is despondent testimony to the fact—seemed capable at times of preserving him in Elizabeth's grace. For Elizabeth disapproved of Puritans no less strongly than she did of Lettice. She disliked their sanctimony and detested their creed which, with its antipathy to her episcopal Establishment and outspoken doubts of the legitimacy of her own royal absolutism, seemed to her to verge on that disrespectful and revolutionary republicanism which it was one day in actual practice to become. Some amongst them forcibly reciprocated her sentiments. Their libels upon her vied in virulence even with those of the hunted Catholics whom they accused her of not hunting zealously enough. At Bury St. Edmunds they hoisted a board with arms painted on both sides to indicate her two-facedness with the legend, " I know thy words, that thou art neither cold nor hot. I would thou wert cold or hot. Therefore, because thou art lukewarm, it will come to pass I will spew thee out of my mouth." Similar displays were widespread through the kingdom. Borrowing an epithet from their Papist foes, they branded her " the woman Jezebel " who " maketh herself a prophetess to teach and deceive my servants to make them commit fornication, and to eat meat sacrificed unto idols." In the face of this only Robert's influence, according to well-informed opinion, persuaded her to tolerate the sect, for the most part loyal to her, at all. Certainly after his death her patience snapped with a loud report and a minimum of delay.

But her quarrel with them was not only general, a clash of temperament and ideas. It was also particular, ranging them against her on the most important issue of her reign. And on this vital and

delicate matter Robert was not only their protector but their spokesman. Across the North Sea the long resistance of the Dutch to
reconquest by Spain was visibly weakening ; across the Channel
in France the Huguenots, already almost penned in against the
south-western coasts, were threatened with extinction by the ultra
Catholic, pro-Spanish Holy League. From the very beginning, in
the 1560's, the more uncompromising of English Protestants had
held that the struggle between Reformation and counter-Reforma-
tion was one war, in which, unless Elizabeth intervened to defeat
the hosts of Rome, her own turn would presently come and find
her standing alone. As the news of the disasters looming over their
co-religionists of the continent poured in, they raised their voices
in a clamour for immediate action. Their accents were different :
some, like Walsingham's immediate followers, summoned her to a
crusade, others, like Leicester, stressed the realm's physical safety
and future greatness ; but together they constituted the most
resolute effort to override her will, and on a matter of supreme
policy, that her personal rule ever knew.

For to her they seemed to be talking the most dangerous
nonsense. Over and over she had declared, with loud and sometimes
vulgar emphasis as their pressure on her grew, that the cause was
none of hers : that her concern was England and that outside it
Protestants and Protestantism could look after themselves. Impatient
with the Dutch as rebels against their lawful sovereign, annoyed
with the Spaniards for provoking them into rebellion over questions
of doctrine, she had fumed at William of Orange, whose belligerent
necessities had naturally not spared her subjects' interests, no less
heartily than at Philip II, of whom she demanded why he could not
let the Lowlanders go to hell in whatever way suited them. Aware,
however, that an outright Spanish victory would lay England open
to invasion, she had not altogether lived up to these sentiments of
irritable neutrality. Her money if not her official blessing accompanied her sea-rovers in their attacks on the sources of Spanish
wealth in the Americas and on the oceans ; she turned a blind eye
upon their Dutch counterparts sheltering and refitting in her ports
and upon the volunteers who, under captains like Sir Humphrey
Gilbert and Sir John Norris, crossed the North Sea to fight on

money subscribed by their co-religionists at home ; her kisses and subsidies to Alençon had been intended as a useful contribution to the cause of Franco-Spanish misunderstanding, on which Dutch survival sometimes depended, and now and then she lent them money outright. But war open and undisguised she hated and was afraid of with good reason. Not long since she had with difficulty expelled a Spanish force from Ireland where virtually the whole population would regard her enemy as their deliverer. In Scotland a strong Catholic faction stood ready to open the border to him. Above all there was the extreme shortage of money, and the consequent unpleasantness of wringing it out of Parliament, to discourage the luxury of taking the troubles of the Dutch upon herself in mortal combat with the first military power in the world.

In accord with her were nearly all the more solid and stable elements in the country—the majority of her ministers, the gentry and even the merchants fearful of the effect of war upon their trade ; indeed Burghley, whose mastery of the art of " throwing the stone without that the hand be seen " made him the ideal executive of her policy, thought that she was not circumspect enough. Against her, acknowledging Leicester as their patron, was a disproportionate, a disconcerting, number of the adventurous, the ardent, the young : men like Drake, Raleigh, Grenville, Sidney, the celebrated scientist, wizard and freethinker John Dee. It was a piquant situation. Long ago prudence had preserved her from the first dangerous temptation to throw in her lot with his, cautioning her to wait on events. Now she was again waiting on events, an anxious defender of things as they were, and he was again imploring her to follow the hazardous course. Perhaps when all was said and done this was his part in her life, to play the tempter to her imagination, representing it, almost being it : unable quite ever to win her over altogether because of the lessons life had taught her, yet holding her by the fascination of the quality in him she cherished all the more for having so sternly to subdue it in herself.

For if she felt that she had to act according to Cecil, she could think in accord with his brilliant and imaginative juniors, else they would scarcely have worshipped her as they did. She was fulfilling

herself not only in still loving Robert but in still magnifying him,
though he opposed her, though he was growing bald and stout and
rosy, though he had dared to marry another woman. There was
obvious pride and satisfaction in her explanation to the latest and
last of the Spanish Ambassadors that she herself could hardly overthrow him " as he had taken advantage of the authority she had
given him to place kinsmen and friends of his in almost every post
and principal place in the kingdom." If there had been resentment
she would have known how to express it more succinctly : when
Walsingham appeared to be cunningly entangling her in his struggle
between Christ and Belial—as he saw it—she flung her slipper at
his head with a shrill cry of " Point de guerre ! Point de guerre ! "
But Walsingham was merely her minister. Robert was her own
creation, the Beloved Adversary whom she had made in a sense
out of herself and delighted in.

It was a delight in which her subjects had never shared. To
them he was still the detested outsider, the greedy, arrogant traitor
in the third generation to her and their weal. It was not a feeling
which, by its nature, could retain its full original intensity for so
long without added stimulus, and it had in fact, as the fear of her
marrying him grew less, tended to become latent rather than active.
But his emergence as a capital political figure infused a ferocious
new vitality into it.

In 1584 there appeared in Antwerp a little book entitled *the
Copye of a letter wryten by a Master of Arts at Cambridge*. From the
colour of its leaves and the general belief that its anonymous author
was a well-known Jesuit priest named Robert Parsons it gained
the popular nickname of *Father' Parsons Green Coat*. But it was
under the name of *Leycester's Commonwealth*, derived from its
theme and affixed to it in later editions that it was destined to
survive, its subject's first and seemingly definitive biography, since
to it he was principally to owe his reputation for all time to
come.

The attribution of the tract to Parsons, though now considered
doubtful, was at the time plausible. He was of the new generation
of Catholics, risen towards the middle of Elizabeth's reign, in whom

burned the purpose of England's redemption by whatever means might be necessary. Many of its members were exiles or sons of exiles ; its priests were mainly young men educated abroad at the Jesuit seminaries of France or the Spanish Netherlands and posted to England to serve their faith not only by preaching and celebrating the Mass, but by working, some of them, for Elizabeth's overthrow through invasion and a few of them even through her assassination. Smuggled by night from one private house to another, relentlessly hunted by Walsingham's spies, occasionally caught and executed with the most infernal tortures, they were of a very different stamp from the Catholics of an earlier style, ready to accept Leicester's protection, as one wrote, in " hope of quietness and being able thereby to lead a good Christian life." Rather they looked upon him as one of the major works of the devil, to be damned by all possible means in this world as he was certain to be in the next.

So far as this world went, they could hardly have hoped to do better. Of its kind " Parsons' " book is a little masterpiece. In vigorous Elizabethan journalese the author piles salacious tit-bit upon sensational detail, with a clever regard for the balance between variety and monotony—now an unexpected charge dramatically introduced, now a previous one hammered in by repetition—and an awful knack of putting in, or leaving our, selected truth so as to keep just on the safe side of the line between the plausible and the incredible. Shrewd psychology converted old fears and prejudices into agreed assumptions between reader and author ; and one assumption was made to lead artfully to the next. The attention was held and conviction wrought because the whole read like a theme argued to its inexorable conclusion.

" You know the Bear's love, which is all for his paunch," strikes the keynote. Related to this first simple truth is a second, that the animal in question, " noble in only two descents and both of them stained with the block," had been " fleshed in conspiracy against the Royall blood of King Henries children in his tender yeares." This was also true : and this being the nature and the rearing of the creature, it is no matter for surprise that he should fatten himself and his relatives upon the best offices of state and in his own interest attempt to subvert the ancient forms of government—nor that he should neglect the opportunity held out by a too willing Queen to satisfy his lusts while—indeed as a means of—satisfying his greed. The speculations of twenty-five years into the relations of the two are rehearsed with a wealth of scabrous detail. What the taproom gossips had said—and much that they had all but forgotten—is offered in testimony of its own truth with the loud and angry authority of print, and the public led on and up to its own fond theory that the unholy infatuation in which Robert held the Queen was alone responsible for England's desperate lack of an heir.

These, which might be called his public crimes, are followed by an elaborately annotated catalogue of his more domestic misdeeds. The list of homicides is impressive for length, but concerning the more familiar ones the writer has little in the way of new information. As Amy's murderer he produces one Sir Richard Verney (later adopted by Scott) who died " blaspheming, saying all the devils in hell did tear him to pieces." The death of Lord Sheffield, Douglass's husband, was procured by " an artificial catarrh that stopped his breath " : that of Essex, Lettice's husband, by an Italian recipe " after learning that his wife was with child by Leicester," and the child, a girl, made away with. To these are now added a miscellaneous list of others well chosen for surprise : the Cardinal de Châtillon, poisoned for fear he would reveal how Robert had thwarted Elizabeth's marriage to Catherine de Medici's son, though French opinion had long had him poisoned by Catherine herself ; Nicholas Throckmorton, whom Robert made away with as a guest in his own house for having many years earlier repeated Mary Stuart's quip about Elizabeth's horse-master ; Doughty, executed by Drake for mutiny during the voyage round the world because he knew too much of Leicester's secrets ; and various additional victims high and low.

Amongst his accomplices, along with Drake, were others scarcely less famous in their time—John Dee, astrologer and alchemist, friend of Raleigh and Marlowe and altogether one of the most curious and remarkable of Elizabethan scientists and philosophers ; Dr. Lopez the Jew, the Queen's own medical attendant whom Robert's step-son Essex later hounded to the gallows, and Dr. Julio the Italian, favourite physician to the nobility, both of them employed " for poisoning and the art of destroying children in women's bellies." Amongst the lesser fry were " Verney for murdering, Digby for bawds (at Digby's house in Warwickshire Dame Lettice lay and other such pieces of pleasure)," Allen " for figuring and conjuring," Doctors Bayly and Culpeper of Oxford, " once papists, now galenists," poisoners so subtle " they can make a man die of any sickness they will and as long afterwards as they like."

The effect of the book was instantaneous, enormous and lasting. The edition was probably small, but copies were swiftly and surreptitiously circulated from hand to hand. Its public was the generation for whom the Earl of Leicester had consistently been the most sinister, dangerous and eye-filling of men, and it gave a wonderfully racy and impressive confirmation of all that, and even more than, had been reported of him in fragments and driblets round the fireside and the parish pump ; nor would any of it have seemed too marvellous to be true to a generation about to provide the audiences for the largest and ablest company of melodramatists the world had ever seen.

In vain did Elizabeth attempt, by an Order in Council, to forbid its circulation, even adding her assurance that the contents were false to her own knowledge. The very fact of her being driven into so remarkable a step as pledging her royal credit in the matter shows what an impression the book made upon her people. Robert's nephew Sir Philip Sidney leaped to his uncle's defence with all the ardour of family loyalty and a prose style of singular beauty. He challenged the author as " a base and wretched tongue that dares not speak his own name " ; he proudly affirmed that though " I am by my father's side of ancient and well-esteemed and well-matched gentry . . . my chiefest honour is to be a Dudley": and shrewdly exposed one after another the lies, the inconsistencies and malignant dissimulation of an author dishonest enough to call himself a Protestant the better to do the dirty work of Papistry. His *Defence* seems to have had no greater effect than Elizabeth's injunction and in fact to have remained long unprinted. But

Leycester's Commonwealth survived to be translated,[1] reissued and treated as documentary material by ballad and fiction mongers and serious historians. Seldom can the attempt to transform a living man into a legendary monster have had such complete and lasting success.

It made no difference, however, to the destiny which events were preparing for him at gathering speed. At about the same time that *Leycester's Commonwealth* appeared, in the same month, July, 1584, that Robert buried his small son, William of Orange was assassinated at Delft. With his death the resistance of which he had been the inspiring force from the very beginning seemed likely to flicker out. The southern provinces, ten out of the whole seventeen, had already given in, and the brilliant soldier now governing the Netherlands for Philip II, his nephew the Prince of Parma, was advancing upon Antwerp, first city not only of the Netherlands but of Europe. In their extremity the Dutch, hopeless of a quick decision from England because of Elizabeth's attitude, overlooked the miserable and treacherous fiasco of Alençon's intervention two years earlier and turned to France for help. But the France of Henry

[1] Upon one household the French edition, entitled *La Vie abominable Ruses, Meurtres, etc., etc., de my lord de Lecestre, Machiavelli . . .* , fell with the force of a calamity. An early copy coming into the hands of the English Ambassador in Paris, now married to Douglass Sheffield, a "very villainous" translation with additions, as he described it in a letter to Walsingham, Stafford was caught in the agonizing dilemma of having either to neglect his duty or violate his wife's peace of mind. The insult to his sovereign and one of her leading ministers could not be allowed to pass unnoticed, yet to notice it was, to risk driving Douglass, who had already been prostrated with "melancholy" by the original edition, quite off her head and possibly into danger of death. So the frantic husband implored Walsingham to tell him what to do "because my nearest have a touch in it which, though between God and my Lord of Leycester's conscience, and almost in the opinion of most Englishmen her conscience be not further touched than an honourable intent and a weak woman deceived," yet the circle in which she moved might cruelly misinterpret her only too prominent role in the story. What Stafford really wanted he made clear in a letter to Burghley of the same date, that the matter should rather "be let alone, as a thing we make no account of, than by speaking of it, or against it, to make think that a galled horse, when he is touched, will wince"—a phrase Hamlet would not be above using. Nor the least important part of Stafford's difficulty was that he should have addressed himself to Robert as the person principally concerned but dared not, as he told Burghley: "If you command me I will send you one (a copy) but else not, for the Earl of Leycester doth not take well what comes from me."

III was too enfeebled by civil war and too erratically governed to be trusted. The Dutch withdrew their embassy in disgust, to the delight of Leicester, who had been working tirelessly to instil contempt for the French and reliance upon England into them, and resolved upon one final appeal to Elizabeth.

They offered her the sovereignty of their country in return for her taking it under her protection. She on her part now accepted the necessity of coming openly to their assistance. Not only was Antwerp of prime importance to her people's trade, it was the most suitable base for an invasion of England should Philip II decide to pay her out for what she had already done underhandedly ; and that he would use if for that purpose if the Dutch succumbed there was no longer room to doubt. The crown she would not accept because of the dishonour of estranging the allegiance of the subjects of a fellow-prince, but she would help them defend the ancient rights his unlawful tyranny threatened—a very medieval point of view still respected in theory. There was nothing very medieval, however, in her approach to practicalities, So many men, so much money, up to what she felt she could afford, with satisfactory security in the form of cities to be held by her in pledge until her outlay had been repaid. The Dutch must also be prepared to help themselves to the limit of their resources, and to provide her with precise information as to what these resources were.

The Dutch cavilled at her terms and even more at her tone. Deeming themselves equals seeking an alliance, they stiffly resisted the implication that they were coming as suppliants. Here Robert was of considerable service. A series of tactful suggestions, fruit of his long experience, to the effect that it " would be unbecoming, and against her reputation, to be obliged to present herself unsought by the other party " persuaded the upright Hollanders to unbend somewhat in the choice and instruction of their delegates. He remained at their elbow while negotiations moved forward with reasonable cordiality until nothing separated the two sides except a narrow difference of figures and Dutch hesitation at handing over Flushing, part of the Orange patrimony. Elizabeth offered to send four thousand foot and four hundred horse, in addition to an immediate force for the relief of Antwerp, on condition that she held Flushing and Brill against repayment of her expenditure after the war ; the Dutch put their immediate need at five thousand foot and a thousand horse. Then news arrived that Antwerp had surrendered. Elizabeth ordered the larger force to be prepared and sent Sir Philip Sidney with a garrison of eight hundred to take over at Flushing. The second and greatest of her differences with Robert had been settled : but this time it was events and not, as with their marriage, she that settled it.

Nor was the next momentous decision altogether hers to make. The name of the commander-in-chief of the expedition had been omitted from the treaty, but in all men's minds it was known beforehand. The Dutch never for a moment considered any one else for the post than the man who had grown into the very symbol of the policy to whose final triumph he had so long and largely contributed. If his military experience was scanty, his invincible hold on Elizabeth's affections seemed the surest guarantee that he would be able to hold her up to the mark when she was tempted to waver and draw back ; and since his task, like William the Silent's before him, would involve the maintenance of orderly rule in a distracted confederation, his religious affinities and his princely magnificence would commend him to the people of the Provinces more than any mere reputation in war. So keen were they to have him, in fact, that Walsingham, confronted with their obstinacy over Flushing and Brill, gathered that " they will make no difficulty if my Lord of Leycester have the charge of the army." In the Privy Council no other candidate was put forward : as early as 1577, when a proposal to aid the Prince of Orange with an expeditionary force was seriously discussed, it was taken for granted that if the force were sent Leicester would lead it.

Of his willingness to go there had been no doubt then and there was none now. He wanted glory, he wanted power, and with these quite genuinely, on the evidence of others as well as of his own letters, wanted to redeem the poor military showing so far of the English volunteers in the Low Countries and to deliver the Dutch from Spain. His eagerness seems to have been tempered less by uncertainty as to whether he would be sent than how Elizabeth would deal with him when he got there.

For he already had premonitions. With her reluctance, often expressed in tears, to part with him, he detected distrust of the Dutch, distrust of having done right in committing her people's blood and treasure to a cause with which she imperfectly sympathised, distrust of him . . . all confessed in his worried communications with his colleagues. She was face to face now with the stark difference between them. He would want to do things on the grand scale, according to his nature, and she on the smallest allowable, according to hers. Already she was regretting, counting, interpreting her commitments, in the thriftiest degree consistent with safety. He, meanwhile, from a couch where a fall from a horse had laid him, was dealing with his bankers for loans in the city secured by mortgages on various of his properties, in the determination to go as speedily as possible, even if she dallied, on the most lavish scale possible to dazzle the natives with his and her splendour.

For a moment he had a shock when Walsingham warned him to hold up preparations. He rose and hurried to see her. " You can consider," he wrote in return to Walsingham, " what manner of persuasion this must be from me to her . . . (I) did comfort her as much as I could, only I did let her know how far I had gone in preparation." He prevailed. She knew that it was in any event too late now to stop him. " I do think for all this she will let me go, for she would not have me speak of it to the contrary to anybody." The following month, October, 1585, she took farewell of him at Richmond with a mixture of emotions which her tears inadequately expressed.

On December 8th he set sail from Harwich after giving London and the towns on the way a brave show with his train of mounted knights, esquires, " musiconners " and 500 troopers from amongst his own tenants, and on December 10th, in a bad temper because his pilots had advised against Brill as an anchorage for his fleet of nearly a hundred sixty-ton vessels, disembarked at Flushing.

Chapter Thirteen

THE NETHERLANDS

THE reception he received would have turned a far less susceptible head than Robert Dudley's. His progress from Flushing to the capital at the Hague was an unbroken triumphal progress through hysterical crowds acclaiming their saviour, their "Messiah." At Middleburgh, his first stop, the provincial Estates assembled to greet him with salutes of gunfire while over the gate of the port flew the Red Cross of England. "A very extraordinary device set off with most wondrous art" had been erected, a castle of crystal founded upon a rock of pearl, with silver firearms flowing round it, in which were represented varieties of fowls, fishes and beasts, some as wounded, some as slain, and others gasping for breath, and over them was a Virgin Lady leaning and reaching out her hands to their assistance. The same thought was rendered in the Latin inscription fixed over the entrance gate of Dort, which the chronicler Holinshed translated :

> The widow countrie wailing in her losse,
> Subject to soldiers and a stranger's crosse,
> By weeping her misfortune sits here alone,
> To think of her pleasures, past and gone,
> But after France and Spain have done their worst,
> Her helpless young ones are by England nurst ;
> Blest be that Virgin Queen that sent this good,
> And blest be he that comes to save our blood,
> Whom to our soules a buckler we maie call,
> And to our countries we crie welcome all.

As he approached Amsterdam with the guard of honour of twenty galleys which Haarlem had given him, "he was received with

sundry sortes of great fishes, as whales and others of great hugeness,"
which towed his ships to the landing stage in the market place.
Bonfires and fireworks lit his way by night, everywhere he passed
he was deafened by shouts of " God save Queen Elizabeth " as if
(he wrote) the Queen herself had been in Cheapside. And every-
where—most dangerous of all to the poise of mind of the pampered,
ambitious, impulsive Favourite—the sight of his own arms inter-
twined with those of his mistress, of the late Prince of Orange, of
the seven Provinces.

His early letters home show him quite drunk with elation. " I
like this matter twenty times better than I did in England," he wrote
Burghley. Of the country, its quaint and thriving cities, its " noble
provinces and goodly havens with such infinite ships and mariners "
he could not exclaim enough ; the little town of Delft was " another London almost for beauty and fairness " whose inhabitants
" have used me most honourably." For country and inhabitants
alike he developed an affection amounting to something like a
passion of possessiveness. He saw it becoming a permanent and
fruitful dependency of England, its citizens devoted and grateful
subjects of Elizabeth, his fame immortally enshrined in their
memory. Under the spell of their ovation, overcome by the sense
that the eyes of all princes and nations were fixed in admiration
(as he reported) upon his Queen and himself for their chivalry to
so noble and unfortunate a people, words almost deliriously reckless
escaped him. At one reception those near him understood him to
say that his house had been unfairly dispossessed of the throne of
England. To Burghley he declared that the Dutch " would serve
under me with a better will than ever under the Prince of Orange ;
yet (though) they loved him well, they never hoped of the liberty
of their country until now." The final expulsion of Spain from the
Netherlands, which the late Stadholder had not achieved in fifteen
years, he expected to accomplish, and so announced, in one sweeping
summer's campaign.

It was in this mood that he was called upon to make the most
fateful decision of his life. On New Year's morning, three weeks
after his arrival, a flourish of trumpets outside his residence at the
Hague announced the arrival of a delegation of notables with an

important communication. Still incompletely dressed, he went to meet them in his " great chamber," where their spokesman " began an oration to me, and, even as he began, one told me in mine ear " what it was about. Flustered, he asked them to accompany him into the privacy of his bed-chamber. There the spokesman proceeded " to offer to me, with many good wordes for her Majesties sake, the absolute government of the whole provinces, and to proclaim the same immediately." As Elizabeth's governor-general he was to exercise supreme authority over their armed forces, their civil government, the raising and expenditure of their revenues, with all the powers ever vested in any previous ruler and the title of Stadholder borne by the late Prince of Orange.

Dazzled but not altogether surprised, he asked for time to think it over. What he had to decide was not whether he would but whether he dared. Elizabeth had sent him as her Lieutenant-General, the leader of an army of auxiliaries with the right to be consulted in certain local matters, chiefly financial, affecting the conduct of hostilities ; there was nothing in her commission about his becoming her Viceroy with the prerogatives and dignity of a virtual monarch at the request, even the ardent request, of those whom he was to govern. The question of a further extension of his authority had been considered before he sailed. The Dutch themselves had openly spoken of the necessity of it. His colleagues of the Privy Council had favoured it as a remedy for the disorder into which Dutch affairs had fallen since Orange's death and which they feared would hamper the successful prosecution of the war. He himself had written to Walsingham before sailing that " I had as lief be dead as be in the case I shall be in if . . . some more authority be not granted than I see her Majesty would I should have." Her feeling in the matter was known to everybody, and to no one better than her favourite. She could not very well forbid him publicly to assume an authority which had not yet been offered him—though she may have done so in private, as she later intimated —but she had made it clear throughout that she would permit no servant of hers to take any oath of allegiance or accept any grant of powers in her name which would involve her in responsibilities beyond those to which she was strictly committed. It was on that understanding that he had, after making his protest, proceeded upon his mission.

But since then, on his own and away from the force of her personality, he had looked on the Netherlands and they on him. The offer, even more splendid than his imagination could have foretold, had actually been made him ; and the reasons for accepting appeared so much more compelling. The only thought in his mind was how to make out the best case for consenting—the only thing he did not do was to write her at once to give his reasons and request her approval, since that entailed too great a risk of being flatly ordered to desist. Instead he consulted with such Englishmen as were available, Bartholomew Clark and Henry Killigrew, the two resident members of the Dutch Council of State, and especially William Davison, Walsingham's successor as Principal Secretary who was temporarily acting as Ambassador at the Hague. Their views chimed with his, as he would have known beforehand. The Dutch system of provincial Estates from which were drafted the Estates-General, who in turn had to refer their decisions back to their separate provincial bodies, was too slow, cumbersome and unworkable in emergencies. The executive Council of State set up after Orange's death was an experimental committee without constitutional definition or popular standing. Some supreme authority was plainly indispensable, and to Leicester's advisers no less than to himself it seemed insufferable that such authority should be exercised over the English deliverers of the country by a native like the nineteen year old Maurice of Nassau, Orange's son, or a foreigner like his nominal lieutenant the German Count Hohenlo, the two obvious alternatives. Finding his own opinions thus sympathetically corroborated, Robert notified the Estates-General of his acceptance and on January 25th solemnly took the oath of office at the Hague.

He had already sent Davison to lay his explanation before Elizabeth. He had written to Burghley, Walsingham and others of the Privy Council to do their best for him before Davison arrived. But Davison, more than apprehensive of what awaited him, dallied at Brill, " detained some 5 or 6 days by the wind and the weather " —actually it was longer and the weather was not unfavourable the whole time—until a sharp letter from Robert put him to sea.

LEICESTER IN THE NETHERLANDS

A posthumous Engraving by R. Vaughan dedicated to Leicester's Widow. By kind permission of The National Museum of Wales.

Meantime the portents from London were anything but favourable. Elizabeth had heard directly from the Estates, and to the offence of Robert's disobedience had been added the neglect of his not even notifying her. From Burghley he heard that she was "so discontent with your acceptance of the government there, before you had advertised and had her Majesty's opinion that, although I, for my own part, judge this action both honourable and profitable, yet her Majesty will not endure to hear my speech in defence thereof." From other sources he learned that she had been particularly outraged at his allowing himself to be addressed by the title of "Excellency." Plaintively he described in return how he was "not only grieved but wounded to the heart. For it is more than death unto me, that her Majesty should be always thus ready to interpret always hardly of my service . . . if some other man had done it, it could not be but it had been much better accepted." As to the use of the "Excellency," he wildly defended himself to Walsingham with an excuse which could not have been worse chosen, that "I refused a title higher than Excellency, as Mr. Davison, if you ask him, will tell you."

As if Davison had not enough to put right already, including his own tardiness, before he could arrive a new and distressing complication had arisen. Lettice had been left behind in London : the town was ringing with the tale that she now proposed to join her consort in a style suitable to his present rank. "It was told her Majesty," reported Robert's servant Thomas Duddeley from Leicester House early in February, "that my lady was prepared presently to come over to your excellency with such a train of ladies and gentlewomen, and such rich coaches, litters and side-saddles, as her Majesty had none such, and that there should be such a court of ladies as should far pass her Majesty's court here." Beside herself with fury, coupling the name of "that she-wolf" and her errant lover "with great oaths," she swore "she would have no more courts under her obeisance than her own, and would revoke you from thence with all speed." It did not matter that the information turned out to be false. If she had not intervened it might have been true, and Elizabeth, without waiting any longer for Davison, sat herself down and dictated a letter to Robert, another to the Estates, and a set of instructions for both, to be delivered by Sir Thomas Heneage, the remaining actor in the little comedy of jealousy played between the same four characters twenty years earlier—documents of such a nature that her ministers implored her to hold them until she had heard Davison.[1]

He went at once to Walsingham who, after warning him that such was Elizabeth's mood she would probably not admit him to her presence, nevertheless went up to speak to her and managed to have him sent for to her " withdrawing chamber." Before he could open his mouth she burst out " in most bitter and hard terms " against Robert for disobeying and himself for not opposing. For a long while she would not let him speak at all. But finally she fell silent and he put in a manful defence of the Earl's conduct, explaining how the discouragement of the Dutch, " the general hatred and contempt of their government," justified him in doing what he had done. She remained unimpressed, appeared at times not to listen, but " broke many times forth into her former complaints ; one while accusing you of contempt, another while of respecting more of your particular greatness than either her honour or service, and oftentimes digressing into old griefs which were too long and tedious to write." A letter which he carried from Robert she refused to receive and abruptly dismissed him. " Next morning Sir Thomas Heneage was dispatched in haste." Again Davison saw

[1] Sir Philip Sidney, too, had been much perturbed by the tale of Lettice's coming and sent a hasty message to his father-in-law, Walsingham, enclosed in one to his wife, to do what he could to stop her. His intervention produced an interesting footnote to the episode. His messenger is "Will, my Lord of Lester's jesting plaier," and the phrase has started much passionate conjecture as to whether the player's surname might not have been Shakespeare, who for all any one knows might well have been in the Nertherlands with many another young actor or member of similar desultory profession in March of 1586. Sidney refers to him as "a knave" who so misperformed his errand as to deliver the letters to Lettice herself and neglect not only to inform his employer of the fact but to answer him at all. There were, however, four actors of the name of Will in the Netherlands, and the likeliest of them to have been used by Sidney seems to have been the comedian Kemp. But the argument is not conclusive, and the utter uncertainty of Shakespeare's whereabouts at the time, coupled with an undoubted firsthand knowledge of battle, gained between the baptism of his twins —results of a shotgun wedding—in February, 1585, and his appearance at the Blackfriar's Theatre in 1589 as a shareholder and a well-known member of Leicester's company of players, would seem to leave him still in the running.

her and " with tears besought her to be better advised, laying before
her the dishonourable, shameful and dangerous affects of so unreasonable and unhappy a message." Stonily she refused, " falling
again into her former invectives." Davison implored her to at least
read Robert's letter. She took it, broke the seal, read a few lines,
then thrust it suddenly into her pocket " to read, as I think, at more
leisure." Perhaps it was the sight of the well-known writing, the
caressing, irresistible phrases ; perhaps it was the stormy interview
with Burghley, who after questioning Davison, turned on her to
her astonishment and threatened to lay down the office of Chief
Minister he had filled for nearly thirty years unless she modified her
orders to Heneage : for one or both these reasons she made her
first concession, that Heneage might withhold the letter to the
Estates.

The letter to Robert—his first direct communication from her—
and instructions stood. They exceeded anything he could in his
darkest moments have feared. The letter, addressed simply to " my
lord of Leycester," without endearment, without even the ordinary
courtesy of " cousin," began straight off:

" How contemptuously we conceive ourself to have been
used by you, you shall by this bearer understand, whom we
have expressly sent unto you to charge you withal. We could
never have imagined, had we not see it fall out in experience,
that a man raised up by ourself, and extraordinarily favoured
by us above any other subject of this land, would have in so
contemptible a sort have broken our commandment, in a cause
that so greatly toucheth us in honour, whereof, although you
have showed yourself to make but little account, in most un-
dutiful a sort, you may not therefore think that we have so little
care of the reparation thereof as we mind to pass so great a
wrong in silence unredressed : and, therefore, our express
pleasure and commandment is, all delays and excuses laid apart,
you do presently, upon the duty of your allegiance, obey and
fulfill whatsoever the bearer hereof shall direct you to do in
our name : whereof fail you not, as you will answer the contrary at your uttermost peril."

As a succinct and unmistakable expression of her feelings it was unsurpassed even by her celebrated " Proud prelate, by God I will unfrock thee ! " The instructions delivered by Heneage at the same time were equally beyond the possibility of misunderstanding. They directed Leicester " to make an open and public resignation in the place where he accepted the absolute government, as a thing done without our privity and consent " and to the Estates administered a stinging rebuke for showing themselves " to have a very slender and weak conceit of our judgment, by pressing a minister of ours to accept that which was refused, as though our long experience in government had not yet taught us to discover what was fit for us to do in matters of state."

There was something positively fiendish in her desire to hurt and humiliate ; a desire born out of her own hurt and humiliation, and exasperated by the fact that she could apparently get none to understand or sympathise with her own plain view of the matter. Against her will, but for the security of her realm, she had agreed to help the Dutch to the extent that her people's resources and their other perils in her judgment allowed. In doing so she had published a proclamation to the world firmly denying any intention beyond this, solemnly pledging her royal honour that she had no design upon the allegiance of the Netherlanders. Her purpose had been mocked, her word dishonoured, her interest placed in jeopardy, and instead of her other servants joining in disapproval of the colleague who had dared to " alter my commission, and the authority that I gave him, upon his own fancies," they one and all, even his long-standing adversaries, seemed to consider that he was perfectly right and she perversely wrong. And that this should have been done to her by the creature she " had raised from the dust," whom she had loved and spoiled yet trusted (as she had said long ago) " to stand by her even if the rest of the world abandoned her " was more than she could bear. It was to hold in " contempt "—the word into which over and over she concentrates the essence of her wrath—her femininity as well as her majesty, treating her as a woman to be coaxed or brow-beaten out of her captious meddling with serious affairs rather than as the queen whose unshared moral and material responsibility derived from God alone. For others to ignore this truth was a slight to be punished, but for Robert to do so was to attack the very foundation upon which she thought her love securely posied. There was perhaps a deeper truth than he realised in his complaint to Walsingham that " if some other man had done it, it could not be but it had been much better accepted."

That she would rebuke him for his presumption, that she might command him to resign his office, he had been prepared to expect by the time of Heneage's arrival with letter and instructions. But not in that language nor in that way—abasing himself like a lackey caught out masquerading in his master's clothes before the very assembly, on the very spot, which had so lately beheld him in his glory. He utterly wilted ; like his father and grandfather before him, when caught out by adversity he broke into cries of self-pity and frantic struggles to transfer the blame to others. He begged to resign : " finding myself very unfit and unable to wade in so weighty a cause as this, which ought to have much more comfort than I shall find or receive "—he hoped he might die and never see his country again—that Elizabeth would send him to some remote spot like the Indies where " by my humble and daily prayer, which shall never cease for her most happy preservation and long continuance " he might serve her without ever offending her sight again. He accused his English advisers in the Netherlands of pressing him against his will and Davison in particular for " over-great slackness to have answered sooner and better for me, as he promised he would." But, at the same time, having delivered these indirect assaults upon Elizabeth's emotions, he turned to more positive measures. He arranged with Heneage, who genuinely sympathised with him, to use Elizabeth's consent temporarily to withhold her letter to the Dutch as a justification for putting off the fulfilment of the remainder of her instructions. And he sent the experienced and amiable traveller and man-of-the-world Sir Thomas Sherley to see if he could do better than Davison had done.

Water will wear away a stone the more easily if the stone has a soft spot for it. Robert's first letter, delivered by Davison, had already touched that spot—for after it Elizabeth had agreed to withhold her own letter to the Dutch, a concession which alone made possible Robert's arrangement with Heneage to stave off the evil moment. More than likely that letter, whose contents she divulged to no one, she read over and over, scanning it hungrily for signs of contrition and affection, as was always her way with his letters. Meanwhile her ministers had been working on her to point out the damage which her humiliation of Robert, whether he had been right or wrong, would do the common cause. Now came Sherley, whose handling of her differed from Davison's as an artist's from an advocate's. Instead of arguing he flattered. He told her that " the world had conceived a high judgment of her great wisdom and providence, which she shewed in assailing the King of Spain at one time both in the Low Countries and also by Sir Francis Drake." When she objected that she could very well answer for Sir Francis since " if need be, the gentleman careth not if I disavow him," Sherley smoothly declared that " even so standeth my lord, if your disavowing of him may stand with your highness's favour towards him." While she was digesting this he tendered her the second of Robert's personal missives. She refused to receive it—perhaps she was afraid to. Nor would she succumb to curiosity when " in divers things she asked of me I seemed more ignorant than I was, and told her that I thought your lordship had written thereof."

A day or two later, seeing her strolling in her garden, he had an inspiration. Obtaining her notice he informed her that Robert, in danger of relapsing into an illness of which her physician Good-rowse had previously cured him, humbly prayed that he be sent over for a time to attend him. " It moved her much and she answered me, that with all her heart you should have him, and that she was sorry that your lordship had that need of him." It was a simple matter then, with the help of Hatton, another of her pets, to induce her to receive the letter, which like the other she perused by herself and put secretly away. The old magic again worked. The watchful eyes round her saw her visibly relenting. Soon Sir Walter Raleigh was able to write, " The queen is in very good terms with you, and, thanks be to God well pacified, and you are again her ' sweet Robin.' " His next letter she accepted without demur, " and after she had read it," reported Burghley, " I found her princely heart touched with favourable interpretation of your actions, affirming them to be only offensive to her in that she was not made privy to them ; not now misliking that you had the authority."

That was all. The determination that no servant of hers should tamper with her commission and in her name break the promise she had given to the world she still adhered to. Robert was to lay down his title but to go on as long as necessary informally exercising the powers which he and her advisers had convinced her could not be abruptly abandoned without damage to her cause ; he was to be allowed to accomplish his change of status quietly because her heart, once he addressed it directly as only he knew how, shrank from the terrible humiliation to which in its first angry hurt it had condemned him. Without sacrifice of principle she had yielded to love and reason, and so told him in the firm, kind and, for her, extraordinarily simple letter in which she communicated her decision :

" Right trusty and right well-beloved cousin and counsellor (it began) we greet you well. It is always thought, in the opinion of the world, a hard bargain when both parties are losers, and so doth it fall out in the case of us two. You, as we hear, are greatly grieved, in respect of the great displeasure you find we have conceived against you, and we no less grieved that a subject of ours, of that quality you are, a creature of our own, and one that has always received an extraordinary portion of our favour above all our subjects, even from the beginning of our reign, should deal so carelessly, we will not say contemptuously, as to give the world just cause to think that we are had in contempt by him that ought most to respect and reverence us, from whom we could never have looked to receive any such measure, which, we do assure you, hath wrought as great a grief in us as any one thing that ever happened to us.

"We are persuaded that you, that have so long known us, cannot think that ever we could have been drawn to take up so hard a course herein, had we not been provoked by an extraordinary cause. But that for your grieved and wounded mind hath more need of comfort than reproof, wherein we are persuaded, though the act in respect of the contempt can no way be excused, had no other meaning and intent than to advance our service ; we think meet to forbear to dwell upon a matter wherein we ourselves do find so little comfort, assuring you that whosoever professeth to love you best taketh not more comfort of your well-doing, or discomfort of your evil doing, than ourself.

" Now to come to the breach itself, which we would be glad to repair in such sort as may be for our honour without the peril and danger of that country, we do think meet that you shall, upon conference with Sir Thomas Heneage and such others whose advice you shall think meet to be used therein, think of some way from the point concerning the absolute title may be qualified, in such sort as the authority may, notwith-standing, remain (which we think most needful to continue, for the redress of the abuses, and avoiding of confusion that, otherwise, is likely to ensue) which, as we conceive, may be performed, if the states may be induced to yield that authority unto you carrying the title of lieutenant-general of our forces, that they now yield unto you under the title of an absolute governor."

But the mischief had already been done. In the concluding portion of her letter Elizabeth authorised Robert to postpone laying down his office if it seemed to him and his advisers " that any such motion for the present may work any peril of consequence to that State," and his formal resignation did not, in fact, take effect until after his final departure. The precaution was useless, for the peril had already been worked. The Dutch had watched with growing misgivings the exposure of an illusion. They had taken Leicester's words to be the expression of Elizabeth's will, and his presence among them her pledge of how she intended to act. It now appeared that he had misrepresented her. If she disapproved the supreme authority over themselves which they had granted him, it followed that she also disapproved of the policy which had made the grant of authority necessary, that of devoting everything to the common purpose of finally delivering the Netherlands from Spain. If it was not in the Queen's mind, it was obviously not within the

Favourite's ability to undertake that the policy should be faithfully carried out, and upon the Dutch leaders there rapidly settled an exasperated sense of having been cheated by both. Between them Elizabeth and Robert had managed to ruin his great mission before it was fairly begun.

Every move of each was henceforth scrutinised with suspicion and distrust. The Dutch, so often hopeful and so often deceived of foreign help, with Alençon's treacherous assault upon the liberties of which he had been styled Defender fresh in their memories, were in no mood to be indulgent. They heard that Elizabeth was treating with Parma for a separate peace and were disposed, not altogether unjustifiably, to believe it. The rumour gained substance from the slowness of her promised remittances. Her troops, unpaid and unprovisioned in consequence, went about like a rabble of starved and sullen ruffians, a disgrace to their country and a danger to the good order of the land they had come to fight for. The state of his army delayed their general's taking the field, which the Dutch, completing the circle, put down to his knowledge that his mistress was trying for a peace which would relieve her of fighting and paying.

It was the very last atmosphere in which a hot-house plant like Robert Dudley could flourish. Optimistic and buoyant, like most of fortune's favourites, he had not been shaped to deal with fortune's reversals. The slow, patient removal of distrust and opposition was not a knack he had ever troubled to cultivate ; distrust he could only counter with dislike and opposition with arrogance. The very notion of the Dutch lawyers and burghers with whom he had to work daring to criticise him transformed them once and for all in his sight from the models of virtue they had been at his coming into a Breughel-like medley of " churls and tinkers." The high task he had so long yearned to get on with became within three months the one thing on earth he yearned to get away from.

He was between the devil and the deep sea. Elizabeth would neither replace him nor adequately support him. The dispute over his title proved to be but the first outcome in action of the profound difference in attitude between them which doomed him to frustration at every turn. His temperament urged him—rightly, according to all the best opinion—to an offensive war without counting the cost, her orders bound him to a defensive one on the strict principle of limited liability. To make sure that her orders were obeyed and her money not squandered, she doled out the £126,000 a year she had promised in slow and tardy trickles. The Dutch, committed to twice the amount, observed, began to doubt and imitated her—a course which naturally drove her to further extremes of caution. Robert expostulated, wheedled, tried to arouse her compassion at the plight of her troops. She replied with demands for accountings of what had already been sent. He could not provide them, at least not satisfactory ones. Close reckoning of money had never been his strong point and the corruption of the time was so luxuriant as to defeat the most exacting scrutiny of every treasury in Europe. The dishonesty of paymasters was the usual motive for their choosing that profession and the system of private recruiting left a wide gap between numbers in a company actually and those ostensibly on the payroll. All Robert could do was to give an example of reckless generosity, borrowing on his properties till they could bear no more, begging endorsements for loans, to relieve the more glaring miseries of his soldiers and reward individual gallantries which he vainly called to official notice. Within three months he reckoned he had disbursed £11,000 and mortgaged his revenues for years ahead. In all bewildered honesty he demanded why he should be accused of having come for ambition's sake when he had given up security and splendour at home for this.[1]

The army on whose fitness for battle everything ultimately

[1] The incredibly involved and tedious details of the finances of the Netherlands campaign are spread over many chapters of Motley's still irreplaceable *History of the United Netherlands* which takes an unfavourable view of Elizabeth's parsimony. The much more recent *Mr. Secretary Walsingham and the Foreign Policy of Queen Elizabeth* of Mr. Conyers Read considerably modifies this view, and the very close and exact study of pledges and actual payments by Professor J. E. Neale in the *English Historical Review*, Vol. XIV, pp. 373-96, strikes a distinct balance of judgment in Elizabeth's favour. That she was tardy with her remittances for fear of being overreached, to the distress of her general and her soldiers, though she eventually met and even exceeded her obligations, seems however unarguable. The estimates and statements of accounts are to be found in the State Papers Domestic and with further details relating to Leicester in State Papers Foreign for the period.

depended meanwhile paid the penalty of its rulers' failure to agree. The numbers swelled while the quality deteriorated ; to the stipulated five thousand foot and a thousand horse had been added a contingent originally enlisted under Sir John Norris, that " chicken of Mars," for the relief of Antwerp and some English volunteers transferred from the Dutch to Leicester's service, with the result that provision lagged still further behind requirements. The human material was poor at best, largely the sort of riff-raff privately recruited in the manner as ably described as caricatured by Falstaff. " In England," wrote Barnaby Rich in 1587, " when service happeneth we disburden the prisons of thieves, we rob the taverns and ale-houses of toss-pots and ruffians, we scour both town and country of rogues and vagabonds." Leicester, looking them over, the fops of the town holding commissions with their hangers-on in attendance and the scourings of the streets whom they had by one means or another impressed into their ranks, wrote to Walsingham :

> " I am ashamed to think, much more to speak, of the young men that have come over. Believe me you will all repent the cockney kind of bringing up at this day of young men. . . . Our simplest men in show have been our best men, and your gallant blood and ruffian men the worst of all others."

Unwilling, like a later Puritan leader, Oliver Cromwell, to retain any whose heart was not in the cause, he offered to release those who could buy themselves out. The result was disconcerting : " the flower of the pressed English bands," men of a little substance, took advantage of the offer and departed, " leaving the remnant supplied with such paddy persons as commonly, in voluntary procurement, men are glad to accept."

They came with as little preparation as heart for the task before them. England, almost boastfully unmilitary by tradition and habit, kept no standing army, and though every able-bodied man was in theory trained to arms, Elizabeth effectively discouraged the employment of the territorial militia overseas with an invasion threatening her own shores. The training, moreover, did not signify in

England what it had come to mean elsewhere. It seemed designed to repeat the victory of 1415 at Agincourt, the nation's last great military memory. Englishmen were still incomparable in the use of the long bow but with little experience of artillery, engineering or even small arms' fire, like Parma's Spanish and Italian veterans. The very pay of an archer was scarcely more than it had been at Agincourt, eightpence a day as against sixpence, with the cost of living immeasurably higher. Out of that they had to provide their own necessities by purchase from a native populace that resented and cheated them : and resented them more when it became more difficult to cheat them as their pay fell three months, then five months, in arrears. Often without food, many literally without shoes and with their coats falling off their backs, mutinous bands left their garrisons and roamed the frozen, hostile countryside for whatever they could lay their hands on. New recruits coming from home often deserted at the very sight of them.

What energy, compassion, graphic letters to his government and the unstinted pouring-out of his own resources could do to build up and hold together this force during an exceptionally bitter winter, its commander did. In the opinion of his subordinates on the spot, civilian and military alike, no man could have done more. The first action seemed to justify his belief that he had accomplished the miracle so often produced with English troops similarly collected and neglected. The general dividing line between the two hostile armies was the River Waal. The allies held its mouth, the Spaniards, occupying Flanders and Brabant to the south and west, certain strong points on the near side of it. Parma's problem was to force the rivers to the north and east so as to penetrate into the territory of the rebellious provinces. Accordingly he had in December advanced to the Meuse and besieged the town of Grave on its left bank. Because of its strategic importance, a wave of panic spread through the Netherlands when he succeeded, despite the fierce resistance of its eight hundred Dutch defenders, after four months of skilful investment, in cutting it off : and Leicester hurried three thousand men under Sir John Norris and Count Hohenlo to its relief. After a savage mêlée on the banks of the river, where the English contingent distinguished itself by its prowess with the pike, the Spanish lines were split and a fleet of hoys run in with provisions sufficient for nine months.

For a start it was promising. Leicester, soaring abruptly from the blackest despondency to the headiest optimism, proclaimed it in all good faith a decisive victory. At Utrecht he dedicated St. George's Day to its fitting celebration. In London he stirred Queen and Privy Council with glowing descriptions of his soldiers' heroism and his jubilant conviction that the enemy had been dealt a mortal blow. Meanwhile at Grave Parma reassembled his battered force and returned to the assault with such vigour that a few weeks later the heroic garrison surrendered and were permitted to withdraw with the honours of war. The staggering reversal was too much for the Governor-General's emotional balance. Instead of facing the truth, or setting about to retrieve the disaster, he obeyed his first blind impulse to divest himself of blame, in his own eyes as well as the world's, by finding a scapegoat. But even his loyal adherents regretted the haste with which he had the commander of the garrison executed for treason, less for the injustice of the act than for the indignation it aroused in his countrymen, all too prone to put the worst construction upon it.

After Grave the rot spread swiftly. He quarrelled not only with the Dutch but with his English advisers until service in the Netherlands became a penance and escape from it a reward. Knowing himself to be confronted with adversaries and rightly suspecting himself to be surrounded by spies who reported ill of him at home, he seemed unable any longer to distinguish between friends and foes. He caused one of the most eminent, and Anglo-phile, of Dutch statesmen to be arrested, only to swallow the humiliation of seeing him released by his compatriots. He tried to have Norris, the ablest English general under his command, recalled but despite his most strenuous efforts failed. His growing irritation and waning prestige became reflected in a constant bickering, and sometimes dangerous brawling, between his Dutch and English officers. Nor were there victories, even abortive ones, to compensate. Bound by Elizabeth's instructions, he could not seek out the enemy in battle, as he desired, but had, though the Spaniards were numerically inferior and almost equally ill-provisioned, to keep his troops to defend various designated and widely dispersed towns. It was autumn before he saw action again, and then only in a series of skirmishes designed to threaten one or another of Parma's similar minor garrisons.

Of one of these, brought about "unawares" by an encounter with a relieving Spanish convoy, a weird affair in which "the better sort" on both sides met in a head-on fray straight out of the pages of chivalry, with Leicester himself, bravely horsed, plumed and armoured, hacking and hewing joyously amongst the foremost, he wrote, "I think I may call it the most notable encounter that it hath been in our age, and it will remain to our posterity famous." He was right, but not for the reason he thought, but because on that field of Zutphen his nephew Sir Philip Sidney received his mortal wound and made his immortal renunciation. His death, not at first expected, nearly broke his uncle's heart and struck from him one of the most tenderly beautiful of Elizabethan letters. It also involved him in a dreary quarrel with the staunchest of his supporters, Walsingham, over the dead man's estate.

Weary of the whole business, only too despondently aware that England had gained nothing from his year in the Netherlands worth Sidney's loss, he sailed for home in November after another brush with Elizabeth, who forbade his departure until the conduct of affairs in his absence was satisfactorily arranged. He must have convinced her that they were, for his welcome was rapturous. Morally she never needed him more. The trial of Mary Stuart the previous autumn for plotting her murder had plunged her into the acutest agony of her life : wanting her enemy dead, she could not bring herself to order the execution of a fellow-queen. He joined his voice forcibly, and as it proved decisively, to those of his colleagues who were urging her to sign the death warrant. After months of swaying she signed, and he alone was spared the terrible reaction which consigned the unfortunate Davison—of whom he had the decency tardily to admit that "my yielding was my own fault . . . whatsoever his persuasions "—to a term of imprisonment for having sent the warrant on to its fatal destination. Meanwhile from the Netherlands news poured in during these fearful days of how one lieutenant after another to whom he had delegated responsibility in his absence had betrayed him—how Sir William Stanley for whom he had expressly asked and to whom he had entrusted Deventer, one of the most important cities in the whole of the Provinces, had delivered it over to the enemy—how his name was abused, his secret instructions opened and his authority contemptuously flouted by the Dutch. He did not want to go back but he had to simply to fill the explosive vacuum his departure had created. But his presence, and his intrigues against the now implacably hostile Dutch leaders, nearly started a civil war when the extreme Calvinist elements amongst the poorer of the working class in various of the towns started forming a Leicestrian party to seize control of the state. After a few months he finally retired, disillusioned and discredited.

The failure was his, but the fault was at least as much Elizabeth's. He himself, recalling in his difficulties the father he had never ceased to venerate, once exclaimed that what the situation required was another Northumberland. But it was precisely her fear of " another Northumberland in him " that caused her to put so impossibly tight a curb on him. Because she refused him adequate powers she doomed his efforts to sterility from the outset : while such powers as he was born with she had already sapped by the long indulgence of her love, leaving him only his ambition, his pride and the ability to support " the charge and dignity " of his office with which to perform a task which would one day all but defy a Marlborough.

Chapter Fourteen

THE END

THE *annus mirabilis*, so long and confidently expected, had arrived—that Climacterical Yeare of the World foretold of the numerical combination 1588 by the Koenigsberg astronomer a century before. In every man's mouth was the ancient octet beginning :

> Post mille exp(l)etos a partu virginis annos
> Et post quingentos rursus ab orbe datus
> Octogesimus octavus mirabilis annus
> Ingruet, in saechum tristia fata feret . . .

in every man's mind the " marvellous and fearful and horrible alterations of empires kingdoms signories and estates with extraordinary accidents plagues and famine . . . (which) should ensue." But that the forthcoming prodigies would include the final separation of Elizabeth and Robert the stars, whose " singular conjunction " had so precisely revealed the linking of their destinies at birth, had somehow neglected to divulge, else his countrymen would have greeted the new year with something more than the lively interest tinged by vague apprehension reported of them. Not even Elizabeth, her knowledge fortified by signs of illness which quickly silenced her stored-up complaints at his return, apparently suspected that the coming crisis of her reign would provide the epilogue to her long love story.

To secure that the kingdom to be overthrown should not include England, she had agreed on a forestalling move to overthrow the empire of Spain in the Netherlands. It had failed ; it was now Spain's turn and no one could any longer doubt that she would seize it. With grim tenacity Philip II had repaired the two mishaps —the death of his designated admiral and Drake's devastating raid on his shipping in Cadiz harbour which had postponed his revenge from 1587 to the year appointed by the prophecies. All reports from Elizabeth's excellent intelligence agents agreed that preparations were complete for a vast armada to sail as soon as the season permitted.

To meet the danger the navy was, of course, the first and principal line of defence. The bulk of it under the Lord Admiral, Howard of Effingham, and his lieutenants Drake and Frobisher lay off Plymouth, and a secondary squadron under Lord Henry Seymour off Dover with Sir John Hawkins in London working feverishly to supply both. But the Navy might fail; the Spanish admiral, the Duke of Medina Sidonia, might succeed in holding it off while he landed an army on the south coast; or, even worse, he might, as some feared, force his way through to the estuary of the Scheldt and embark Parma's veterans for an assault upon some stretch of the more vulnerable east coast. Since every possibility could not be provided for, a choice had to be made. Sir John Norris, appointed on April 6th to supervise the defences of the maritime counties from Norfolk to Dorset, took up his headquarters at Weymouth to organise the defences of what prevailing opinion took to be the most threatened area. The famous system of fire-beacons was arranged to direct the militiamen to their assembly-points and give them their line of march. Trained pioneers hurried in with spade and pick-axe to construct forts and trenches, artillerymen to rear their gun platforms. At Warham Bridge a barrier was prepared in the event of retreat, when the roads were to be cut and the water let in, while special companies of petronels—horsemen armed with pistols—drove off the cattle and burned everything that could not readily be carried away. To persons not in actual service orders were issued forbidding them to leave their towns and villages without express permission. By June, when the Armada was expected to sail, 27,000 infantry, 2000 light and 500 heavy cavalry waited in the south to resist a landing or, if it succeeded, to oppose the enemy's progress inland.

They formed part of an available total of over 130,000—according to the returns made by the Lord Lieutenants of the counties in answer to a circular issued by the Privy Council on April 2nd—the largest host ever mustered in the island and one far exceeding the Crown's ability or the willingness of their native shires and boroughs to maintain on a war footing. Nevertheless by June, after frequent exchanges between ministers and local authorities of letters of abuse and appeal, three further armies had been assembled. One, of fourteen regiments each 2000 strong under the Earl of Huntingdon, waited in East Anglia and did not much enter into the picture. Another, under the Earl of Leicester, of 20,000 foot and 2000 horse, covered the mouth of the Thames and the approaches to London. A third, of 34,000, under Lord Hunsdon, lay to the west of London to act as a mobile striking force when the actual site of the invasion was known, and in addition to guard the person of the Queen and put down internal insurrection—a very real danger if the widespread fear of a Catholic rising once the Spaniards had gained a foothold was realised.

To these dispositions Robert took vehement exception—and not only because of the comparatively subordinate role to which they reduced him. Not believing for a moment that the 20,000 troops reported on board the Armada could achieve a landing in the face of resistance before joining up with Parma, he implored his colleagues not to concentrate the country's main strength in the south and not to disperse the rest with the invasion assuredly coming from the east. " I beseech you," he wrote Walsingham, " assemble your forces and play not this kingdom away by delays." His own intelligence from the Netherlands, superior perhaps to the Privy Council's because of his special connections there, made it certain, he declared, that " the Prince (Parma) is looked to issue out presently : he hath suffered no stranger this six or seven days to come to him or see his camp and ships, but hath blindfolded them " and, if the Duke of Sidonia got through, " will play another manner of part than is looked for."

He was right, as events in the Channel even as he wrote were beginning to prove, and as the Spanish archives would one day confirm. Meantime in his own area of responsibility he worked literally day and night to fit his command for the supreme ordeal he felt convinced was before it. Conferences in London with Norris and other generals at three in the morning would be followed by hasty notes dispatched at dawn before dashing out to camp for inspections and manœuvres. Once at ten in the evening he rode from Leycester House to Tilbury to examine a lighter and chain which had been relied upon to block the river at that point, taking with him an engineer from the royal dockyards at Deptford, and anxiously reported that " I find it a thing most assured that they will not do the good that is expected, unless they be strengthened with a competent number of masts before them ; for otherwise if two or three ships made of purpose should come against it, with a full tide and a good strong gale of wind, no doubt they would break all and pass through." This deficiency ordered to be put right, next morning he was at Gravesend to see to the construction of gun-platforms still lacking for artillery which had been sent, a little later back to Tilbury to inspect the forts and see that the work on the masts had been started. He gave personal attention to the drafts as they passed into his camps, estimating their worth, struggling to procure them the food of which they were painfully short and to protect them against the leeches who hurried to profit from the situation which meat and beer mercilessly overpriced ; a detachment of a thousand recruits on its way from London he met and sternly returned because they had been sent inadequately provided for. And on top of all this he had the general duties of a Privy Councillor to attend to, including the incessant labour which he took on himself of seeing that the navy obtained the powder and shot and other absolute necessities for which its leaders were urgently crying. " They have put me to more travail," he wrote Walsingham as the Armada came up the Channel, " than ever I was in (in) my life."

Certainly never in his life did he rise to an occasion as on this, the greatest of all its occasions. His vanity excepted, taking the form of repeated complaints that his authority was insufficient— which was, after all, true if his military conception was right—the other characteristic faults so disastrously vented upon the Netherlands seemed for the moment to have been placed under an iron control. In the numerous letters scrawled " in haste " during those weeks of terrific tension there is scarcely a trace of easy optimism, petulance or recrimination over blame : " there is no looking back now," he advised the Council on July 24th, " to any oversight past." Instead one feels throughout a cool and steady force both in act and judgment.

It impressed itself alike upon his colleagues and Elizabeth, whose affection for and confidence in him that May and June struck observers as being as complete as ever. His advice was listened to : more men, including some of the best trained bands in service, were sent him, and on July 24th, as it became plain that the Armada was trying to fight its way through the Straits of Dover to the Flemish coast, he was made " Lieutenant and General of the Queen's Armies and Companies." She wanted to make him Lieutenant-General of England and Ireland as well in the event of anything happening to her, but on this point, necessarily involving the delicate question of the succession, her other ministers fell into disagreement and the patent was never signed.

He not only cajoled her now, he all but commanded. A letter he wrote her at the very height of the crisis, on July 27th, displayed not only the understanding of her which had only once failed him, but something like a masterfulness upon which he had never before ventured. There had been worried dispute in the Council as to where Elizabeth should remain until the issue of the battle in the Channel were known, for if she were taken, all would have been over. Some wanted her to remove herself far inland, she herself was determined to be virtually on the spot where the invasion occurred :

" Now for your person," wrote Robert, " being the most sacred and dainty thing we have in this world to care for, a man must tremble when he thinks of it ; specially finding your Majesty to have that princely courage, to transport yourself to the utmost confines of your realm to meet your enemies and defend your subjects. I cannot, most dear Queen, consent to that ; for upon your well being consists all the safety of your whole kingdom ; and therefore preserve that above all. Yet will I not that, in some sort, so princely and so rare a magnanimity should not appear to your people and the world as it is. And thus far, if it please your Majesty, you may do, to draw yourself to your house at Havering : and your army being about London, at Stratford, East Ham, and the villages thereabout, shall be always not only a defence, but a ready supply to these counties, Essex and Kent, if need be. And in the meantime your Majesty, to comfort this army, and people of both counties, may, if it please you, spend two or three days to see both the camp and the forts. It is not fourteen miles at most from Havering, and a very convenient place for your Majesty to lie by the way and so rest you at camp. I trust you will be pleased at your Lieutenant's cabin and with a mile there is a gentleman's house where your Majesty may be. You shall comfort not only these thousands, but many more that shall hear of it. And thus far, and no further, can I consent to venture your person. And by the grace of God, there can be no danger in this, though the enemy should pass by your fleet . . ."

The advice to withdraw to Havering had not to be considered, for word came that the battered Armada had been driven into Calais Roads. But the invitation was accepted, to Robert's joy— " I see most gracious Lady, you know what will most comfort a faithful servant . . ."

She arrived at Tilbury Fort by barge on August 8th, where Robert received her to a royal salute from the Block House, the flags flying, the fifes and drums playing. Escorted by 1000 horse and 2000 foot, he attended her in a coach

" ornamented with diamonds, emeralds and rubies in checker-wise . . . by strange invention with curious knots embroidered with gold "

to the camp and the house he had chosen for her. Next day she saw a sham fight by the troops and later inspected them drawn up in parallel lines, carrying a truncheon and walking " sometimes with a martial pace, sometimes like a woman." The following afternoon she returned to St. James's Palace after calling the sergeant-major of the camp and giving him a message for the troops which appears to have been a version of the immortal Tilbury speech. An echo of it appears in the letter which her host wrote a few days later to the Earl of Shrewsbury describing how her visit had " so inflamed the hearts of her good subjects as I think the meanest person amongst them is able to match the proudest Spaniard that ever dares to land in England."

The test never came. Drake's fire-ships drove the Armada out of Calais Roads into the North Sea, where a raging gale dispersed it and contrived that the only Spaniards who landed in England would be survivors of its wreckage. Robert, still fearing that it might reassemble and complete its task of conveying Parma, tried hard to persuade Elizabeth to keep her army in being. But Elizabeth was not to be budged from her own profound instinct to save expense and ordered the troops to be paid off as soon as possible. At a great thanksgiving in London she rode in a chariot through the streets draped with blue cloth through " the Companies of the City standing on both sides with their banners in goodly order " to the service at St. Paul's, hung for the occasion with flags captured from the wrecked and captured galleons of the enemy. Robert meanwhile, his affairs at camp wound up, left for the holiday he had been wistfully promising himself since spring, intending to go by way of Kenilworth to take the waters at familiar Buxton or nearby Leamington.

And on the way, anti-climactically, one might almost say irrelevantly, he died. On August 27th, at the very height of the national rejoicing, he sent Elizabeth a note from Maidenhead asking a favour for an old servant. A few days later, from Rycott, home of Sir John Norris's parents, where they had in the past spent pleasant days together during more than one of her progresses, he wrote her in his characteristic vein :

" I most humbly beseech your Majesty to pardon your poor old servant (the two o's in ' poor ' drawn as always in his familiar letters like two eyes : ⊙ ⊙) to be thus bold in thus sending to know how my gracious lady doeth and what ease of her late pain she finds, being the chiefest thing in this world I do pray for, for her to have good health and long life. For my own poor case, I continue still your medicine and find it amends much better than with any other thing that hath been given me. Thus hoping to find perfect cure at the bath, with the continuance of my wonted prayer for your Majesty's most happy preservation, I humbly kiss your foot, from your old lodging at Rycott this Thursday morning, ready to take my journey . . . "

A postscript acknowledged a gift she had sent after him.

That was the last time she ever heard from him. On September 4th, at Cornbury, near Oxford, and very near Cumnor where Amy's body had been found twenty-eight years before almost to the day, he succumbed to " the continual fever "—another authority says " cold rheums," but they were probably the same thing—which had been troubling him at the beginning of the year.

His legend, more powerful than the truth in his life, very soon took charge also of his death. It produced testimony, widespread if confused, to corroborate in one version or another the tale that he had planned to poison his wife and Sir Christopher Blount, his handsome and very youthful Gentleman of the Horse, on discovering that they were lovers, but that Lettice anticipated his intention and neatly turned the tables on him by giving him a poisoned cordial after a heavy meal at Cornbury. The story has its variations and ignores the fact that there was a post-mortem and that Robert loved his wife to the day of his death ; but Lettice did in fact later marry Blount. There was no arguing with the legend after that.

They buried him in the Lady's Chapel of the Collegiate Chapel at Warwick where the " noble Impe " already lay and to his memory erected a monument at a cost of £4000 with his effigy in armour lying on its back, his earl's coronet on his head, an effigy of Lettice beside him, and a Latin inscription setting forth his offices, dignities and ancestry. But the monument and inscription were, as usual with such things, other people's after-thoughts ; his will, dictated the previous year in the Netherlands, proved more honestly revealing about him. For though he left the bulk of his property " to my most dear, well-beloved wife," an earlier clause declared that " first of all, and above all persons, it is my duty to remember my most dear and gracious princess, whose creature under God I have been, and who hath been a most bountiful and princely mistress to me." To her he left, together with a prayer " that she may indeed be a blessed mother and nurse to this people," a jewel with three great emeralds with a fair large table diamond in the middle and a rope of fair white pearls to the number of six hundred on which to hang the jewel, both having been earlier acquired against her coming to Wanstead on a visit that never took place.

Of the property so long and grandly accumulated comparatively little remained as Elizabeth and the lesser creditors closed in. The proud title of Leicester, passing to another Robert, Sir Philip Sidney's younger brother, shortly became extinct. Soon little remained but the legend and the memory in the heart of an ageing queen, who wrote upon the brief note from Rycott " His last letter " and put it in a chest by her bedside where she might read and re-read it even while she hounded the writer's widow for her due and cherished the widow's son as the darling of her old age until he presumed too much and paid for his presumption with his young head.

FINIS

INDEX